# Evolutionary Biology of Aging

# Evolutionary
# Biology of Aging

## MICHAEL R. ROSE

Professor of Evolutionary Biology
University of California, Irvine

New York    Oxford
OXFORD UNIVERSITY PRESS
1991

## Oxford University Press

Oxford   New York   Toronto
Delhi   Bombay   Calcutta   Madras   Karachi
Petaling Jaya   Singapore   Hong Kong   Tokyo
Nairobi   Dar es Salaam   Cape Town
Melbourne   Auckland

and associated companies in
Berlin   Ibadan

## Copyright © 1991 by Michael R. Rose

Published by Oxford University Press, Inc.,
200 Madison Avenue, New York, New York 10016

Oxford is a registered trademark of Oxford University Press

Library of Congress Cataloging-in-Publication Data
Rose, Michael R. (Michael Robertson), 1955–
Evolutionary biology of aging / Michael R. Rose.
p. cm.   Includes bibliographical references.
ISBN 0-19-506133-0
1. Aging.   2. Evolution.   I. Title.
[DNLM: 1. Aging.   2. Evolution.   WT 104 R797e]
QP86.R59   1991   574.3'72—dc20
DNLM/DLC   90-6787
for Library of Congress

1 3 5 7 9 8 6 4 2

Printed in the United States of America
on acid-free paper

*To my son Darius*
*who helped me write this book*

# PREFACE

In 1952, Sir Peter Medawar published an essay on aging titled "An Unsolved Problem of Biology." At the time, few would have disputed his view that the fundamental biological causes of the progressive deterioration of the older adult were not known, even in outline. A subject of intense medical interest had not yet been illuminated by the light of scientific understanding.

It cannot be said that this lack of illumination was due to a lack of scholarly attention. The father of academic biology, Aristotle, began the biological study of aging millennia ago with his *De Longitudine et Brevitate Vitae*, posing the following problems:

> . . . it is not clear whether in animals and plants universally it is a single or diverse cause that makes some to be long-lived, others short-lived. Plants too have in some cases a long life, while in others it lasts for but a year.
>
> Further, in a natural structure are longevity and a sound constitution coincident, or is shortness of life independent of unhealthiness? (Ross, 1908, p. 464b)

After the Renaissance, other authors took up Aristotle's biological perspective on aging, the most notable being Francis Bacon, the English philosopher of science and statesman, in his *Historia Vitae et Mortis* of 1645 (Spedding et al., 1889). An important feature of Bacon's writing was his insistence on the value of skepticism: "With regard to the length and shortness of life in animals, the information to be had is small, observation careless, and tradition fabulous" (Spedding et al., 1889, p. 233), where the word fabulous means "as from fables." This problem has certainly been perennial in aging research.

Since the 1930s, particularly in the United States, the field of gerontology has made the study of aging a commonplace part of the spectrum of biomedical research (vide Shock, 1987). Yet for some, the darkness surrounding aging continues. In his synoptic review of the field, Alex Comfort (1979, p. 9), the noted gerontologist and sexologist, declared that:

> In almost any other important biological field than that of senescence, it is possible to present the main theories historically and to show a steady progression from a large number of speculative ideas to one or two highly probable, main hypotheses. In the case of senescence this cannot be profitably done.

From Comfort's standpoint, aging would have to be considered still an unsolved problem of biology.

The chief purpose of this book is to argue that aging can now be regarded as a problem that is well on its way toward a scientific solution. This immediately raises two questions of definition. First, what is meant by *aging?* This is a theory-laden problem, which will be addressed primarily in Chapter 2. For the time being, aging can be taken to refer to the autonomous process of deterioration that the adults of most species seem to undergo with increasing chronological age. Second, the term *solution* is also a problematic one. Evidently, science does not furnish us with cut-and-dried conclusions that exhaust all possibility of further discovery. Scientific problems do not have solutions like those of chess endgame puzzles, in which White has to checkmate Black in two moves, beyond any chance of escape by Black. Thus it cannot be the case that the final answers to all scientific questions about aging will soon be found.

Medawar's expression, "an unsolved problem of biology," must refer by negation to biological problems that are thought to have been solved in some limited sense. For an evolutionary biologist obvious examples of such solutions to problems are (1) the solution of the problem of adaptation by the theory of natural selection and (2) the solution of the problem of heredity by the theories of genetics. No serious evolutionary biologist would suggest that the last words have been said on the topics of adaptation and heredity, but it is apparent that firm foundations for work on these problems have been laid down. To use a metaphor of military conquest, where these two problems are concerned, our base of operations has been secured, and we are now moving forward wherever we find resistance crumbling. In these terms, then, it is argued here that we now have the foundations for a solution of the problem of aging in the same sense as we might say that we have one for the problem of adaptation.

The basis of this solution is the theoretical result that the force of natural selection tends to decline with age in organisms that do not reproduce by fission. Starting from this central finding, presented in Chapter 1, the book attempts to cover the biology of aging as a whole from the perspective of evolutionary biology. The first step in this synthesis is a reformulation of the definition of aging and a critique of methods for studying aging, provided in Chapter 2. After that, the empirical literature bearing on the evolution of aging is discussed in Chapters 3, 4, and 5. Chapters 3 and 4 are experimental in subject matter, while Chapter 5 deals with the comparative data. All this material is directly related to the evolutionary theory of aging, including the genetic mechanisms that underlie the evolution of aging.

In Chapters 6, 7, and 8, the theoretical and empirical results of the first five chapters are used to develop an evolutionary perspective on physiological research on aging, the domain of gerontology. While it is not argued that the evolution of aging is the only profitable avenue for research on aging, it will be argued that it provides the essential foundation for aging research, with respect to both theory and experimental systems. That is to say, it is argued that the evolutionary biology of aging, rather than, for example, cell biology, should be the intellectual core of gerontology. This is not to deny the value of techniques and experimental results that have already been developed within gerontology. Rather, it is to assert that they have lacked the indispensable focus that the evolutionary biology of aging can provide to the field as a whole.

In broadest outline, then, this book attempts to do two things. First, to present evolutionary research on aging: theoretical, experimental, and comparative. This is not a controversial goal, nor is it a particularly difficult task, given the relative clarity of both theoretical and empirical conclusions concerning the evolutionary biology of aging. Second, to overthrow the present intellectual order of gerontology, and to replace it with one based on evolutionary and genetic foundations. This second goal will of course be controversial. Many biologists interested in aging have been impatient with gerontology's lack of progress, and they have long sought an unseating of the present order. On the other hand, many dedicated gerontologists will resent the idea that the foundations of their field might need to be wholly recast. For my part, I can only say that I think that in the long run everyone will be happier once the rate of progress in gerontology accelerates substantially. Specifically, I think that the problem of postponing aging will become a soluble one by building upon the accomplishments of a new gerontology that can readily define and achieve its experimental goals. My conviction is that this new gerontology will arise from the change in the foundations of the field argued for here. This change will require some intellectual retooling, but not too much in the way of new experimental systems, techniques, or materials. As changing ideas is not as expensive as changing laboratories, except where our intellectual vanity is concerned, only our judgment of the truth or falsehood of the alternatives should be weighed in the balance between the two intellectual systems of present-day gerontology and gerontology reformulated in terms of evolutionary biology. I hope that those who are now committed to the extant intellectual system of gerontology will try the road not taken.

*Irvine, Calif.*                                                                                                          M.R.R.
*February 1990*

# ACKNOWLEDGMENTS

The original impetus for my work on aging was supplied by Brian Charlesworth in 1976. He cajoled me into working on the problem when I, as a naive graduate student, still thought of it as more or less intractable. In the summer of 1982, Monty Slatkin suggested that I write a book on the evolution of aging, and ever since I have been working on the project by fits and starts. Monty Slatkin and David A. Wake were also my first editorial patrons, commissioning the book for their *Evolution* series.

Over the five years that I have been producing drafts of this book, it has been read by a number of my colleagues. The manuscript was read in third draft by S. Abrams, B. Charlesworth, J. Gallant, P. H. Harvey, R. B. Huey, T. E. Johnson, L. S. Luckinbill, G. M. Martin, L. D. Mueller, G. Payne, M. Slatkin, P. M. Service, A. J. Shaw, D. A. Wake, and G. C. Williams. Portions of the fourth draft were read by C. E. Finch (Chapters 5, 6, and 8), J. E. Fleming (Chapter 7), D. Harrison (Chapters 6 and 8), D. Reznick (Chapters 3 to 5), and R. S. Sohal (Chapter 6). My editor at Oxford University Press, William Curtis, subjected the entire fourth draft to careful scrutiny. The quality of the criticism that the manuscript received has been great indeed. I doubt that I have been able to achieve the goals that my readers have set for me, partly because I have on occasion ignored their advice. The book's limitations and deficiencies are undoubtedly my own.

I have received bibliographic, graphical, and other assistance with manuscript preparation from Cheryl Grandy, Cindy Kunz, Ernest Novaczek, and Alex Olvido.

The following publishers have given permission to use copyrighted material: Academic Press, Blackie and Son, Cambridge University, Company of Biologists Ltd., Dover, Elsevier Publications, Genetics Society of America, Gerontological Society of America, S. Karger Publishers, Macmillan Magazines, Pergamon Press, Proceedings of the National Academy of Sciences, Society for the Study of Evolution, Springer-Verlag, University of Chicago Press, Van Nostrand Reinhold, John Wiley and Sons, Williams and Wilkins Company.

# CONTENTS

# Evolutionary Biology of Aging

No one has yet produced a satisfactory explanation of the whole process,
and probably no one ever will.
F. M. Burnet, 1976, p. 82

# 1

# The Evolutionary Theory of Aging

Nothing in biology makes sense except in the light of evolution.
TH. DOBZHANSKY, 1973

Aging is a puzzling phenomenon for the theory of evolution by natural selection. The basic intuition of Darwin was that adaptation could be explained by the enhanced survival rates of individuals with heritable attributes that fostered survival and reproduction. Therefore, these heritable attributes should spread through species because of their higher rates of transmission. Mathematically, it has been shown that, in the absence of unusual patterns of selection, natural selection often acts so as to increase the mean fitness of a population (Nagylaki, 1977; Ewens, 1979). This result formally illustrates the validity of Darwin's basic idea. So how does it happen that evolution has so frequently produced organisms with survival and reproductive rates that decline with adult age?

It is not enough to assert that evolution by natural selection cannot achieve perfection, and thus aging is a reflection of the limits to its success in enhancing survival and reproduction. Certain types of organisms, such as some coelenterates and all prokaryotes, are not known to undergo any type of life-span limitation, as discussed in Chapter 5. Therefore, there is no absolute limit to natural selection on aging; organisms can evolve indefinitely long life spans.

It is the evolutionary theory of aging that resolves the apparent paradox of evolution producing so many organisms that undergo aging. In outline this theory proposes that, in the absence of fissile reproduction, the force of selection is greatly diminished at later ages. Before presenting the evolutionary theory of aging in detail, a few general comments might be useful by way of explaining how the organization of the chapters reflects the different levels of theory and experiment in this area. Some orientation for those who are not evolutionary biologists might also be helpful.

Evolutionary theories are quite different from those in other parts of biology. Indeed, much of the thinking of evolutionary biology has affinities with that of physics. From a few, seemingly inconsequential, axioms, both mathematical physicists and mathematical population geneticists can spin extensive webs of mathematical theory that seem to be wholly devoid of empirical significance. The evolutionary theory of aging is a theory of this kind; it is hypothetico-deductive in character, not inductive. In this chapter, an attempt will be made to present the main

3

features of the deduction of the theory from its simple axioms, within a framework provided by the history of the development of this theory. No attempt will be made to "derive" this theory from experimental findings.

But this lack of induction in theory formulation does not preclude contact with empirical findings. Such abstract, mathematical theories can, in principle, be tested with far greater stringency than the inductive theories of much experimental biology. This is possible because experimental tests of the direct corollaries of formal scientific theories put such theories at risk of wholesale falsification (Popper, 1959). Regrettably, this is true in physics much more often than in evolutionary biology, for reasons that are probably due to the greater potential for theory defense (Lakatos, 1970) in evolutionary biology. In the case of the evolutionary theory of aging, fortunately, it is in fact possible to develop experiments that subject the theory to critical test. Such experimental tests are discussed in Chapter 3. Even more unusual is the fact that there are comparative corollaries of the theory that provide equally good, if not better, opportunities to test the theory, as discussed in Chapter 5.

One aspect of the study of the evolution of aging that may be confusing is that a variety of particular population genetic mechanisms may underlie the same general evolutionary outcome of aging. Here the general evolutionary theory of aging is discussed separately from the particular population genetic mechanisms that might underlie the evolution of aging, which are discussed in Chapter 4. Experimental tests of the population genetic mechanisms are also reviewed in Chapter 4. In Chapter 5 comparative tests at both levels of the theoretical hierarchy are discussed, although an attempt is made to keep their consequences distinct. It is hoped that this somewhat elaborate structure will help the reader understand the distinctions between the different levels of theory and the distinctions between the different kinds of evidence.

## Early Development of the Evolutionary Theory of Aging

### Wallace

The earliest Darwinian explanation of aging known is one put forward by Alfred Russel Wallace, one of Darwin's contemporaries and a co-discoverer of natural selection, in a brief note written between 1865 and 1870, but published only in 1889, as a footnote to the 1889 English translation of Weismann's 1881 essay, "The Duration of Life."

> . . . when one or more individuals have provided a sufficient number of successors they themselves, as consumers of nourishment in a constantly increasing degree, are an injury to those successors. Natural selection therefore weeds them out, and in many cases favours such races as die almost immediately after they have left successors. (quoted in Weismann, 1889, p. 23)

This note antedates theoretical population genetics, which originated in the period 1915–30 (Provine, 1971), and thus Wallace's delineation of the selection

## *Weismann*

ugust Weismann, the great German theorist of nineteenth-century biology, pres-
nts a much more difficult case (Kirkwood and Cremer, 1982). Weismann's (1889)
The Duration of Life" was his first analysis of the evolution of aging. An impor-
nt starting point for Weismann was the rejection of the view that biological
ngevity is determined by the body's physicochemical attributes in a simply me-
hanical fashion: "Physiological considerations alone cannot determine the duration
f life." Instead, "duration of life is really dependent upon adaptation to external
onditions, that is length, whether longer or shorter, is governed by the needs of the
pecies" (Weismann, 1889, p. 9). This starting point of Weismann's divorced the
volutionary approach to aging from the physiological approach, the latter becom-
ng modern gerontology, at the very inception of evolutionary work on the problem.
   The evolutionary mechanism for aging that Weismann first proposed was group
election:

> . . . in regulating duration of life, the advantage to the species, and not to the
> individual, is alone of any importance. This must be obvious to any one who has
> once thoroughly thought out the process of natural selection. It is of no importance
> to the species whether the individual lives longer or shorter, but it is of importance
> that the individual should be enabled to do its work towards the maintenance of the
> species. (Weismann, 1889, p. 10)

n subsequent passages of this essay, Weismann discusses the natural history of
birds, mammals, and insects in a way that is partly founded on a perception of
species welfare as a major focus of selection.
   Weismann did not consider the older organism positively harmful, however. His
view was rather that immortality would be simply neutral: "the unlimited existence
of individuals would be a luxury without any corresponding advantage" (Weismann, 1889, p. 24). In later essays, Weismann expanded on this idea, using a
parallel with the loss of vision of cave animals, particularly propelled by the inferences he drew from his theory of the separation of the soma from the germ line:
"The perishable and vulnerable nature of the *soma* was the reason why nature made
no effort to endow this part of the individual with a life of unlimited length" (1889,
p. 154). Weismann referred to this as the principle of panmixia, which is effectively
that of the evolutionary deterioration of a neutral character (Kirkwood and Cremer,
1982), most explicitly connecting it with his theory of aging in German publications
that have not been translated into English. At this later stage, Weismann dropped his
group-selectionist explanation of aging altogether (Kirkwood and Cremer, 1982).
Indeed, he did not reiterate it later than 1883, in German, while he also cryptically
refers to earlier errors in the English editions of his essays (1889–92). Even in the
1883 German essay, which briefly refers to the possible "injuriousness" of the old,
Weismann discusses positive selection for prolonged life:

> I would emphasize the fact that a lengthening of life is connected with an increase
> in the duration of reproduction, while on the other hand there is no reason to expect

mechanism is unclear. In the past Wallace's theory has been interpre
group selection (e.g., Wilson, 1974; Rose, 1983). The term *group se*
to selection acting at the level of populations or species, in which the p
wholesale extinction of populations provides the differential "reproc
drives the process of selection. In evolutionary theories group selectior
distinguished only when its action is thought to be contrary to the ac
vidual selection, the classical form of selection (vide Williams, 1966
sage quoted above resembles a group-selection hypothesis, with the old
disposing of themselves to make way for the young, in order that the spe
more successful.

However, a case can be made that this is not what Wallace was sug;
full argument that Wallace presents begins on a very abstract level, by hy
the existence of an organism that does not reproduce, but could live fore'
points out that the accidental death of this organism would extinguish
Hence, natural selection would favor reproduction. But immortal reprod
nisms would lead to a Malthusian crisis of food depletion, Wallace supp
argument evidently ignores the possibility of predator-limited populatic
The crucial passage is then as follows:

> The deficiency of nourishment would lead to parts of the organism no
> renewed; they would become fixed, and liable to more or less slow decomp
> as dead parts within a living body. The smaller organism would have a
> chance of finding food, the larger ones less chance. That one which gave off
> small portions to form each a new organism would have a better chance of l
> descendants like itself than one which divided equally or gave off a large
> itself. Hence it would happen that those which gave off very small portions
> probably soon after cease to maintain their own existence while they would l
> numerous offspring. (quoted in Weismann, 1889, p. 23)

There is some fanciful biology here, but there is also the kernel of an impo:
immortality sacrificed for increased reproduction at the level of the ir
However confused, this is not a group-selection hypothesis. The phrase '
those successors," in the first quotation, follows the second quotation in
original note. The possibility is that he meant *injury* in a generalized sen:
thing that "causes a partial or entire loss of something of value" (*Webster's
ary of Synonyms*, 1951, p. 457), rather than an injury in the specifically
sense. Certainly the former was a typical Victorian usage. Thus this "injur
refer simply to a reduction in an individual's total production of successor
accords better with the gravamen of the second quotation. On this interp
Wallace's theory was not one of group selection, at any point.

It should be understood that Wallace could not have had a modern under:
of the importance of distinguishing between group and individual selecti
therefore his thinking was necessarily confused. However, while it is tem
condemn Victorian Darwinian usage of terms like *survival of the species* or
*tage to the race*, as group selectionist, as would be appropriate today, this is l
legitimate approach to the founders of Darwinism.

life to be prolonged beyond the reproductive period; so that the end of this period is usually more or less coincident with death. (Weismann, 1889, p. 155)

Weismann goes on to suggest:

> . . . it is easy to imagine the operation of natural selection in producing such alterations in the duration of life, and indeed we might accurately calculate the amount of increase which would be produced in any given case if the necessary data were available . . [i.e.] the statistics of destruction, that is, the probabilities in favour of the accidental death of a single individual at any given time. (Weismann, 1889, p. 156)

Here Weismann seems to be intuiting the idea of a mathematical analysis of the force of natural selection with respect to age. This approach was in fact taken by W. D. Hamilton in 1966, as will be discussed, and lies at the heart of present evolutionary analysis of aging.

A third element in Weismann's thinking was that somatic mortality might give enhanced individual fitness. The source of enhanced benefits Weismann left open:

> Perhaps it was in a better performance of their special physiological tasks, perhaps in additional material and energy available for the reproductive cells as a result of this renunciation of the somatic cells; or perhaps such additional power conferred upon the whole organism a greater power of resistance in the struggle for existence . . . (Weismann, 1889, p. 141)

Thus, like Wallace, Weismann effectively suggested that potential somatic immortality was sacrificed for the sake of enhanced reproductive output and/or enhanced realized survival rates. This idea too would be echoed many decades later by Medawar (1946, 1952) and, with greater emphasis, by Williams (1957), as will be detailed in Chapter 4.

While Weismann compiled some comparative data concerning longevity and reproduction, as has been common in works on aging since Aristotle, he apparently did not test his evolutionary theories of aging experimentally.

## Fisher and Haldane

To perform the kind of analysis that Weismann intuited, the mathematical apparatus of population genetics is necessary. Unfortunately for Weismann, this apparatus was not available during his lifetime. Population genetics was born just about the time Weismann died, in 1914 (Provine, 1971). The first allusions to the evolution of aging within population genetics came from R. A. Fisher, one of the three co-founders of population genetics. In his 1930 work, *The Genetical Theory of Natural Selection*, Fisher took organismal fitness to be given by the Malthusian parameter, which is in turn the implicit solution for $r$ in the following equation:

$$\int_0^\infty e^{-rx} l(x)m(x) \, dx = 1, \tag{1.1}$$

where $e$ is the natural exponential; $l(x)$ is the "survivorship," the probability of survival from birth to age $x$; and $m(x)$ is the fecundity per individual of age $x$. These variables require some introduction for those with little background in population biology. The survivorship function $l(x)$ is the most difficult to absorb intuitively. Its value ranges from 1.0 at birth at age 0 to 0.0 at the age beyond which no individuals survive, say $d$. Between 0 and $d$, $l(x)$ is always declining, never rising. This pattern occurs because death is irreversible. To be alive at age $y$, one has to be alive for all ages from 0 to $y$. The fecundity variable $m(x)$ is more natural. It has only positive values, including zero. In almost all organisms, $m(0) = 0$ and $m(d) = 0$, with $m(x) > 0$ for some intermediate values of $x$. From these basic features of the demography of populations, the crucial evolutionary determinants of aging follow.

The other feature of Eq. (1.1) that needs to be explained is the Malthusian parameter $r$. It should be clearly understood that $r$ is the *solution* to the equation. We need to be given the $l(x)$ and $m(x)$ functions as data; $r$ is the unknown that we obtain from the equation. What interpretation can we place on this solution? In a homogeneous population with a specified set of $l(x)$ and $m(x)$ values, the Malthusian parameter gives the rate of population growth after enough time has elapsed. Equation (1.1) effectively states this. Mathematically, it asks what "pressure" reducing population size would have to be used to eliminate net population growth due to the expected reproductive output of each newborn individual. That is why the term $e^{-rx}$ appears in the equation. It is a declining exponential that "pushes" downward more with age as $r$ increases in value. Once $r$ has been found, the ultimate population growth equation is given by

$$n(t) = n(0)e^{rt}, \tag{1.2}$$

where $n(t)$ gives the total population size at time $t$ and $n(0)$ gives the population size after enough time has elapsed.

One point may need clarification: the "after enough time" requirement for the population to grow at the rate given by the Malthusian parameter. The time required is the time needed to achieve the stable age distribution associated with the particular $l(x)$ and $m(x)$ functions. If we artificially create a population solely of individuals who have just reached reproductive maturity, the initial population growth rate will be very large. After a while, however, there will be older, often less fecund, individuals, as well as many prereproductive juveniles. The result of this demographic shift will be a lower reproductive rate, per capita, relative to that of the hypothesized initial population. This shifting in age structure will eventually decrease in amplitude. After some time has passed, the population will normally approach a stable composition of age classes, at which point the population growth rate will be given by Eq. (1.2), with $r$ obtainable from Eq. (1.1) (Charlesworth, 1980, Chapter 1). Before this stable age distribution is achieved, the population growth rate may be quite different from that assumed in Eq. (1.2).

Figure 1.1 illustrates two different types of age distribution, indicating the different population growth patterns that are to be expected with each one.

Fisher's use of the Malthusian parameter as the determinant of fitness probably reflected the work of J. B. S. Haldane (1927) and H. T. J. Norton (1928), two other

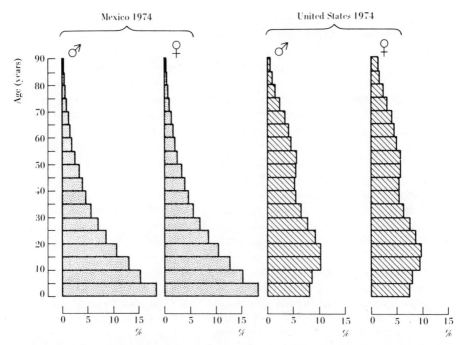

FIGURE 1.1. Age distributions for two different human populations. The age distribution for Mexico is that of a rapidly growing population, with many young individuals. The age distribution for the United States is more uniform over ages, with more older people, and it gives rise to slower population growth. Data from United Nations, Dept. of International Economic and Social Affairs, *Demographic Yearbook 1974*.

important British population geneticists, who had shown that the Malthusian parameter was tantamount to fitness in the one-locus two-allele model when $l(x)$ and $m(x)$ are time-independent functions of genotype. (As was his habit, Fisher did not cite their work in his book.) Indeed, this problem of the appropriate measure of fitness in populations with age structure lies at the core of the evolutionary theory of aging. It will be examined again later in this chapter.

Fisher's discussion of the evolution of aging grew out of an equation related to Eq. (1.1). What Fisher was interested in was a way of calculating the "value" that individuals of different ages have where the growth of the population as a whole is concerned. The equation of interest defines a variable $v(x)$ that Fisher (1958, p. 27) called "reproductive value," given by

$$v(x) = \int_x^\infty e^{-rt}\, l(t)m(t)\, dt\; e^{rx}/l(x). \tag{1.3}$$

The integral term gives the remaining reproductive output of individuals alive at age $x$, in proportion to the growth of the population as a whole, as reflected in the $e^{-rt}$ term. If the population is growing rapidly, then reproduction at late ages makes a relatively small contribution to an individual's reproductive value, and conversely if the population is declining rapidly. The term outside the integral can be understood by rearranging it as follows:

$$e^{rx}/l(x) = [e^{-rx}l(x)]^{-1},$$

which is the inverse of the proportion of the population surviving to age $x$. Thus $v(x)$ gives the expected future reproductive contribution of individuals of age $x$, relative to the total reproductive output. Whatever the values of $r$, $l(x)$, or $m(x)$, $v(0) = 1$, so that $v(x)$ is effectively scaled relative to the value of newborns. Reproductive value is thus a kind of economic concept that includes both depreciation, in the $e^{-rx}$ term, and accumulation of future value, given by the entire integral term, weighted by representation in the population, the nonintegral term.

Figure 1.2 shows a graph of the reproductive value of Australian women given by Fisher (1958, p. 28). Evidently, after age 19 their reproductive value declines steeply. Fisher (1958, p. 29) then commented:

> It is probably not without significance in this connexion that the death rate in Man takes a course generally inverse to the curve of reproductive value. The minimum of the death rate curve is at twelve, certainly not far from the primitive maximum of the reproductive value; it rises more steeply for infants, and less steeply for the elderly than the curve of reproductive value falls, points which qualitatively we should anticipate, if the incidence of natural death had been to a large extent moulded by the effects of differential survival.

In his typically elliptical fashion, Fisher seems to be saying that aging and infant mortality are molded by natural selection according to the magnitude of the reproductive value. The intuitive justification for this is that one might expect natural selection to use some "economic" system of accounting for the demographic value of different individuals in the population, such as that embodied by the age-specific

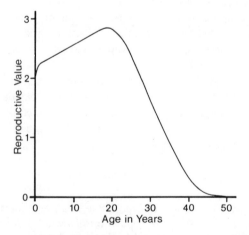

FIGURE 1.2. Fisher's reproductive value, calculated for Australian women from demographic data obtained in 1911. (From Fisher, 1958, p. 28.)

reproductive values. This is the earliest unambiguous analysis of the evolution of aging from the standpoint of natural selection acting on the individual.

In 1941 J. B. S. Haldane discussed the case of Huntington's chorea, the catastrophic disease of neural degeneration that is caused by a dominant allele with high penetrance. Haldane (1941, pp. 192–94) pointed out that the average age of onset of Huntington's chorea is 35.5 years, and thus the "present age of onset of that disease may merely mean that primitive men and women seldom lived much beyond forty, so postponement of onset beyond this age had no selective advantage." Here we have Weismann's idea of the evolutionary irrelevance of the old recast in population genetic terms.

## *Medawar*

Neither Fisher nor Haldane dealt directly and at length with the problem of aging in their extant publications. It was Sir Peter Medawar (1946, 1952) who directed a concerted attack on the problem, more than 60 years after Weismann's first paper. Medawar developed his argument verbally and graphically, using hypothetical populations with a constant likelihood of survival per unit time. Drawing on Fisher and Haldane, Medawar said that, "What is important from our point of view is that the contribution which each age-class makes to the ancestry of the future decreases with age" (1946). Thus

> . . . the force of natural selection weakens with increasing age—even in a theoretically immortal population, provided only that it is exposed to real hazards of mortality. If a genetical disaster . . . happens late enough in individual life, its consequences may be completely unimportant. Even in such a crude and unqualified form, this dispensation may have a real bearing on the origin of innate deterioration with increasing age. (Medawar, 1952)

From this basic deduction, Medawar went on to develop further hypotheses concerning the population genetic mechanisms of aging, which will be taken up in Chapter 4. However, the foregoing constitutes the kernel of his thought, particularly the idea of the force of natural selection declining with age. While elements of this idea are present in the writings of Weismann, Fisher, and Haldane, Medawar (1946, 1952) was the first to develop this insight at any length.

In addition, it is clear that Medawar clearly saw the implications of his analysis for our basic understanding of aging. For him, the declining force of natural selection was a feature of evolution of the most profound consequences for our understanding of aging. Of course, underscoring this opinion will be a central concern throughout this book.

## Theoretical Population Genetics of Aging

Until 1966 evolutionary analysis of aging was largely verbal, with only piecemeal algebraic and graphical formalization. From 1966 to 1980, W. D. Hamilton and

Brian Charlesworth made the evolutionary theory of aging mathematically explicit from beginning to end.

## Hamilton

W. D. Hamilton (1966), otherwise known as one of the intellectual leaders of sociobiology and cognate disciplines, began the research program. He assumed, following Fisher, that fitness was given by the Malthusian parameter of a genotype, designated by $r$ in Eqs. (1.1)–(1.3). (The importance of this assumption will be discussed further in the section on Charlesworth's work.) In his model, he also took

$$l(x) = P(0)P(1)P(2) \cdots P(x-1), \tag{1.4}$$

the $P(t)$ values giving the proportion of organisms who have already reached age $t$ that then achieve age $t+1$. In the case of man, an example of such a $P$ value would be $P(50 \text{ years})$, which would give the likelihood of survival of a 50 year old to age 51. The population is thereby divided into discrete age classes, so Eq. (1.1) becomes

$$\sum_{x=1}^{\infty} e^{-rx} l(x)m(x) = 1, \tag{1.5}$$

$m(x)$ once again representing age-specific fecundity, with the summation proceeding to infinity. [With infinitesimally small age-class durations, Eq. (1.5) is equivalent to Eq. (1.1).] The critical results that Hamilton derived concern the dependence of the Malthusian parameter $r$ on age-specific changes in survival probability $P(x)$ and fecundity $m(x)$.

What Hamilton was interested in was the effect on fitness of perturbations to both age-specific survival probabilities, the $P(x)$ values, and age-specific fecundities, the $m(x)$ values. Since the age-specific $P(x)$ values act multiplicatively to determine $l(x)$, the equation for the effect of survival probability changes is simplest when $\ln P(x)$ is used in place of $P(x)$. This change of scale gives the effect of a proportionately uniform perturbation to age-specific survival probabilities. In systems with many variables, the effect of a perturbation of one of these variables on another is evaluated mathematically using partial derivatives. Thus in order to evaluate the effect on fitness $r$ of a change in another demographic variable, we take the partial derivative of $r$ with respect to that demographic variable. In cases in which we are considering age-specific perturbations, we want to obtain a partial derivative that has the age of perturbation incorporated explicitly in the result. Here, if $a$ is the age at which the perturbation to $P(x)$ takes place,

$$\frac{\partial r}{\partial \ln P(a)} = \frac{\displaystyle\sum_{x=a+1}^{\infty} e^{-rx} l(x)m(x)}{\displaystyle\sum_{x=1}^{\infty} xe^{-rx} l(x)m(x)} \tag{1.6}$$

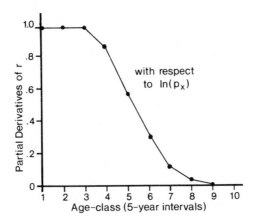

FIGURE 1.3. Age-specific partial derivatives of $r$ with respect to $\ln p_x$ for demographic data drawn from the United States human population of the 1939–41 census. (From Charlesworth and Williamson, 1975.)

[Equation (1.6) is equivalent to Hamilton's (1966) Eq. (8).] The age of perturbation $a$ appears as the index at which the sum in the numerator of the right-hand side begins. Thus, once reproduction has started, so that the $m(x)$ values are greater than zero, the magnitude of this sum *decreases* with age, because fewer positive terms are included. Once $a$ reaches the last age at which $m(x)$ is greater than zero, the end of reproduction, Eq. (1.6) becomes zero, remaining at that value for all subsequent ages. Assuming that $r$ constitutes fitness, this shows that the force of natural selection acting on survival is indeed attenuated with age, reaching zero at the end of reproduction, as Medawar (1946, 1952) proposed. Figure 1.3 illustrates the fall in the intensity of natural selection on survival predicted by Eq. (1.6).

Hamilton (1966) also gave the parallel result for age-specific fecundity effects:

$$\frac{\partial r}{\partial m(a)} = e^{-ra}\, l(a)/ \sum_{x=1} xe^{-rx}\, l(x)m(x) \tag{1.7}$$

equivalent to Hamilton's Eq. (25). The survivorship function $l(x)$ decreases with $x$, since an organism has a decreasing likelihood of being alive as time passes. Hence, for positive, zero, or small negative values of $r$, Eq. (1.7) should decrease in size as $a$ increases. Figure 1.4 shows the predicted fall with age in the intensity of natural selection acting on fecundity. An interesting difference between this result and Eq. (1.6) is that this equation can decrease before the onset of reproduction, whereas Eq. (1.6) only decreases with the onset of reproduction. However, since Eq. (1.7) predicts the intensity of natural selection on age-specific reproduction, if there is no reproduction, then there will be no observable aging.

Another difference arising from Eq. (1.7) is that it allows the numerical possibility of natural selection *rising* in intensity under certain unusual conditions. If $r$ is negative, we have

$$e^{-ra} = e^{ka},$$

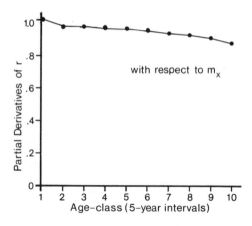

FIGURE 1.4. Age-specific partial derivatives of $r$ with respect to $m_x$ for demographic data drawn from the United States human population of the 1939–41 census. (From Charlesworth and Williamson, 1975.)

where $k$ is greater than zero, making this term an *increasing* function of $a$. If it increases rapidly enough, it may counterbalance the decrease with age of $l(a)$, making the product $e^{-ra} l(a)$ increase with age. Thus, in a population sharply declining towards extinction, selection on fecundity may *increase* in intensity with age. However, since such populations will normally be at low densities or extinct, most observed populations should have $\partial r/\partial m(a)$ decreasing with age. In addition, $l(x) = 0$ for all $x \geq d$, $d$ being the greatest age to which individuals survive, so that Eq. (1.7) must converge on 0 as $x$ approaches $d$. Thus selection on fecundity will normally be attenuated with age in a fashion broadly similar to selection on survival, when fitness is determined by the Malthusian parameter.

Hamilton (1966) demonstrated at some length the divergence of the implications of his Eqs. (1.6) and (1.7) from those of Fisher's reproductive value, where the force of natural selection is concerned. In fact, Hamilton showed that it is possible to have the force of natural selection, as given by Eq. (1.6), decreasing exponentially while reproductive value increases exponentially. This can occur, for example, when age-specific fecundity increases exponentially from the onset of reproduction. If reproductive value is in fact the correct measure of the force of natural selection, such organisms should not undergo age-related deterioration, while Hamilton's equations for the force of natural selection suggest that they would. Organisms like trees may come close to such exponentially increasing fertility with age, yet they age in cases without vegetative reproduction, as discussed in Chapter 5. This suggests that Hamilton's equations give the correct force of natural selection. Therefore, Fisher's analysis must be incorrect, at least as a direct explanation of the evolution of aging. In any case, as will be shown below, direct derivation of the force of natural selection yields Hamilton's results.

A further disparity between Hamilton's equations and Fisher's reproductive value arises for selection on survival probability among juveniles. Hamilton's Eq. (1.6) suggests that selection on juvenile survival should be uniform, in the absence of parental care, while Fisher's reproductive value suggests that, in the absence of parental care, it should become stronger closer to the onset of reproduction. Here the empirical evidence is mixed, in that juvenile mortality is sometimes greater closer to the onset of reproduction. However, this may be explicable in terms of the phenotype of the adult, particularly in cases with parental care, like the human population, or in terms of a period of increased risk during development, a problem discussed in Chapter 2.

## Charlesworth

Brian Charlesworth is the population genetics theorist who has done most to provide a mathematically explicit analysis of the evolution of aging, this having been his main area of research during the 1970s. Charlesworth essentially followed the lines of analysis started by Haldane (1927) and Norton (1928), developing a population-genetic theory for age-structured populations, with results concerning the effects of selection, attainment of Hardy–Weinberg equilibrium, and so on. Here discussion is confined to the relevance of Charlesworth's work for the basic evolutionary theory of aging.

In this respect, Charlesworth addressed the critical question of the extent to which the Malthusian parameter of a genotype is in fact tantamount to its fitness (Charlesworth, 1970, 1974, 1976, 1980). For single-locus systems, independent of the number of alleles, the gene frequency dynamics with age structure are similar to those with discrete generations, the Malthusian parameter constituting fitness, providing selection is weak (Charlesworth, 1974; 1976; 1980, pp, 154–63). Near stable equilibria with respect to the action of selection, the continuous-time, two-allele, single-locus age-structured model is evolutionarily equivalent to the discrete generation model (Norton, 1928), with the Malthusian parameter approximating fitness. In age-structured models with two loci and weak selection, tight or loose linkage makes the dynamics of selection approximate discrete-generation models, with the Malthusian parameter playing the role of fitness (Charlesworth, 1974; 1976; 1980, pp. 163–65). Other than the continuous-time age-structured diallelic one-locus model analyzed by Norton (1928), all these models have dynamics that are not well specified by the Malthusian parameter when selection is intense (Charlesworth, 1974, 1976, 1980). Finally, it should be said that nonrandom mating, density dependence, and differences in selection on the sexes can all engender major deviations from the evolutionary dynamics inferred from the Malthusian parameter (Charlesworth, 1980).

The question now becomes what does this theoretical work tell us about the material validity of Hamilton's (1966) assumption that the Malthusian parameter of a genotype is the determinant of its evolutionary success? One answer that can be given to this question is that Hamilton's assumption is incorrect, in a mathematically strict sense. The exceptions to it are numerous and widespread, even in fairly simple mathematical models. From the inception of work on this problem (e.g., Charlesworth, 1970), it has been shown that the Malthusian parameter is not an adequate guide to the evolutionary dynamics in a variety of circumstances. Present-day work on age-structured populations has generalized Hamilton's work on

the strength of natural selection with respect to age under conditions in which the
Malthusian parameter is not fitness; Hamilton's (1966) original results re-emerge as
special cases in this analysis (Abugov, 1986).

However, this misses the essence of the problem. Hamilton's concern was
selection on age-specific life-history characters, particularly aging, as opposed to
selection on fitness without age specificity. In light of subsequent research, Hamilton's (1966) assumption that the Malthusian parameter of a genotype would be the
determinant of its evolutionary fate can be seen as a reasonable working assumption
for the evolution of most populations. It can be expected to fail in many cases,
where exact numerical prediction of evolutionary trajectories is concerned. However, we will not usually know exact values for genotypic Malthusian parameters, to
say nothing of the fact that we usually do not know the structure of the relevant
genetic system itself. Insofar as we can form any simple conclusion about the
evolution of age-specific fitness components, the working assumption that their
effects on the Malthusian parameter determine their evolutionary destiny is a reasonable one, even though this is likely to be quantitatively incorrect in many instances.


## Conclusion

Since Weismann gave up his early invocation of group selection, all evolutionary
theorists who have published on the causes of aging have agreed that the ultimate
cause is the declining force of natural selection with age. This is the essential
evolutionary theory of aging. From the 1880s to the 1980s, this idea has been
formulated in a progressively more explicit and formal fashion, culminating in the
mathematical treatment of Charlesworth (1980). Given age-structured populations
and genetic variation in life histories, aging is a straightforward corollary of population genetics theory.

This does not show that the evolutionary theory of aging is correct. That must be
decided empirically. But the theory itself is only a natural development of some of
the most basic elements of population genetics. To the extent to which population
genetics is accepted as the formal basis for evolutionary theory, then evolutionary
theories of aging must be formulated in population-genetic terms. Conversely, one
of the more striking results of theoretical population genetics is that the force of
natural selection should normally decline with age, which then provides an obvious
explanation for aging. This joint necessity and sufficiency of population-genetic
theory in explaining the evolution of aging suggests that this result has a preeminent
claim to be considered in any analysis of the evolution of aging.

Finally, the fact that evolutionary theory can explain the existence of aging in a
strikingly *a priori* fashion, unlike any other theory of aging, suggests that it war-
rants serious examination as a theoretical foundation for the study of aging. However, the first step in such an examination should be rigorous empirical tests of the
validity of this theory. The intellectual appeal of a scientific theory is never a
sufficient guide to its truth. After treating the foundations for experimental research
on aging in Chapter 2, the discussion will proceed to consider experimental tests of
the evolutionary theory in Chapter 3.

# 2

# Observation of Aging

One way to discuss a phenomenon is to begin with a definition of it, and then proceed to explain theoretically how the phenomenon has arisen. The problem with this manner of proceeding is that definitions can beg questions and so preclude certain types of answers. For this reason the present book began with theory, glossing over the problem of a definition by using a rough "common-sense" definition of aging. However, it is not always going to be the case that common-sense ideas of aging will suffice for an empirical evaluation of the evolutionary theory of aging or its implications. Therefore, it is now necessary to consider the problem of defining the phenomenon of aging in such a way that sources of ambiguity are reduced in importance.

Once that task has been discharged, the chapter moves on to consider some of the concrete problems involved in measuring aging. The discussion should reveal the extent to which the interpretation of observations as artifactual depends on theoretical assumptions. A related concern is the range of factors that modulate aging, since a lack of understanding of such factors will render the interpretation of many empirical findings moot.

It will not be possible to provide any simple recipes for the reliable observation of aging. The hope must be that enough cautionary material will at least improve the prospects for obtaining results useful in the experimental evaluation of alternative theories. Sir Karl Popper, the great Austrian philosopher of science, has a wonderful metaphor for this problem:

> Science does not rest upon solid bedrock. The bold structure of its theories rises, as it were, above a swamp. It is like a building erected on piles. The piles are driven down from above into the swamp, but not down to any natural or "given" base; and if we stop driving the piles deeper, it is not because we have reached firm ground. We simply stop when we are satisfied that the piles are firm enough to carry the structure, at least for the time being. (Popper, 1959, p. 111)

## Definition of Aging

All exercises of definition in science are unsatisfying to some extent. Part of the problem is that the entities and processes of scientific theories are usually highly

17

abstract. This makes it hard to use everyday words for the phenomena under discussion. An example from evolutionary biology is the term *fitness,* a word that has caused no end of misunderstanding. A major part of this problem is that such terms are often taken from conventional vocabulary and then used in a technical sense, sometimes with an unconscious accretion of specific interpretations.

Terms also acquire implicit theoretical content. For example, the very term *evolution* in biology is frequently used in a way that is restricted to a Darwinian understanding of the term, in spite of alternative uses of it. Thus professional biologists almost always mean Darwin's theory of evolution by natural selection, usually taking into account the contributions of population genetics and the "modern synthesis" from the period 1918–59 (Mayr, 1982), when they use the term *evolution.* But the term could equally well refer to a completely different idea of progressive change in living things, even a Bergsonian vitalism. However, as it would become impossible to preclude all the erroneous interpretations of a particular usage in every case, in practice such potential ambiguities are neglected.

An even greater pitfall is essentialist disputes about definitions of terms. Such disputes revolve around the "true" definition of a term, as if there is some unique metaphysically valid usage (cf. Popper, 1959; Mayr, 1982). Consider a particular definition of the term *species,* the one from population genetics based on reproductive isolation (e.g., Dobzhansky, 1937). This definition is also sometimes called the "biological species concept," a considerable act of arrogation. This definition supposes that species are delimited by barriers to genetic exchange, such as the inability to hybridize or the failure of hybrid zygotes to develop (Dobzhansky, 1937; Futuyma, 1986). A taxonomist could ask if this is in fact the "true" definition of species, especially given its origins in the usages of Aristotle and Linnaeus, who did not generally delimit species on the basis of reproductive isolation. There are no neat and final solutions to problems of this kind.

Most terms in biology are partly matters of arbitrary convention and partly appeals to intuition. As such, like most words, they are somewhat ambiguous and so sometimes misleading. Perhaps the best that can be done is to offer an explicit definition, while acknowledging its difficulties.

## Aging and Senescence

The words *aging* and *senescence* are full of meaning in everyday language, in which they have no clear distinction. Aging has the broader range of associations, in that it includes the notion of maturation or development, in worked metals as well as organisms. Butter and cars are both commonly said to age. Moreover, the term *aging* is not irretrievably linked to the notion of deterioration. As wine and liquor age, they are thought to get better. In contrast, senescence has a clear association with deterioration as time passes, perhaps because the Latin root of *senex* or *senis,* meaning simply old, is shared with the emotionally charged word *senile,* which refers to the decay and especially the supposed imbecility of old age. Senile has no association with an improved maturation, and senescence similarly rarely does. It would be convenient to be restrictive about senescence, using it alone to refer to processes and aspects of organismal deterioration with age, as opposed to a purely chronological aging, with no deteriorative connotation associated with aging. However, this would be at variance with the overwhelming precedent of American biological research, in which the term *senescence* is rarely used compared with the term *aging,* and both have an association with deterioration.

A further problem with the scientific usage of the term *senescence* is that it is used to refer to the "senescence" that individual flowers and leaves are said to undergo by botanists (vide Thimann, 1980). The cases referred to are usually those of autumnal defoliation in deciduous trees, loss of flowers at the end of flowering seasons, or turnover of new leaves for old in the course of plant growth and maintenance. This can be a profound source of confusion in the context of biological research, as opposed to geriatrics and its cognate fields.

In view of present conventions and the potential confusion involving plant senescence, the term *aging* will normally be used here in preference to *senescence,* the somewhat ambiguous common usage of aging notwithstanding. The main exceptions will be the use of the verb *senesce* in place of *age,* since in some contexts the latter can be a source of grammatical confusion. Nonetheless, in quotations and other contexts, unless otherwise indicated, the term *senescence* can be taken as equivalent to *aging.*

## Definitions of Aging in Gerontology

Gerontologists generally define aging in terms of increases in the likelihood of death. For example, over three editions, Comfort's *The Biology of Senescence* (1956, p. 17; 1964, p. 22; 1979, pp. 21–22) defines aging "as a progressive increase throughout life, or after a given stadium, in the likelihood that a given individual will die, during the next succeeding unit of time, from randomly distributed causes . . . ." Whatever the specific variant of phrasing, the idea is generally that of an increase in the likelihood of death with age or its converse, a decrease in the likelihood of survival with age. All such definitions thus focus upon death and the deterioration that leads to it.

What is left out of this definition is any explicit consideration of reproduction. Medawar has repeatedly pointed out that the decline and loss of reproductive capacity with age, as illustrated by mammalian menopause, is almost as widespread a phenomenon as a decline in the likelihood of survival (Medawar, 1952, 1955; Medawar and Medawar, 1983). Declining reproductive rates are often introduced casually into gerontological discussions of aging. But given the explicit definition in terms of mortality, this is incoherent, since reproduction is if anything antagonistic to survival in *Drosophila* (Maynard Smith, 1958; Partridge and Farquhar, 1981), salmon (Robertson, 1961), and soybean (Leopold, 1961). (This is discussed further in this chapter and in Chapters 4 and 6.)

## Definitions of Aging in Evolutionary Biology

Evolutionary biologists have followed the lead of Medawar, treating decreases in both age-specific survival rates and age-specific reproductive rates as aging (Hamilton, 1966; Charlesworth, 1980, Chapter 1). This is natural for evolutionary biologists, in that the organism is of importance insofar as it reproduces copies of its genes, by its own reproduction or the facilitation of the reproduction of individuals with which it shares genes by descent (Hamilton, 1964a,b). In other words, evolutionary definitions of aging cover age-dependent declines in components of fitness, and, as discussed in Chapter 1, this fitness is given by the Malthusian parameter in the best understood cases, while the fitness components are survival probabilities and age-specific fecundities, which quantitatively determine fitness.

The formal definition of aging to be used here is *a persistent decline in the age-specific fitness components of an organism due to internal physiological deterioration.* This last phrase bars fitness-component deterioration due to (1) fluctuations in reproductive opportunities, (2) deterioration in the quality of the organism's environment, and (3) phenotype-dependent, and thus possibly age-dependent, changes in externally imposed mortality, when the relevant phenotypic change is not due to endogenous physiological deterioration. Each of these three points requires some elaboration.

First, the exclusion of fluctuations in reproductive opportunities is important in the case of sexual organisms that are denied mating opportunities at some later point in life. Under such conditions, age-specific fecundity will decline for lack of fertilization. However, this does not mean the exclusion of an internal physiological decline in the capacity to obtain mating opportunities, which could be an important part of the senescent decline of males in species with polygyny.

Second, the problem of deterioration in the environment is primarily a problem for scientific observation when the deterioration is slow and persistent. Some sudden deterioration in the environment, such as that brought about by extreme weather in field populations, can cause increased death rates and reduced fertility but is normally not a difficulty for the observation of aging. An organism might also be subjected to a slow deterioration in its immediate environment, which has the same effect as a drastic environmental disruption, but is more recondite. Moreover, it is possible that a nesting animal such as a bird, a large plant such as a tree, or the like could itself cause localized cumulative deterioration in its environment, giving rise to ostensible aging. This is excluded as well.

Third, a developing organism may suffer an increased risk of death due to predation or disease at particular stages in the developmental process, possibly as well as diminished reproductive opportunities. When these risks arise from growth or some other nonsenescent change, these effects are excluded from the proposed definition of aging. Excluded, for example, are increases in predation that arise from the attainment of a predator's preferred size (Elner and Hughes, 1978), in which growth is the internal physiological process that has led to increased mortality. Another sort of mortality increase that would be excluded is that of periods of acute vulnerability during organismal development, such as those of exoskeleton shedding in arthropods, fledgling flight in birds, initial growth of seedlings, and the early juvenile period of many different types of organism. Finally, the progressive accumulation of parasites would be excluded from the aging process, providing there is no differential in resistance between young and old organisms.

# Measurement of Aging

## Field Studies

As defined here, aging is extremely difficult to observe in the natural habitats of most organisms. One of the few methods that might be used is systematic exclusion of all organisms known to have suffered any life-threatening or constraining injury or disease, leaving only those individuals in which deterioration could not be attributed to exogenous factors. Leaving aside the problems of continuous monitoring of all individuals, from birth to death, it is doubtful that many individuals would remain for study at the age at which laboratory populations exhibit aging. Most wild populations with iteroparous reproduction, in which the first breeding episode is *not* followed shortly by death, show little increase in the adult mortality rate with age. Indeed, it has been argued that vertebrate adult mortality rates in the wild often decrease on average (Comfort, 1979, pp. 142–43). On the other hand, some methods of extrapolating adult survivorship data that contrast nonsenescent with observed mortality patterns indicate significant increases in mortality rates in wild vertebrate populations (Neese, 1988). This result has been interpreted as evidence for material aging in the wild (Neese, 1988), particularly among large mammals. The available invertebrate data are too sketchy to provide much useful information. However, since wild iteroparous vertebrates generally are subject to lower mortality rates than invertebrates, it seems less likely that aging would be detectable in iteroparous invertebrate populations in the wild, though there are a few cases in which it appears to be detectable (e.g., Edmondson, 1944, 1945).

The great exception to the general rarity of aging in the wild is the dramatic deterioration exhibited by semelparous organisms after their single bout of reproduction. (*Semelparous* refers to organisms that reproduce only once during their lifetime, such as Pacific salmon, univoltine insects, and monocarpic plants.) Some do not like to refer to aging in semelparous organisms. Comfort (1979, p. 140) calls it "pseudosenescence." Kirkwood and Cremer (1982) suggest that in "these cases it is better to talk of programmed *death,* rather than aging." In the evolutionary definition adopted here, there is no fundamental distinction between the deterioration of semelparous organisms after reproduction and that called *aging* in iteroparous organisms that reproduce more than once per lifetime. Thus the most readily observed type of aging in the wild is that of semelparous organisms. Such aging is discussed further in Chapter 6.

## Laboratory Artifacts

Inasmuch as chemists rarely find it convenient to perform their experiments outdoors during thunderstorms, most biological experiments are also performed in laboratories, rather than in the field. The reasons for this are manifold. Critical environmental factors, such as ambient temperature, are readily controlled. With such control of the environment, it is possible to use delicate instruments that provide data of great precision. With organisms cultured in the laboratory, it is possible to pair experimental and control organisms when manipulative treatments are performed. Furthermore, it is often possible to repeat such experiments as often as desired under reproducible conditions. All told, the laboratory is a haven for most empirical scientists.

In evolutionary biology, unfortunately, the laboratory can also be a source of treacherous artifacts. One problem is that the laboratory environment can be a novel selective regime for populations newly sampled from the wild. With novel selective regimes, populations are not at evolutionary equilibrium. Their properties cannot be interpreted in terms of theoretical results applicable only to such equilibria, while most general theoretical results are confined to such cases. Therefore, under novel selective regimes, evolutionary biologists will not usually be able to analyze the population genetics of the characters of interest. Indeed, there are few characters for which these problems are greater than they are for fitness components. Since aging is a protracted decline in survival probability or reproductive output, it is essentially a composite fitness-component character. Thus we should expect aging to be particularly subject to problems of novel selection in the laboratory environment. The consequences of this problem will be discussed further in the following, particularly in Chapter 3.

However, this does not exhaust the list of potential artifacts. Since aging is a phenomenon of fitness-component deterioration, as defined here, the most important source of laboratory artifacts will be deficiencies in the laboratory environment. Disease and parasitism can often spread readily under laboratory conditions because of the opportunities for infection that the proximity of successive hosts affords. Inadequate nutrition may hasten death or impair reproduction, possibly in interaction with disease. Such inadequate nutrition can arise from insufficient provision of the organism's dietary requirements, overcrowding, or from the unpalatability of its food. On the other hand, overfeeding could give rise to obesity or chronic gastrointestinal tract infection. Animals housed together at high density may attack one another, causing stress, injury, or death. Poor mating conditions in sexual species could lead to an artifactual decline in reproductive output. Inadequate exercise due to cramped conditions could cause cumulative impairment of circulatory functions and wastage of muscle tissue. All such deficiencies in laboratory experiments could give rise to a pattern of "aging" that is not intrinsic to the population, in the sense that better laboratory conditions would abolish it.

Most gerontologists do not consider declining reproductive output as a primary senescent attribute, conforming to the medical focus on survival, making them often negligent about the reproductive state of their organisms. A common procedure in assays of survival patterns is to keep the sexes apart, preventing reproduction altogether. Deficient conditions for reproduction are perhaps the most important source of artifacts in research on aging, often in ways that are not obvious. If *Drosophila* females are kept virgin, they lay fewer eggs and live much longer (Maynard Smith, 1958). The mutant *grandchildless*, in which the daughters of homozygotes lack ovaries, similarly gives rise to increased longevity in such daughters (Maynard Smith, 1958). These effects are shown in Figure 2.1. On the other hand, if *Drosophila melanogaster* males are given abundant mating opportunities, they may die sooner than males with fewer mating opportunities (Partridge and Farquhar, 1981). But denying protozoa the opportunity to mate can lead to a

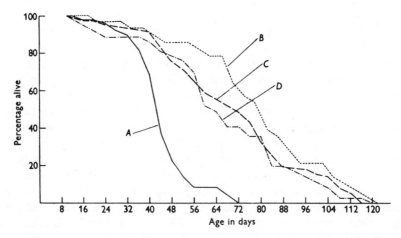

FIGURE 2.1. Effects of mating and reproduction on survival in *Drosophila subobscura*. A: Normal mated females. B: "Ovariless" females that lack ovaries and lay no eggs. C: Virgin females, which may lay some eggs, but fewer than normal. D: Mated females that have been sterilized by maintenance at high temperatures. The normal mated females lay most eggs and die sooner. (From Maynard Smith, 1958.)

decline in cell division rate and, ultimately, to cell death (Sonneborn, 1957, 1958; Bell, 1988). These examples all show that the laboratory context provided for reproduction can have substantial effects on aging. In addition, if a particular culture regime does not standardize the opportunities for reproduction, then it will be difficult to obtain consistent measurements of aging.

All the foregoing amounts to a case for the use of laboratory organisms whose culture requirements can be readily provided and reliably controlled. In particular, if experimenters are unable to maintain an organism in the laboratory for an indefinite number of generations, then there is little reason to place much confidence in their observations of aging. Any such decline in fitness components could reflect an environmentally imposed breakdown. In this regard, it is worth mentioning that Lansing's famous experiments on aging in rotifers, in which cultures reproduced from older females had accelerated "aging," used stocks that eventually died out (Lansing, 1947). Such experiments are irrelevant from the present standpoint. Indeed, it is an open question how many of the experiments measuring fitness components over "natural" lifetimes have been properly designed.

The history of biology leaves few grounds for "good-faith" confidence in freedom from artifacts when scientists do not have a well-defined theoretical basis for their empirical inferences. One poignant example of this is Charles Darwin's credulous reiteration of reported cases of the inheritance of acquired characters, which led him to his theory of pangenesis. The development of Mendelian genetics led to the spread of exacting standards in the experimental study of heredity, which in turn led to the demolition of Lamarckism, Darwin's pangenesis, and many other views (Mayr, 1982). Similarly, questions of artifact in experimental design arising from a lack of theoretical background will play a prominent role in this book.

## Demographic Measurement

The evolutionary definition of aging given in the preceding section incorporates the gerontological definition, in that age-specific survival probability is a fitness component. The empirical problem is that an individual organism's survival probability, as such, is impossible to measure directly. There is only one piece of evidence that is indisputably relevant to a possible decline in age-specific survival probabilities: the age at which an organism dies. The death event suggests that the probability of continued survival has become low, a patently indirect inference.

This problem is often finessed by proceeding smoothly to the age-specific mortality rates obtained from population life tables: "The probability that an individual organism, which has survived to time $x$, will die before time $x + 1$ depends on the *rate of mortality* ($q$) per 1,000, meaning the number, out of 1,000 individuals living at time $x$, who have died by time $x + 1$" (Comfort, 1979, p. 21). Implicit in this approach is the biological equivalence of all individuals used to calculate $q(x)$. Not only must all individuals be genetically identical with respect to their likelihood of death, they must also lack any developmental variation having effects on this likelihood. Empirical work that uses such measures as $q(x)$ as if they are equivalent to an individual organism's likelihood of death dismisses intraspecific variation from the outset of the research study, however inadvertently.

In principle, age-specific male and female fertilities, or the equivalent in hermaphroditic and asexual forms, are readily observable. In practice, they are extremely difficult to observe because of their intrinsic dependence on offspring viability and fertilization success. Female, or asexual, fertility is more straightforward to measure than male or hermaphroditic fertility, because parentage is rarely in doubt in females that set seed, lay eggs, or bear live offspring. Aquatic females that shed many eggs in an ejaculatory fashion, as do many fish, approximate the male in difficulty. The greatest problem in the measurement of asexual or female fertility arises when the offspring depend on the mother to survive or develop. This makes offspring viability a function of maternal phenotype, and thus genotype. The dependence of juvenile viability on maternal genotype could be direct. For example, the female could determine egg size during egg development, before oviposition. Or the dependence could arise indirectly, as a result of pleiotropic genetic effects on both adult female fecundity (here taken as the rate of production of progeny irrespective of their viability) and progeny viability. Leaving offspring viability aside, however, female or asexual fecundity will usually be the age-specific fitness component that is most readily measured on individual organisms.

Age-specific male, or hermaphroditic, fertility rates are more difficult to measure for a variety of reasons. The dependence on offspring viability remains, with all its attendant obscurities. In addition, there is the problem that there is often no simple analog of female fecundity. In species that (1) shed gametes in mating aggregations, (2) have external fertilization, and (3) lack male–male competition for shedding opportunities, an equivalent of female fecundity may be available in total sperm production, providing sperm fertilization rates do not vary. In strictly monogamous species, if such exist, male fecundity may be measured from the couple's joint production of offspring, and similarly for strictly self-fertilizing hermaphrodites. For the remaining species, "male fecundity" will not normally be measurable, as such. Reproductive male fitness components will depend on mating rates and fertilization rates, which in turn are frequently dependent on competition between males for access to ova. (The male function in outcrossing hermaphrodites is equivalent in all respects.) Often, genetic marking and the scoring of resultant progeny will be the only reliable way to infer male fertility (vide Brittnacher, 1981).

With all these difficulties lying in the way of fitness-component measurement on individuals, it is not surprising that gerontologists have typically fallen back on demographic measurement of entire populations to infer the attributes of the hypostasized organism. If one is concerned with differentiation between populations arising from different gene frequencies or different environmental treatments imposed on the population as a whole, then demographic measurement of aging has much to recommend it. Since differences between population means will be used to test the significance of the genetic or environmental effects of interest, there can be no objection to observing aging using demographic statistics like $q(x)$, the age-specific death rate for the population, or $m(x)$, the age-specific fecundity. While the attributes of individuals may be obscured by such measures, and some, like male fertility, may be left unexamined, basic information about mean age-specific survival probabilities and mean age-specific reproductive rates is made available. Such information may be of exactly the type required to test population-level hypotheses.

Perhaps one root cause of the problems with previous aging research has been reliance on an implicitly medical model of the organism, despite continuing dependence on observations of populations of organisms. Medical geriatrics, on one hand, and evolutionary research on aging, on the other, avoid this conceptual incoherence. The former is geared toward the pathologies of the individual and collects such data. The latter is founded upon population genetic hypotheses and tests such hypotheses using population data. But most gerontological research is formulated in terms of organismal, cellular, and molecular hypotheses, while relying on aging cohorts of individuals or proliferating cell-culture populations for testing.

## Physiological Measurement

As almost all attempts to measure fitness components directly will be subject to a plethora of operational difficulties, an attractive strategy is to seek physiological measures of aging that are less subject to such operational problems. Comfort (1979, pp. 34–35) provides a characteristically trenchant critique of some of the elementary errors that have often been made in pursuit of this strategy:

> An overcommon practice has been to keep a single specimen, a bird or a bullfrog, for ten or twenty years, and, when it is found dead, having been so for hours or possibly days, to describe histological appearances in its tissues in a note entitled "Senile changes in the nervous system of *Passer* (or *Bufo*)." (Comfort, 1979, p. 34)

Comfort also mentions in passing that measures of aging must be distinguished from "mere measures of chronological age," such as those provided by growth rings in trees. That is, the adduced aging changes must be causally related to the probability

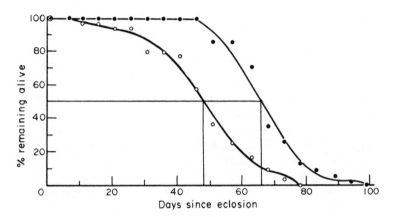

FIGURE 2.2. Male survival patterns of Canton-S (open circles) and Oregon-R stocks of *D. melanogaster*. The Oregon-R stock clearly lives longer, on average. Reprinted with permission from *Experimental Gerontology* 13, Ganetzky, B. and J.R. Flanagan. On the relationship between senescence and age-related changes in two wild-type strains of *Drosophila melanogaster*. Copyright 1978, Pergamon Press plc.

of survival, in his terms, or survival and reproduction, in the evolutionary approach to aging.

Indeed, the problem of discovering appropriate physiological measures of aging is quite difficult. Ganetzky and Flanagan (1978) made an experimental study of this problem that raises many of the most pertinent issues. They selected two wild-type strains of *Drosophila melanogaster*, *Oregon-R* (OR) and *Canton-S* (CS), which have appreciably different male survivorship curves, as shown in Figure 2.2, OR males living about 20 days longer at 21.5 °C. Since it had already been found that alcohol dehydrogenase (ADH) activity decreases with age in a hybrid strain of *Drosophila* (Burcombe, 1972), Ganetzky and Flanagan (1978) set about measuring the ADH activity level trajectories in the OR and CS males. The results, shown in Figure 2.3, are exactly the reverse of what might be expected; the longer-lived strain shows an earlier decline in ADH activity levels. A variety of other biochemical characters studied by Ganetzky and Flanagan also did not behave according to "the view that any age-dependent change could serve as an indication of physiological age with respect to aging, and that any effect that specifically alters the senescence process should have a proportional effect on the appearance of these landmarks." They suggest, instead, that many physiological indicators decline with age but play no causal role in the events leading to death. Thus the problem of identifying physiological indices is not solved by simply finding an attribute that declines with organismal age.

Ganetzky and Flanagan (1978) suggest an experimental strategy for establishing physiological measures of aging: identifying age-dependent physiological changes that occur later in genetically longer-lived populations compared with those that are genetically shorter lived. The only measure like this that Ganetzky and Flanagan found was the time taken for 10 out of 20 flies knocked to the bottom of a glass vial to leave the bottom of the vial, the results being shown in Figure 2.4. One interest-

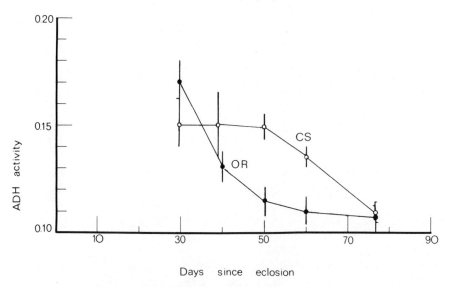

FIGURE 2.3. Mean level of alcohol dehydrogenase activity as a function of age in Canton-S and Oregon-R stocks of *D. melanogaster*. Note that the activity level declines more rapidly in the Oregon-R stock, in spite of its greater average longevity. Reprinted with permission from *Experimental Gerontology* 13, Ganetzky, B. and J.R. Flanagan. On the relationship between senescence and age-related changes in two wild-type strains of *Drosophila melanogaster*. Copyright 1978, Pergamon Press plc.

ing thing about the study of Ganetzky and Flanagan is that the only character that can be plausibly viewed as a measure of general physiological capacity in their study, locomotor activity, proved to be a suitable measure of senescence. Enzyme activities did not prove to be useful indicators of aging. Another interesting thing about the results is that the longer-lived strain had a higher level of locomotor activity at early ages, as well as a later onset of locomotor decline.

Somewhat similar studies have been performed on selected *D. melanogaster* populations of different mean longevities (Rose et al., 1984; Service et al., 1985; Service, 1987). (The creation of these populations is discussed in Chapter 3.) The longer-lived populations were designated O and shorter-lived populations were designated B, with fivefold replication, giving $O_1$–$O_5$ and $B_1$–$B_5$ populations. In these studies, the focus was on differences in physiological measures that were associated with the O populations, because these were consistently longer lived. A number of different characters were studied, with the results shown in Table 2.1. As may be seen from the table, not all general physiological measures need be enhanced in populations that are genetically predisposed to live longer.

One of the differentiated characters, resistance to desiccation, declines with age in both males and females, as shown in Figure 2.5, conforming to the standard ideas of how a physiological measure of aging should behave. Another character, resistance to starvation in females, does not behave in this fashion, as shown in Figure 2.6. Rather than declining with age, it *increases* with age. Yet genetic enhancement

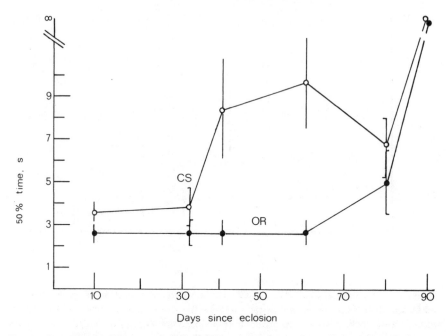

FIGURE 2.4. Level of locomotor incapacitation, as measured by the amount of time, in seconds, it takes for 50 percent of a sample of *D. melanogaster* to climb up the sides of a vial. Higher values indicate greater incapacitation. Note that flies from the Oregon-R stock preserve their locomotor capability longer. This is also the stock that has a greater average longevity. Reprinted with permission from *Experimental Gerontology* 13, Ganetzky, B. and J.R. Flanagan. On the relationship between senescence and age-related changes in two wild-type strains of *Drosophila melanogaster*. Copyright 1978, Pergamon Press plc.

of starvation resistance is associated with genetic enhancement of longevity (Service et al., 1985). These results suggest that the physiological measurement of aging requires careful interpretation.

Associated with the rapid increase in age-specific death rate at later adult ages is the type of survival curve exhibited by the normal flies of Figure 2.1. The conven-

TABLE 2.1.   Differentiated characters in longer-lived populations
of *D. melanogaster* studied in Rose (1984b), Rose et al. (1984),
Service et al. (1985), and Service (1987).

| Enhanced characters | Depressed characters |
| --- | --- |
| Later fecundity | Early fecundity |
| Starvation resistance (all ages) | Early ovary weight |
| Desiccation resistance (all ages) | Early metabolic rate |
| Ethanol resistance (all ages) | Early locomotor activity |
| Later locomotor activity | |
| Lipid content (all ages) | |

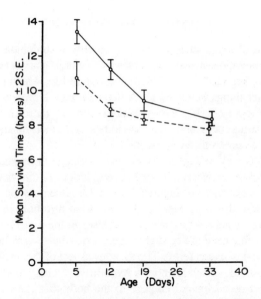

FIGURE 2.5. Mean survival times under desiccation for female *D. melanogaster* from longer-lived (———) and shorter-lived (– – –) stocks. While both exhibit declining age-specific desiccation resistance, flies from longer-lived stocks tend to survive desiccation longer at most ages. (From Service et al., 1985.) © 1985 by the University of Chicago.

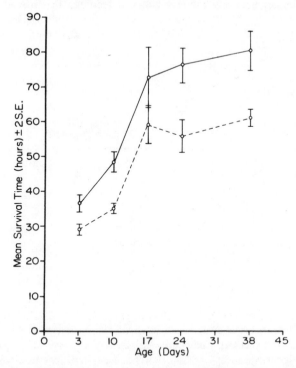

FIGURE 2.6. Mean survival times under starvation for female *D. melanogaster* from longer-lived (———) and shorter-lived (– – –) stocks. While both exhibit increasing age-specific starvation resistance, flies from longer-lived stocks tend to survive starvation longer at most ages. (From Service et al., 1985.) © 1985 by the University of Chicago.

tional association of organismal survival probability with demographic death rates leads to the interpretation of survival curves as "vitality" curves (vide Lamb, 1977, p. 3). The idea is that vitality is the ability to sustain life, which is supposed to fall with age, all other things being equal. A diagrammatic representation of this concept is given in Figure 2.7. It is easy to make Figure 2.7 more elaborate, in order to account for the differences between individuals and variation in environmentally imposed threats to survival, as in Figure 2.8.

The problem is how to explain an *increase* with age in resistance to starvation, given the correlations between this attribute and longevity (Service et al., 1985), in terms of diagrams like those of Figures 2.7 and 2.8. One possible solution is shown in Figure 2.9. Here the hypothesis is that the death threshold increases with age, continued survival requiring progressive increases in the hypothetical vitality character. Individuals that have lower vitality trajectories die sooner, in spite of a steady increase in the vitality character(s). The dubious aspect of this model is the increase in the death threshold, which is entirely hypothetical. One possible source of such an increase might be accidental damage to the body that cannot be repaired. For example, in fruit flies it is common to find frayed wings and lost tarsi in older flies (cf. Rockstein, 1966). Such damage could make it more difficult for the fly to move between sources of nourishment, resting sites, and so on. Continued survival might then come to depend on an increased ability to withstand greater nutritional stress arising from longer intervals between bouts of feeding. This use of the "vitality

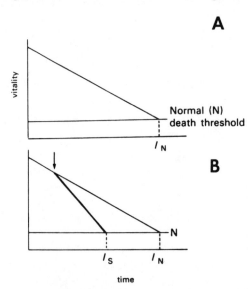

FIGURE 2.7. Graphs showing the basic ideas of the "vitality threshold" model of senescence. The assumption is that death occurs when the vitality line meets the death threshold line. In the simplest model (A), vitality decreases linearly with age, and the death threshold lies at a single, age-independent value, $l_N$. However, many variations are possible, including those in which the rate of decline of vitality increases (B), because of some stress, giving an earlier age at death, $l_S$. (From Lamb, M.J. 1977, *Biology of Aging*, Blackie, Glasgow and London, p. 74.)

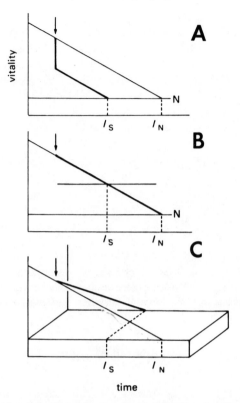

FIGURE 2.8. Graphs showing elaborations on the "vitality threshold" model of senescence. In these variants of the basic model, there is a downward shift in vitality at some point (A), the death threshold is elevated (B), or some other trauma gives rise to a new type of deterioration that leads to an earlier crossing of the death threshold (C). (From Lamb, M.J. 1977, *Biology of Aging*, Blackie, Glasgow and London, p. 74.)

model" does not exhaust the set of conceivable variations on it. While the model is versatile, the degree to which it has to be elaborated to account for such data as are already available, to say nothing of the data that might be collected in the future, indicates that the concept of vitality as a converse of aging is problematic.

It is not easy to find straightforward physiological measures of aging. Still, it is possible to find physiological measures of aging with some reliability in specific settings. In fruit flies, resistance to starvation does not appear to be a good measure of the likelihood of death of the individuals of different ages *within* populations, in that older females are more resistant to starvation but more likely to die (Service et al., 1985). Nevertheless, resistance to starvation does appear to be a guide to differences in rates of aging *between* populations. Resistance to desiccation is a good guide to both. The only sensible conclusion is that physiological measures of aging must be appropriately calibrated, in the most general sense of the term, before being used.

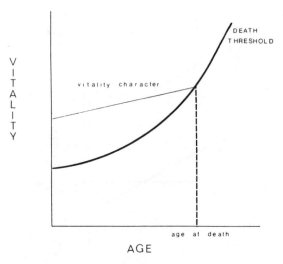

FIGURE 2.9. A vitality threshold model for aging in which the death threshold rises with increasing age. This is proposed to account for deaths among individuals that seem to exhibit increases in vitality measures, as is true of starvation resistance, as shown in Figure 2.6.

## Modulation of Aging

### Environmental Effects

However it is measured, aging is not an absolute property of a species, even in the absence of external stresses, like contagious disease and radiation. In poikilotherms, those organisms that lack endogenous control of their body temperatures, a host of environmental factors are known to affect longevity, from temperature to crowding (Lamb, 1977; Comfort, 1979). Of course, the sensitivity of reproductive output to environmental conditions is even more apparent (e.g., Partridge, 1986). Perhaps the only source of limits to lists of environmental factors affecting aging is ignorance.

Drosophila species serve as good examples of environmental dependence in poikilotherms, because few aspects of their biology have escaped attention. Variation in all of the following factors have been shown to affect fecundity or survival: oxygen level (Kloek, Ralin, and Ridgel, 1976), light regime (Allemand, Cohet, and David, 1973; Allemand, Cohet, and Savolainen, 1976; Allemand, 1977), temperature (Hollingsworth, 1966, 1969; Miquel et al., 1976; Parsons, 1978), nutritional biochemistry (Herrewege, 1974, 1975), larval crowding (Lewontin, 1955; Lints and Lints, 1969), and culture "ecology" (Robertson and Sang, 1944; Sang, 1949a,b,c; Mueller, 1985). What this range of findings suggests is that almost all aspects of a fruit fly's environment may influence its pattern of aging. We know as much or more about the biology of Drosophila as about that of any other invertebrate genus. This plethora of environmental variables affecting in aging Drosophila suggests that, in the absence of evidence otherwise, the possibility of a comparable range of environmental influences should be allowed for in the study of other invertebrate genera. Two particularly well-studied environmental influences are worthy of detailed review here: temperature and nutrition.

## TEMPERATURE

There is an abundance of evidence suggesting that poikilotherm life span depends on ambient temperature. One of the earliest reports was that of Loeb and Northrop (1917), working with *Drosophila melanogaster;* they found that life span varied inversely with ambient temperature over the range of 10 to 30 °C. Although there has been some controversy about the physiological basis of this effect (Maynard Smith, 1963; Lamb, 1968; Miquel et al., 1976; Lamb, 1977), which will be discussed in Chapter 6, it has been reproduced many times in *Drosophila* species (Alpatov and Pearl, 1929; Maynard Smith, 1963; Strehler, 1961, 1962; Clarke and Maynard Smith, 1961a,b; Hollingsworth, 1966, 1968, 1969; Lamb, 1968; Miquel et al., 1976; Parsons, 1978). (See Chapter 6 for illustrative data.) Similar results have been found for other invertebrates, such as the cladoceran *Daphnia magna* (MacArthur and Baillie, 1929) and the nematode *Caenorhabditis elegans* (Klass, 1977). So far as can now be told, life span is inversely correlated with temperature for invertebrate poikilotherms that undergo aging, at least over that part of the temperature range that sustains life.

## NUTRITION

Nutrition is the other variable that is well known to have major effects on life span. The best data come from studies on rodents: mice, rats, and hamsters. The classic experiments are those of McCay and colleagues (McCay and Crowell, 1934; McCay et al., 1939; McCay, Sperling, and Barnes, 1943; and McCay, Pope, and Lunsford, 1956). Rats fed on calorie-restricted diets as juveniles suffer retardation of growth. When they are subsequently provided with sufficient food to grow to adult size, they live much longer than control rats fed sufficient calories for rapid maturation. The resulting survivorship patterns are shown in Figure 2.10. A number of chronic diseases have decreased incidence under these conditions as well. There has since been a series of experiments of generally similar design, with variation in the species used, as well as variation in the timing or nutritional nature of diet restriction (e.g., Ross, 1961, 1976; Miller and Payne, 1968; Stuchlíková, Juricobá-Horiková, and Deyl, 1975; Weindruch and Walford, 1982, 1988; Yu, Masoro, and McMahan, 1985; Yu, 1987). The prolongation of rodent life span has been readily reproducible, providing that diet restriction commenced after weaning (Widdowson and Kennedy, 1962).

Comparable results have been obtained with invertebrates. For example, starved *Daphnia longispina* exhibit a substantial prolongation of life span (Ingle, Wood, and Banta, 1937). With insects, there is inconsistency, Comfort (1979, p. 182) suggesting that hemimetabolous species (species that do not undergo extensive metamorphosis between larval and adult stages) exhibit genuine prolongation of life with reduced food intake, while holometabolous species (those that do undergo full metamorphosis) seem to exhibit only prolonged larval life in response to dietary restriction. Holometabolous adult survival seems to be enhanced by increased feeding (Rockstein, 1959). This is probably an area that could benefit from further

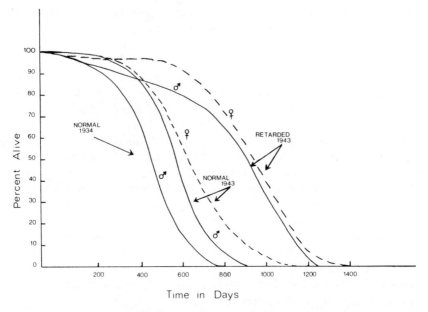

FIGURE 2.10. Survival patterns of "normal" rats, fed ad libitum, and "retarded" rats, which were subjected to nutritional restriction that delayed reproductive maturation. Retarded rats live significantly longer. (From McCay, Sperling, and Barnes, 1943.)

research. Nonetheless, there is a wide range of animal species that exhibit increases in total life span under dietary restriction, making such postponed aging one of the most reliable results of gerontological research.

One thing that should be mentioned in this context is that reduced nutrition is also known to reduce fecundity in *Drosophila* (Robertson and Sang, 1944), an observation that suggests the possibility that reduced fecundity may be part of the physiological mechanism underlying enhanced longevity. (This type of relationship between fecundity and longevity is discussed in detail in Chapters 4, 5, and 6.) The general problem of physiologically accounting for the dependence of longevity on nutrition will be taken up in the following, particularly in Chapter 6.

## USE OF CONTROLS

Temperature and nutrition are features of an organism's environment that have been amply shown to affect longevity in many species. Similarly, in view of the list of environmental influences detected in *Drosophila,* there is good reason to allow for the possibility that aging in any particular species could be sensitive to environmental factors other than nutrition and temperature. The problem is that such factors may often be unknown or uncontrolled. Fecundity in *Drosophila,* for example, is notoriously difficult to control (Bell, Moore, and Warren, 1955; Rasmuson, 1956). All these results strongly underscore the conclusion that patterns of aging are not "species characteristics," unlike such characters as chromosome number. Rather, they have significance only relative to appropriate controls. Thus the measurement of aging may be of necessity always a problem of comparative measurement, in which experimental treatment of one group gives rise to a pattern of aging that is only meaningfully evaluated relative to a control group handled as similarly as possible to the experimental group, with the sole exception of the treatment imposed on the latter.

## Genetic Effects

The genetics of aging will be of primary interest in Chapters 3 and 4, where they will be discussed in some detail. However, some genetic effects on aging belong in a special category, as they are specific to contrived laboratory settings and may give rise to misleading results when they influence the observation of aging. These are the genetic effects that arise from deleterious alleles that are normally rare.

### INBRED LINES

The first systematic experimental study of the effect of inheritance on life span was that of Raymond Pearl and his colleagues (Pearl, 1922; Pearl and Parker, 1922; Gonzales, 1923) using *D. melanogaster*. They were able to show definitively that survivorship patterns, and thus longevity, are inherited, by creating inbred lines that expressed abnormal morphological phenotypes in association with characteristic survivorship patterns. However, the longevities associated with the distinct phenotypes were often quite low. $F_1$ hybrids between such lines had mean longevities like those of outbred populations, with the $F_2$'s segregating so as to produce longevity patterns matching the appropriate abnormal phenotype, suggesting that depressed longevity was associated with a recessive Mendelian gene, either by genetic linkage or by pleiotropy. In effect, inbreeding appeared to have produced fixation of a recessive deleterious allele affecting longevity.

Similarly, Clarke and Maynard Smith (1955) found that crossing inbred lines of *Drosophila subobscura* produced a substantial increase in longevity among hybrids, although the inbred lines were not morphologically distinct. The results of these experiments are summarized in Figure 2.11. Again, these results are readily interpretable in terms of recessive deleterious gene action and the population genetics of inbreeding (Crow, 1948; Wright, 1977). In the course of inbreeding, the theoretical expectation, and the commonplace finding, is that recessive deleterious alleles, normally present at low frequency because of a balance between selection and mutation pressures, will become fixed by finite-population sampling effects due to chance. Distinct inbred lines will normally be fixed for recessive deleterious alleles at different loci. Thus crossing of individuals from different inbred lines will result in the elimination of most deleterious genetic effects, because of regained heterozygosity at most loci that were homozygous for the recessive deleterious allele in one or the other parental inbred line. In effect, the hybrid progeny recover something approaching the condition of the original outbred population. (This cannot be a complete return to initial conditions, because of the rapid genetic drift of small populations and possible selection for gene combinations that epistatically

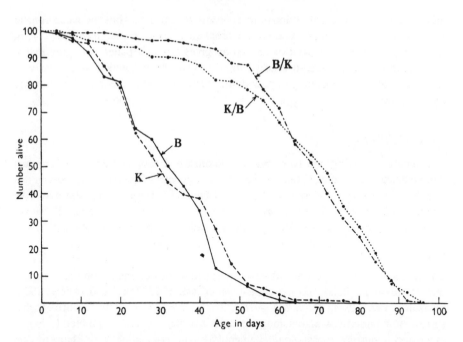

FIGURE 2.11. Survival patterns of two inbred lines of *D. subobscura*, B and K, together with their two reciprocal crosses, K/B and B/K. The hybrid lines evidently live much longer, on average, thereby exhibiting "hybrid vigor." (From Clarke and Maynard Smith, 1955.)

mitigate the effects of homozygosity.) Thus the biology of aging in inbred lines will be highly variable from one line to the next, in that it will depend primarily on the particular set of deleterious alleles fixed by the inbreeding process.

As in *Drosophila*, inbred lines of *Mus musculus* exhibit large reproducible differences in longevity (Russell, 1966; Storer, 1966). Since a great deal is known about the morbid pathology of mammals, it has been possible to associate the characteristic life span of such strains with strain-specific abnormalities in identifiable organ systems (Sprott, 1983, 1987). Also as in *Drosophila*, $F_1$ hybrids of inbred strains are usually longer lived than the parental strains (Russell, 1966). This again suggests a pattern of hybrid vigor resulting from regained heterozygosity of recessive deleterious alleles. The interest of the mouse work is that the aberrant nature of the causes of death in inbred lines is more apparent.

Not only do the physiological genetics of aging in inbred laboratory populations bear little clear relation to aging in outbred populations, they also have little bearing on the genetics of aging in populations that are inbred in the wild. The nematode *Caenorhabditis elegans* has two forms: male and hermaphrodite, the latter typically self-fertilizing (Brenner, 1974). Males are rare products of nondisjunction. Most reproduction is by self-fertilization. Thus wild animals of this species, when sampled from nature, are already homozygous at most loci. Crosses of inbred strains in this species do *not* exhibit hybrid vigor (Johnson and Wood, 1982). The inbreeding depression exhibited by longevity in laboratory strains of normally out-bred populations is an artifact that has no bearing on the evolutionary or physiologi-cal basis of aging in wild populations, whether these are normally outbred *or* inbred. Rather, such inbreeding depression appears to involve losses of function at loci essential for the maintenance of life, such functions normally operating well in the vast majority of individuals within populations that are not artificially inbred.

## GENETIC DISEASES

In this context, human progeroid diseases in which there is the superficial ap-pearance of greatly accelerated aging, like Hutchinson–Gilford syndrome and Werner's syndrome (Martin, 1978; Salk, 1982; Brown, 1987), can be seen as parallels of the pathologies of inbred strains of *Mus* or *Drosophila*. These are rare disorders. Hutchinson–Gilford syndrome is only known in about 20 cases world-wide. Its symptoms begin in early childhood, with severe growth retardation, loss of epidermal tissue, failure of sexual maturation, abnormal skeletal development, and widespread atherosclerosis. The median age at death is 12 years. Werner's syn-drome manifests in early adolescence, with cessation of growth, multifold epider-mal pathologies, hypogonadism, widespread atherosclerosis, and frequent neo-plasms. Patients normally die in their 30s. Only 6 Werner syndrome patients are known in the United States. Both the patients with these genetic diseases and inbred laboratory animals exhibit aging brought about by deleterious genotypes that are normally rare.

In the case of human progeroid disease, these genotypic effects may arise from alleles that are normally dominant, as has been suggested for Hutchinson–Gilford syndrome (Brown and Wisniewski, 1983), or due to an autosomal, deleterious, recessive allele, as has been suggested for Werner's syndrome (Epstein et al., 1966; Brown and Wisniewski, 1983). In the case of experimental animals, such syn-dromes come to light primarily when they become prevalent as a result of fixation, or near fixation, due to inbreeding. In the case of man, they come to light because of the medical profession's focus on pathological impairment, irrespective of rarity. In either case, the aging patterns are rare in natural populations.

## MUTATIONS OF LARGE EFFECT

*D. melanogaster* is in some ways an instructive intermediate. Visibly aberrant mutations have received more attention in this species than any other, because of their use in genetic analysis. As a consequence, numerous grossly pathological mutant forms are known in this species (vide Lindsley and Grell, 1968). Some of these are known to have greatly reduced life spans (e.g., Bozcuk, 1981) or to be wholly incapable of reproducing. Such mutants probably suffer from syndromes that have little or nothing to do with the physiological basis of aging in "wild-type" flies: "reduced lifespan is not a sufficient criterion to recognize those mutants of most interest . . . mutants that lead to an altered lifespan through changes in those processes that normally lead to senescence" (Ganetzky and Flanagan, 1978).

None of this is to say that the deleterious alleles detected by inbreeding or mutagenesis are irrelevant to the evolutionary biology of aging. That is an issue that will be taken up in detail in Chapter 4. However, the measurement of aging in organisms suffering from the effects of markedly deleterious alleles will *not* be a useful guide to senescence in the majority of individuals within populations that have not been artificially inbred. Most individuals in natural populations do not have such genetic syndromes.

## Conclusion

The conventional demographic definition of aging used in gerontology, declining survival probability, poses difficulties with respect to the problem of observing the survival probability of individuals and with respect to the neglect of age-specific fertility, which also tends to decline with age in many species. The definition proposed here is *a persistent decline in the age-specific fitness components of an organism due to internal physiological deterioration.* As such, this definition is explicitly focused on the characters treated by the evolutionary theory of aging, discussed in Chapter 1. This definition also lends itself to experimental research of the type often performed within evolutionary biology, in which populations are the basic units of observation.

The measurement of rates of aging is subject to a number of severe difficulties. Observation of aging in the wild will normally be confined to the spectacular aging exhibited by semelparous organisms like Pacific salmon and soybean. In the laboratory, measurement of aging is compromised by handling artifacts and by responses to the novel selective pressures engendered by the laboratory environment. Fertility characters are often hard to observe, particularly for males. Physiological measurements of aging have the problem of adequate calibration, in that arbitrarily chosen indices of aging are not reliable indicators of longevity. These cautionary points do not, however, necessarily mean that the measurement of aging is a hopeless task.

A wide range of environmental factors influence aging. Two of the better known factors are temperature and nutrition, especially the former among poikilotherms. In rodents and some invertebrates nutritional restriction appears to increase life span.

Measurements of aging can be vitiated by the use of inbred or mutant stocks in species that normally outbreed. Progeroid diseases are problematic as models of "genetically accelerated" aging. They are more likely to be pathologies due to highly deleterious alleles present in low frequencies in natural populations. In general, aging due to such alleles is probably a side effect of a pervasive collapse in fitness components, quite unlike the decline in fitness components characteristic of aging.

# 3

# Experimental Tests of the Evolutionary Theory of Aging

There are two ways to test a scientific theory: test its assumptions or test its predictions, corollaries, and consequences. The latter is preferable, since it effectively tests not only the assumptions of a theory, but also the cogency of the deductive reasoning used to derive the theory's corollaries once its assumptions were adopted.

This chapter begins with experimental tests of those assumptions of the evolutionary theory of aging that can be regarded as specific to the theory and empirically contingent. Some of the empirically contingent assumptions of the theory are general to a vast range of biological research and will not receive any attention here. Mendelian inheritance is an example of such an assumption. Other assumptions are well-known to vary from species to species, where this variation is part of the structure of the theory. The most important assumption of this kind is age structure, in which adults potentially survive reproduction to reproduce again. The critical assumptions that are left concern patterns of genetic variation and covariation for survival and reproduction.

The best experiments for testing the evolutionary theory of aging are selection experiments in which the action of natural selection at different adult ages is manipulated. These experiments have produced some dramatic corroborations of the evolutionary theory in some cases. In other cases, ambiguous results have inspired further experiments.

On the whole, however, it is striking how closely experiment and theory can interact where the evolution of aging is concerned. By the standards of both evolutionary biology and gerontology, it is an exceptionally fertile area for strong inference in the prosecution of the experimental method.

## Genetic Variation Affecting Aging

The evolutionary theory of aging depends on only a few assumptions. First, it assumes the validity of population genetics, which is itself dependent on the validity of Mendelian theories of inheritance. It would not be appropriate to examine this assumption here. Second, it requires the existence of genetic variation affecting adult survival and reproduction. Third, it requires that not all genetic variation affecting aging positively covary with fitness. This third assumption will be discussed further shortly. The immediate concern will be the second assumption.

The general rule of thumb in quantitative genetics is that there will be genetic variation for almost every character in an outbred population (Falconer, 1981; Roff and Mousseau, 1987; Mousseau and Roff, 1987). The few characters for which this is not true were unlikely to have such genetic variation, because of the biology involved. For example, in a few cases it has been difficult to select upon sex ratio of offspring or upon biased handedness (Falconer, 1981).

The genetics of aging are no exception to this general rule. Indeed, knowledge of genetic variation affecting aging has been available for most of this century (e.g., Pearl, 1922). To take man as an example, the progeroid genetic syndromes, discussed in Chapter 2, provide dramatic evidence of the dependence of human aging patterns on genetics (Brown, 1987; Albin, 1988). The most abundant data, however, come from *Drosophila*. Many of the Mendelian alleles of *Drosophila* affect aging when tested (e.g., Bozcuk, 1981). However, such pathological mutants, like those responsible for progeroid disease, do not necessarily provide a good guide to the genetic variation that predominates in outbred populations.

Research with both *Drosophila* and *Caenorhabditis elegans* has provided a great deal of evidence for the presence of quantitative genetic variation in aging. Work with somewhat inbred lines of *Drosophila* has revealed abundant variation between lines for longevity and reproductive aging (Gowen and Johnson, 1946; Clarke and Maynard Smith, 1955; Giesel, 1979; Giesel and Zettler, 1980). Recombinant inbred genotypes have also revealed large genetic effects on aging in both *Caenorhabditis* (Johnson and Wood, 1982; Johnson, 1986) and *Drosophila* (Hiraizumi, 1985; Hughes and Clark, 1988). Quantitative genetic experiments without inbred stocks have also revealed genetic variation affecting aging in *Drosophila* (Maynard Smith, 1959; Rose and Charlesworth, 1981a).

Once discussion moves beyond the premier metazoan genetic models, *Drosophila* and *Caenorhabditis,* the nature of the evidence is far weaker. Different mouse strains are known to have different aging patterns (Sprott, 1987), although these differences have no obvious extrapolation to outbred mouse populations. Otherwise, the range of evidence bearing on the genetics of aging is not impressive, chiefly consisting of sporadic studies on species of practical importance, like honeybees (e.g., Rinderer, Collins, and Brown, 1983; Milne, 1985), rather than the evaluation of fundamental theories.

In any case, there is little doubt that patterns of aging are subject to genetic variation. The critical assumption that remains for evaluation is the *nature* of that genetic variation.

## Genetic Covariation of Fitness and Aging

The intellectual seductiveness of the equations giving the decline in the force of natural selection with age leads the unwary to suppose that genes affecting specific age classes naturally exist. While the evolutionary theory of aging absolutely requires the existence of such genes, they need not exist. Instead, the genetic effects on survival and reproduction might be uniform with respect to age, all alleles simply being better or worse for the functioning of the organism at every stage and in every respect. In this case, natural selection would have the same effectiveness in molding late life-history characters that it has in molding early life-history characters. All life-history characters would then be inseparable, positively correlated, components of fitness, evolving as fitness evolves (Giesel, 1979; Giesel and Zettler, 1980). Aging would simply reflect the failure of natural selection to overcome the many sources of damage that impinge on the continuation of reproduction and survival (cf. Cutler, 1976).

Thus we have a fundamental dichotomy. Either aging genetically covaries directly with fitness or it does not. Only in the second case can the declining force of natural selection allow the evolution of aging. Therefore, evidence bearing on the genetic covariation of fitness and aging requires careful attention.

The key parameters in the corpus of evidence bearing on this question are the genetic correlations between life-history characters. Genetic correlations are quantitative measures of the similarities, in both magnitude and effect, of the breeding values of the alleles affecting the correlated characters. Breeding value is a quantitative genetic concept that reflects the effect of an individual of a particular genotype on the mean value of a character in a population. Such breeding values are functions of *both* the genetic effects of particular alleles and the frequencies of the different genotypes present in the population. As such, their mathematical specification can be quite complex (vide Falconer, 1981). When genetic correlations are positive, the breeding values affecting the two characters positively covary, being high together or low together. Conversely, when genetic correlations are negative, the breeding values will tend to be opposed in sign. When genetic correlations are zero, the breeding values will not quantitatively correspond. Thus the scientific issue at stake is whether or not the genetic correlation between fitness, particularly early reproduction, and later survival or reproduction is near one.

In addition, there are other types of genetic evidence that bear on patterns of covariation of allelic effects. Mutations may have positively or negatively covarying effects. Likewise, covariation among clones may provide some indication of patterns of covariation.

## Aging as Genetically Unitary with Fitness

There is a large body of data that seemingly corroborates the hypothesis of positive genetic covariation between fitness and aging. The first type of corroborative evidence comes from mutations of large effect. To the extent that these mutations shorten adult life, they also generally reduce survival likelihood among juveniles and diminish early reproduction. The most dramatic illustrations of this are to be found among some of the human progeroid diseases discussed in Chapter 2. Both Hutchinson–Gilford syndrome and Werner's syndrome drastically increase the likelihood of death and reduce the rate of reproduction (Brown, 1987), leading to a substantial reduction in organismal fitness. Natural selection will act to eliminate alleles engendering such syndromes and thereby act to postpone aging as well. Less dramatic genetic diseases, like hemophilia, can be viewed in the same light.

The *Drosophila* literature is also replete with studies of alleles that have deleterious effects on fitness, as well as hastening death and the cessation of reproduction (Pearl, 1922; Gonzales, 1923; Bozcuk, 1981). Alleles of large effect, such as *white*, which seriously impairs visual function, have deleterious effects on many components of fitness, effects analogous to those of human genetic diseases, like cystic fibrosis. The *Drosophila* literature also affords a number of surveys of the nature of the mutations affecting components of fitness (e.g., Hiraizumi, 1961; Temin, 1966; Simmons and Crow, 1977; Giesel, 1979; Giesel and Zettler, 1980; Simmons, Preston, and Engels, 1980). The work of Giesel and Zettler is illustrated in Figure 3.1. This large body of evidence indicates that low-fitness alleles and new mutations depress multiple fitness components simultaneously. In addition, work with outbred *Drosophila* newly caught from the wild revealed positive genetic correlations between life-history characters (Murphy, Giesel, and Manlove, 1983; Giesel, 1986). There is apparently abundant support for the view that "natural selection must favor the evolutionary accumulation of longevity factors" (Giesel, 1979); aging is thus the obverse of fitness.

Beyond the cases of man and *Drosophila*, the evidence bearing on this point is much less direct, normally lacking identified genetic loci. Several strictly phenotypic studies have clearly shown a positive association between early reproduction and longevity (Hogstedt, 1981; Smith, 1981). Correlations between longevity and age-specific fecundity in clones of the rotifer *Platyias patulus* tended to be positive, as shown in Figure 3.2 (Bell, 1984a). Similar results were obtained with comparable data from *Daphnia pulex* (Bell, 1984b), as shown in Figure 3.3. Thus there is evidence outside *Drosophila* and *Homo* that corroborates the view that aging

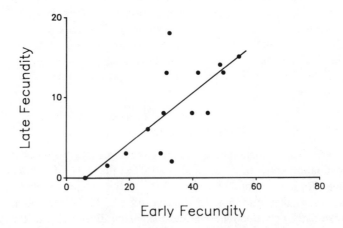

FIGURE 3.1. Strain mean values for first-third-of-life mean fecundity per day versus last-third-of-life mean fecundity in *D. melanogaster*. The graph clearly shows a positive genetic correlation between early and late fecundity over the strains used. (From Giesel and Zettler, 1980.)

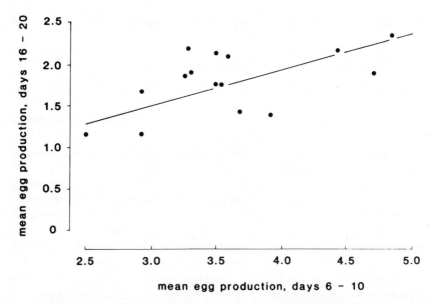

FIGURE 3.2. The sum of eggs produced during days 16 to 20 is plotted against the sum of eggs produced during days 6 to 10 in *Platyias patulus* under laboratory conditions. The results are ostensibly evidence against a cost of reproduction. (From Bell, 1984a.)

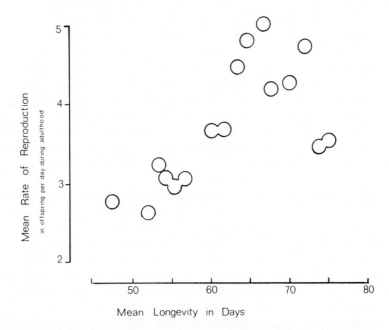

FIGURE 3.3. Clonal means for rate of reproduction versus longevity in *Daphnia pulex* reared in the laboratory. There is a significant positive correlation between the two variables, at least under these conditions. (From Bell, 1984b.)

simply reflects the limited accomplishments of natural selection in enhancing fitness, of which adult survival and reproduction are major components.

## Aging as Genetically Distinct from Fitness

One can also find examples of genetic variation in aging that is not a direct reflection of genetic variation in fitness.

As before, the best evidence comes from *D. melanogaster*. Consider the evidence that does not come from quantitative genetics first. Tradeoffs have been found between longevity and egg production among some long-established laboratory populations, such that individuals from populations that tended to have higher early fitness also tended to die sooner (Gowen and Johnson, 1946). Allelic variants maintained at high frequency in equilibrium cage populations that had deleterious effects on larval viability had no net effect upon fitness itself, indicating that "the detrimental effects on viability of mutations from an equilibrium population are offset by pleiotropic effects on other components of fitness" (Simmons, Preston, and Engels, 1980). Hybridized chromosomes from a variety of inbred *D. melanogaster* lines gave strains with a negative association between early fecundity and longevity, with more fecund strains dying sooner (Hiraizumi, 1985). Samples of chromosomes of *D. melanogaster* had significant patterns of covariation over fitness components (Hughes and Clark, 1988). Some combinations gave rise to negative associations between early and late fitness components, while other combinations lacked significant covariation.

Turning to the quantitative genetic evidence, studies of correlations between relatives in *D. melanogaster* have revealed negative genetic covariation between early virility and fecundity, on one hand, and late fecundity and female longevity, on the other (Tucić, Cvetković, and Milanović, 1988). Other genetic covariation between fitness and aging characters was nonsignificant. Scheiner, Caplan, and Lyman (1989) studied tradeoffs between life-history characters in *D. melanogaster* using sib analysis at two different temperatures. The experiment was very small in scale, with few significant results, but they found some weak evidence for negative genetic covariation between early and late life-history characters. There was little evidence for a strong positive association between longevity and early reproduction. Overall, the *Drosophila* data indicate a weak pattern of negative covariation between early reproduction and longevity.

Perhaps it would be instructive to give explicitly one particular set of *Drosophila* results that can be compared with others of differing technique. Table 3.1 gives the additive genetic correlation estimates for a suite of female adult life-history characters studied in a sib analysis of outbred, laboratory-adapted, *D. melanogaster* (Rose and Charlesworth, 1981a). There is little evidence in these results that the alleles responsible for these genetic correlations act in the same direction at all ages in *Drosophila,* like the results just surveyed. If anything, they suggest that beneficial effects at early ages are associated with deleterious effects at later ages.

Outside *Drosophila,* the genetic evidence for evolutionary independence of later survival and reproduction from fitness is extremely thin. In man, it has been argued that female carriers of Huntington's chorea, which dramatically accelerates the age

TABLE 3.1.   Estimated additive genetic correlations for adult female life-history characters in *D. melanogaster*

|  | *Fecundity days 1–5* | *Fecundity days 6–10* | *Fecundity days 11–15* | *Longevity* |
|---|---|---|---|---|
| Fecundity days 1–5 | — | −.16 | −.48 | −1.43 |
| Fecundity days 6–10 | −.16 | — | .51 | .30 |
| Fecundity days 11–15 | −.48 | .51 | — | −.71 |
| Longevity | −1.43 | .30 | −.71 | — |

Rose and Charlesworth, 1981a.

of death, have enhanced fertility (Albin, 1988). It has also been suggested that other disorders that shorten life, such as idiopathic hemochromatosis, might be associated with equal or enhanced early reproduction (Albin, 1988), but the quality of evidence for these conclusions is rather poor.

Turning to plants and invertebrates, vegetative clones of annual meadow grass, *Poa annua,* that have high early reproduction also have reduced later survival and reproduction (Law, 1979). The seaweed fly, *Coelopa frigida,* appears to have a stable inversion polymorphism in which one karyotype gives rise to greater longevity and fecundity but suffers slower development, which reduces fitness by postponing reproduction (Butlin and Day, 1985). In Darwin's finches, small body size gives rise to a selective advantage among juveniles but a selective disadvantage among adults (Price and Grant, 1984), again suggesting a lack of correspondence between early and late genetic effects upon life-history characters. A *Caenorhabditis elegans* mutant, *age-1,* appears to convey increased life span along with reduced fertility (Friedman and Johnson, 1988). All together, these results are miscellaneous in taxa and experimental methodology, but they do seem broadly in accord with each other and the corresponding *Drosophila* results. While this body of evidence could be larger, it does at least indicate the possibility that the evolution of aging is uncoupled from the evolution of early age-specific fitness components.

## Methodological Problems in the Genetics of Aging

The reader may be forgiven for concluding that "the jury is out" on the question of whether or not aging is distinct from fitness at the genetic level. However, some resolution can be found for these apparently contradictory results bearing on the genetic relationship between aging and fitness, in that some of this evidence is problematic and has been widely criticized as such (Rose and Service, 1985; Reznick, Perry, and Travis, 1986; Clark, 1987). There are three major methodological problems that need to be taken into account: (1) disparity between phenotypic and genetic correlations, (2) inbreeding depression, and (3) genotype–environment interaction.

### PHENOTYPIC AND GENETIC CORRELATIONS

The first problem is intuitively straightforward: Total phenotypic correlations between characters may arise from external environmental factors or accidents of

TABLE 3.2.   Estimated phenotypic correlations for adult female life-history
characters in *D. melanogaster*

|  | Fecundity days 1–5 | Fecundity days 6–10 | Fecundity days 11–15 | Longevity |
|---|---|---|---|---|
| Fecundity days 1–5 | — | .66 | .50 | −.22 |
| Fecundity days 6–10 | .66 | — | .54 | .17 |
| Fecundity days 11–15 | .50 | .54 | — | .21 |
| Longevity | −.22 | .17 | .21 | — |

Rose and Charlesworth, 1981a.

organismal development, rather than genetic effects (Rose and Service, 1985; Reznick, Perry, and Travis 1986). These nongenetic effects may give rise to phenotypic correlations that are positive *or* negative. A period of acute starvation or disease may depress both reproductive output and longevity in any organism. Alternatively, virginity and a resultant lowering of reproductive output may prolong life span, as is common among *Drosophila* females (Maynard Smith, 1958). Similarly, increased mating opportunities can depress male longevity, at least in *Drosophila* (Partridge and Farquhar, 1981). Depending on the circumstances of data collection, phenotypic correlations between life-history characters could be quite spurious.

This is illustrated in Table 3.2, which gives the *phenotypic* correlations obtained from the same *Drosophila* data as those used to obtain the *genetic* correlations of Table 3.1. While the entries in Table 3.1, which gives additive genetic correlations, are for the most part negative, those of Table 3.2 are mostly positive. Evidently, phenotypic correlations cannot be used directly to infer genetic correlations.

Yet this has often been the practice in studies of covariation between life-history characters (e.g., Bryant, 1979; De Steven, 1980; Smith, 1981; Browne, 1982). [This is not meant to exclude the use of phenotypic correlations between relatives in the estimation of genetic correlations, the standard method of quantitative genetics (Falconer, 1981).] Some known genetic sampling structure, such as chromosomes, clones, or siblings, must be present to allow appropriately genetic inferences concerning the evolution of aging. Thus the solely phenotypic evidence on either side of the question must be dismissed from consideration.

### INBREEDING DEPRESSION

The second methodological problem in the study of life-history genetics, inbreeding depression, has already been mentioned in Chapter 2. Inbreeding, particularly incestuous mating, is well known to have deleterious consequences for most sexual species; many organisms have evolved mechanisms for avoiding it (Charlesworth and Charlesworth, 1987). Some studies of the genetics of aging and fitness (e.g., Giesel, 1979; Giesel and Zettler, 1980; Giesel, Murphy, and Manlove, 1982) primarily rely on inbred lines and/or homozygous chromosomes. It has been suggested that these experiments constitute a survey of low-fitness alleles, the effects of which are expected to be similar over all ages (Rose and Charlesworth, 1981a). The logic behind this argument was that inbreeding depression is generally deleterious, over all fitness characters. As a group of inbred lines is expected to vary in the extent to which they suffer from homozygosity of recessive deleterious alleles, they will accordingly vary in the degree to which they suffer inbreeding depression. But as the degree of inbreeding depression affecting the lines varies, so will the degree to which each fitness component is depressed. This variation will thus be positively correlated over characters. Some inbred lines will be generally "sicker" than others. This will then give rise to a pattern of positive genetic covariation for fitness components, including longevity. Others have reiterated this argument (e.g., Clark, 1987).

This explanation of the positive genetic correlations obtained in experiments on inbred lines was tested in a study in which inbred lines of *D. melanogaster* were derived from an outbred population (Rose, 1984a), the outbred population having the estimated genetic correlations shown in Table 3.1. The results are shown in Table 3.3. (Only the results for the same characters as those of Tables 3.1 and 3.2 are shown.) As expected, the correlations obtained with the inbred lines are predominantly positive, unlike those obtained directly from the outbred population, shown in Table 3.1. This clearly indicates that the process of inbreeding the derived lines changed the signs of some of the genetic correlations from negative to positive values. Results from experiments on the genetics of aging that use inbreeding, at least in outbreeding species (cf. Johnson and Wood, 1982), are likely to be misleading.

## *de novo* mutations

Closely associated with the problem of inbreeding depression is that of the relationship between new mutations and established alleles in populations at genetic and selective equilibrium, since inbreeding makes manifest the homozygous deleterious effects of some recessive alleles (Simmons and Crow, 1977; Simmons, Preston, and Engels, 1980). Here several studies of *D. melanogaster* have revealed the relationship between the evolution of a population and the genetic correlation between different fitness-related characters. Chromosomes that retard development, in homozygous or heterozygous combinations, enhance fertility providing that flies having these chromosomes are above a certain threshold for developmental speed (Hiraizumi, 1961). Below this threshold, among slowly developing larvae, fertility increases with developmental speed, although not significantly so. In another series of experiments, genetic tradeoffs arose between fitness characters among alleles that were at high frequency in laboratory cage populations, but positive correlations

TABLE 3.3.  Mean correlations for adult female life-history characters over inbred lines of *D. melanogaster*

|  | Fecundity days 1–5 | Fecundity days 6–10 | Fecundity days 11–15 | Longevity |
|---|---|---|---|---|
| Fecundity days 1–5 | — | .62 | −.11 | .01 |
| Fecundity days 6–10 | .62 | — | .34 | .50 |
| Fecundity days 11–15 | −.11 | .34 | — | .23 |
| Longevity | .01 | .50 | .23 | — |

Rose, 1984a. © 1984 by the University of Chicago.

occurred between fitness characters in newly arisen mutations (Simmons, Preston, and Engels, 1980). Since most new mutations that have a detectable effect upon fitness will be of low fitness (Simmons and Crow, 1977), these results fit with Hiraizumi's (1961): Markedly deleterious alleles tend to have positively correlated pleiotropic effects over all fitness characters. (This is exactly in line with the effects of human progeroid syndromes, discussed in Chapter 2.)

Those alleles that are at high frequency in randomly mating populations will usually have high fitness. It is among this set of alleles that positively correlated pleiotropic effects are less predominant, from the available evidence. The alleles that determine the results of experiments that utilize inbreeding, contrived homozygosity, or *de novo* mutations in normally outbred species are normally rare, recessive, and deleterious. These alleles are quite unlike the beneficial alleles that determine the pattern of correlation between characters like fitness and aging in outbred populations. Evidently the results from experiments that employ inbreeding or mutagenesis will normally be spurious from the standpoint of the evolution of aging. (See also Chapter 2.)

## GENOTYPE–ENVIRONMENT INTERACTION

The third problem is that of genotype–environment interaction, particularly in the analysis of genetic correlations between the fitness characters of organisms recently brought into the laboratory. The phenomenon of genotype–environment interaction arises when genotypes that perform well in one environment perform poorly in another environment, relative to the other genotypes in the population. In a characteristic experiment, first-generation descendants of *D. simulans* females captured in the wild and brought into the laboratory were used for quantitative genetic analysis (Murphy, Giesel, and Manlove, 1983). Substantial genotype–environment interaction was found over different temperatures, while all significant genetic correlations between early and late life-history characters were positive. Experiments with rotifer life-history characters yielded positive genetic correlations among life-history characters in rotifers sampled from the wild but assayed in the laboratory (Bell, 1984a,b). Experiments on *Drosophila* populations that have been outbred in the laboratory for many generations did not yield positive genetic correlations, as shown in Table 3.1 (Rose and Charlesworth, 1981a). Analogously, field experiments on a field population did not yield consistently positive genetic correlations (Law, 1979). There seems to be a problem arising from studying in environment B samples of a population that evolved in environment A. It seems likely that this problem is genotype–environment interaction.

In order to make this problem clear, a number of fine points of practical experimental design must be discussed. It is rarely the case that experimental organisms are observed without any type of handling. Often laboratory insects are placed on special media for the observation of oviposition rate, media that may elicit a greater rate of egg laying than that exhibited normally. Similarly, a field population of vertebrates may be studied by regular weighings or extraction of blood samples. Plants growing in their natural habitats may be stripped of a flowering structure for an assay of gamete production. To the extent to which such observations reflect the initial physiological state and capacities of an organism, then their relative artificiality is not worrisome. Problems arise only when observation is repeated or protracted *and* such observation substantially alters the physiological or morphological basis of life history.

The suspicion arises that experiments performed in such a way that the physiology of life history is altered are subject to vitiating genotype–environment interactions. Such interactions arise when segregating alleles from a population subjected to a sufficiently novel environment are more likely to have effects of the same direction on all life-history characters than they were in their original environment. Upon transfer to a novel environment, variation between alleles with respect to the extent to which they are suited to the novel habitat largely determines patterns of variance and covariance. Alleles that are fortuitously preadapted to the new environment will tend to enhance all characters, while those that are not will tend to depress a broad range of characters, producing positive genetic correlations (Rose and Service, 1985; Reznick, Perry, and Travis, 1986; Clark, 1987).

Indirect evidence in support of this interpretation is available in studies of *D. pseudoobscura* (Dobzhansky, Lewontin, and Pavlovsky, 1964) and *D. robusta* (Etges, 1989). Flies were sampled from nature and brought into the laboratory, as in the life-history studies under review here. Comparing the initial with the subsequent year of laboratory cultivation, one study found large changes in life-history characters, although there was a lack of controls (Dobzhansky, Lewontin, and Pavlovsky, 1964). In the other study, significant changes in chromosomal inversion frequencies were observed after only 4–5 generations of culture in the laboratory (Etges, 1989). These results indicate that, for small invertebrates like *Drosophila*, the laboratory environment may be radically different in selection pressures from the natural habitat. This in turn suggests a great deal of potential for "novel-environment" effects on fitness-related characters.

The critical test of the novel-environment artifact is whether or not additive genetic correlations are increased, not in magnitude but toward $+1$ from $-1$, when genetic correlations between fitness-related characters are measured in a novel environment. Such an experiment was performed on an outbred *D. melanogaster* population that had been established in the laboratory for some time (Service and Rose, 1985). In the normal laboratory environment, the additive genetic correlation between early fecundity and starvation resistance was $-.913 \pm .027$ (mean plus or minus standard error). In a novel laboratory environment, with different temperature, light regime, and culture medium, the additive genetic correlation for these characters was $-.453 \pm .178$, a statistically higher value than that in the laboratory regime under which the flies had been maintained for more than 200 generations. Thus it appears that genetic correlation estimates obtained in novel environments may sometimes be biased towards positive values, making them suspect as estimates of the true underlying pattern of pleiotropy.

## The Balance of the Evidence

The only evidence that reliably addresses the question of the evolutionary relationship between aging and fitness is that obtained from populations allowed to breed in their natural fashion and studied in their evolutionarily normal environment. If laboratory experiments are necessary for reliable life-history observation, as will usually be the case with mobile metazoa and protozoa, then the population(s) studied must be at or near evolutionary equilibrium in the relevant laboratory environment. Conversely, if inferences are to be drawn from field populations, then they must be studied in the field. Other types of experiment face potentially grave artifacts due to inbreeding or genotype–environment interaction (Rose and Service, 1985; Reznick, Perry, and Travis, 1986; Clark, 1987).

As things now stand, there is no incontrovertible genetic evidence that aging is evolutionarily bound to fitness. All the studies that claim to support this conclusion (e.g., Giesel, 1979) have major methodological flaws (Rose, 1984a; Rose and Service, 1985; Service and Rose, 1985; Reznick, Perry, and Travis, 1986; Clark, 1987).

On the other hand, some genetic studies using *Drosophila* (e.g., Rose and Charlesworth, 1981a; Tucić, Cvetković, and Milanović, 1988; Hughes and Clark, 1988) and other species (e.g., Law, 1979; Friedman and Johnson, 1988) indicate that aging and earlier fitness components may be genetically distinct from each other, such that alleles enhancing early reproduction may not necessarily enhance longevity. If there is to be a provisional conclusion drawn, it must surely be that aging and fitness are genetically distinct to that extent.

However, the evolutionary independence of fitness and aging does not directly follow from the genetic independence of aging and fitness. The point is that the logical progression from genetic independence to evolutionary independence is theory laden, the theory of course being that of population genetics. The application of this theory to the evolution of aging depends on approximations, simplifying assumptions, and the extrapolation of results from one or two loci to many loci. Fortunately, this application can also be tested empirically, independently from the estimation of genetic correlations characterizing segregating genetic variability. These tests involve ascertaining whether or not the evolution of aging, as contrived in laboratory settings, in fact follows the patterns predicted by the evolutionary theory. Such tests are the concern of the next section.

## Response to Selection on Aging

If aging is evolutionarily independent of fitness in some fashion, then it should be possible to contrive circumstances in which selection can mold it in a way different from its action on fitness. Indeed, the basic evolutionary theory of aging has as a simple corollary the evolutionary dependence of aging on mortality and reproductive opportunities. For example, Eq. (1.6), giving the intensity of natural selection acting on age-specific survival probability, does not indicate a decrease in the intensity of natural selection until the first age at which $m(x)$ is greater than zero, the first age of reproduction. If this age is postponed substantially by the direct intervention of an experimenter, then natural selection will remain at full intensity for a longer part of the organism's lifetime. Over a number of generations, this should lead to an evolutionary postponement of aging.

Similar arguments apply if adult survivorship is kept relatively higher as a result of experimental, or other, intervention. Conversely, if all individuals over a certain age are killed or otherwise removed from a breeding population, over a number of generations, the force of natural selection estimated by Eq. (1.6) would be truncated at that age. This would allow the evolution of accelerated aging, in a population with appropriate genetic variability.

The first clear statement of these corollaries was that of Edney and Gill (1968):

> The [evolutionary] hypothesis requires that it should be possible to prolong the life span of a species by breeding it in an environment where the hazard factor is lower than normal. Such an experiment would be difficult to carry out, because genetically controlled senescence, already present in a population, would limit the extent to which environmental improvement could immediately extend specific longevity.
>
> A quicker answer might be obtained by the reverse procedure—in which the experimenter would impose an additional severe hazard by decreasing the normal life span for several generations. Then, according to the hypothesis, the subsequent life span of the experimental population should be shorter than that of a control population when both are tested in the environment of the control population.

Both types of experiment have been done: selection for postponed aging with *Drosophila* species and selection for accelerated aging with both *Drosophila* and *Tribolium*. Each will now be discussed in turn.

## Laboratory Selection for Postponed Aging

Working before the ideas of Edney and Gill (1968) were published, Wattiaux (1968a,b) performed experiments in which *Drosophila* cultures were maintained using adult females that had survived a number of weeks before being allowed to contribute eggs to the next generation. It should be pointed out that, in all experiments of this design, males and females are allowed to mate normally from the onset of adult life. In the *Drosophila subobscura* experiment, there was a 6 to 8 week postponement of reproduction (Wattiaux, 1968a), while the *Drosophila pseudoobscura* experiment involved a four week postponement of reproduction (Wattiaux, 1968b). The control lines were maintained using females within a few days of a week from adult eclosion. In effect, the selected lines were subjected to regimes of laboratory natural selection in which the force of natural selection was substantially increased at later ages. In the control lines, selection on life-history characters was intense only at early ages. After a number of generations, the selected lines were compared with the controls for longevity and inversion polymorphism in both experiments. In the *subobscura* experiments, Wattiaux (1968a) also compared age-specific female fecundity and early male mating success.

The results from the *D. subobscura* experiment are shown in Figures 3.4 and 3.5 for females and males, respectively. Longevity increased significantly in the "late-reproduced" population compared with the "early-reproduced" population, among both females and males. Later female fecundity was also significantly increased in the late-reproduced population, relative to the control. These results suggest that aging can indeed evolve separately from fitness, especially as the early-reproduced

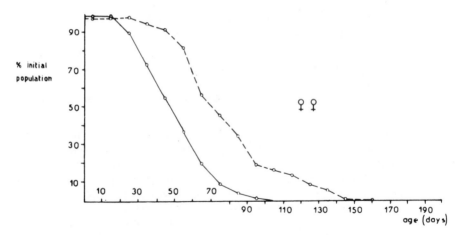

FIGURE 3.4. Female survival patterns of stocks of *D. subobscura*. The stock that was reproduced using young females is plotted as a solid line. The late-reproduced stock is the
dashed line; it has greater longevities. (From Wattiaux, 1968a.)

population underwent more generations in the laboratory than the late-reproduced
population, allowing more opportunity for adaptation to laboratory conditions.

On the other hand, a freshly caught sample of wild *D. subobscura* had substantially greater early fecundity than either the late-reproduced or early-reproduced
populations, as well as substantially greater male longevity relative to either "experimental" population. (Female longevity was similar to that of the late-reproduced
population.) This suggests that inbreeding depression could have been involved in
these results, particularly as the founder laboratory population consisted of 9 males

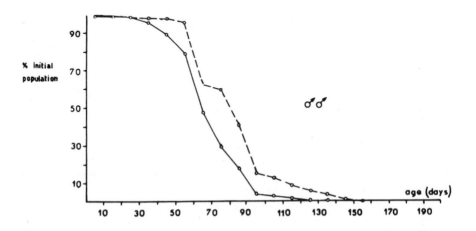

FIGURE 3.5. Male survival patterns of stocks of *D. subobscura*. The stock that was reproduced using young females is plotted as a solid line. The late-reproduced stock is the
dashed line; it has greater longevities. (From Wattiaux, 1968a.)

and 62 females. Since the early-reproduced line underwent 14 more generations in the laboratory before the data of Figures 3.4 and 3.5 were collected, relative to the late-reproduced line, it may have been more inbred. Thus, the lower longevity of the early-reproduced population could have been an artifact of inbreeding depression.

The *D. pseudoobscura* experiment involved three pairs of selected and control lines, according to inversion karyotype: Chiracahua (CH) monomorphic, Arrowhead (AR) monomorphic, and AR/CH inversion polymorphism (Wattiaux, 1968b). With comparison of males and females, this gives six tests for successful postponement of aging. Four of six times there was a statistically detectable postponement of aging after just a few generations of culture reproduction at later ages. Since these were apparently long-established laboratory populations, inbreeding depression is unlikely to have been a major factor in these results. The two failures of corroboration might have been due to a lack of sufficient generations for selection to act. On the whole, Wattiaux's (1968a,b) experiments seem to have given results largely in line with those corollaries of the evolutionary theory of aging that were adduced by Edney and Gill (1968), although the corroboration is not striking, and artifacts may have been involved in some of the significant results.

Wattiaux's late-reproduction type of experiment was repeated in the late 1970s with a *D. melanogaster* population known to possess abundant genetic variability for life-history characters (Rose and Charlesworth, 1981a) and systematically outbred in the laboratory for more than 50 generations before the start of the experiment. As before, a late-reproduced line was bred using adults that had survived at least 21 days from pupal eclosion (Rose and Charlesworth, 1980, 1981b). After twelve generations, the longevity of this late-reproduced culture was about 10 percent greater than that of the control, early-reproduced, population, a statistically significant increase. As in the *D. subobscura* study (Wattiaux, 1968a), late fecundity was also significantly increased.

A similar experiment was independently performed beginning around 1980, also using *D. melanogaster* (Luckinbill et al., 1984). In this case, there was twofold replication of the late-reproduced and early-reproduced populations. Unlike the assays of the earlier experiments (Wattiaux, 1968a,b; Rose and Charlesworth, 1980, 1981b), the longevities of flies from selected and control lines were assayed without synchrony, controlled rearing densities, or standardized maternal ages. In addition, the age at which females were used to produce eggs for the next generation in the late-reproduced populations was progressively increased, from generation to generation. As shown in Figure 3.6, the resulting increase of longevity in the late-reproduced cultures was so great that it overcame the measurement problems arising from the lack of parallel longevity assay of the two types of population. Later fecundity was also substantially increased in females from late-reproduced populations (Luckinbill et al., 1984).

Also beginning in 1980, another late-reproduction experiment (Rose, 1984b) was performed on the *D. melanogaster* population that had been studied extensively in the 1970s (Rose and Charlesworth, 1980, 1981a,b). There were five separate populations subjected to each procedure, early or late culture reproduction, but only three populations of each type were assayed in the data of the first published study

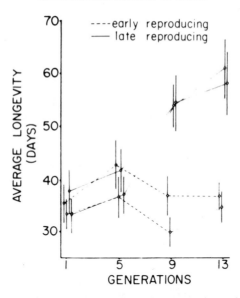

FIGURE 3.6. The sequential pattern of mean longevity change in stocks of *D. melanogaster* maintained using older females, compared with controls. Mean longevity consistently increases in the late-reproduced lines. (From Luckinbill et al., 1984.)

(Rose, 1984b). Again, the age at which females contributed eggs to establish the next generation in the late-reproduced lines was progressively increased, until the late-reproduced culture generation length was 70 days, as compared with 14 days in the early-reproduced cultures. The female survival patterns after 15 generations are shown in Figure 3.7. Both male and female longevities are significantly greater in the late-reproduced cultures (Rose, 1984b). Late fecundity was also increased significantly. (See Chapter 4 for more detail on fecundity data from experiments of this kind.)

These populations have since been repeatedly examined for longevity differentiation of all ten populations developed in the course of the experiment (Rose, 1984b). For example, after an additional 11 generations the mean longevities of the ten populations had achieved the values shown in Table 3.4 (Hutchinson and Rose, 1990). In this assay, the early- and late-reproduced populations were reared and handled as pairs, with assays for each pair beginning on separate days. This made the appropriate method of data analysis one of five pairwise differences. The late-reproduced longevities were significantly greater. Additional work with these populations has also shown that they have not been subject to inbreeding depression, making the interpretation of results obtained from them straightforward (Hutchinson and Rose, 1990).

Overall, the results from experiments conducted by three independent laboratories with three different *Drosophila* species indicate that aging can be postponed when selection is made to act with greater force at later ages by postponing culture reproduction, as predicted by Edney and Gill (1968). This prediction in turn is a straightforward corollary of the basic theoretical result that the force of natural

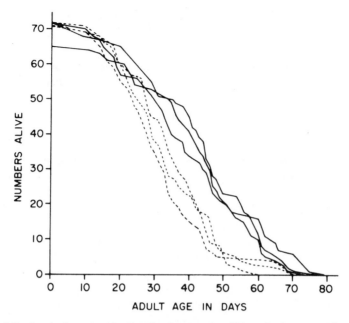

FIGURE 3.7.  Survival patterns for females from stocks of *D. melanogaster* maintained using females of different ages. Stocks reproduced using older females are plotted as solid lines. Stocks reproduced using younger females are plotted as dashed lines. (From Rose, 1984b.)

selection acting on survival probability begins to fall once reproduction starts. Therefore, the experimental results with selection for postponed aging are clearly corroborative of the evolutionary theory of aging.

However, this interpretation has been queried on the grounds that the longer-lived stocks could have been selected for reproductive restraint, rather than postponed aging as such (Partridge, 1987). This criticism is founded on work showing the importance of reproductive activity in determining mortality patterns (Partridge et al., 1986, 1987). Service (1989) has shown that the differentiation that

TABLE 3.4.  Mean longevities from pupal eclosion,
in days, of early-reproduced and late-reproduced
*D. melanogaster* populations after 25 generations
of late reproduction, as in Rose (1984b).

| Late-Reproduced Populations | Early-Reproduced Populations | Difference |
|---|---|---|
| 71.3 | 60.7 | 10.6 |
| 55.1 | 46.7 | 8.4 |
| 64.4 | 49.5 | 14.9 |
| 59.6 | 47.2 | 12.4 |
| 62.2 | 46.3 | 15.9 |

Data of Hutchinson and Rose (1990).

evolves under the early- and late-culture regimes does not depend on reproductive activity; late-culture flies kept as virgins throughout their lives still exhibit postponed aging relative to control flies handled in the same manner. Therefore, there seems little reason to doubt that the fundamental physiology of these flies has been altered. This is a point that will be discussed further in Chapter 8.

## Laboratory Selection for Accelerated Senescence

The second of Edney and Gill's (1968) two proposed tests of the evolutionary theory of aging requires measuring the effects of senescence of truncating the effective life span of individuals in a laboratory population over a number of generations. This has been done twice with *Tribolium*. The first study of this kind used *Tribolium castaneum* strains that had been in the laboratory for some time (Sokal, 1970). Two pairs of selected and control strains were used, one phenotypically "wild-type," the other homozygous for the autosomal *black* allele. The control strains were kept in mass culture, allowing prolonged adult survival with contribution to subsequent generations by older beetles. Selected lines were derived from the controls and subjected to 40 generations of culture maintenance involving discrete generations in which "recently eclosed adults were permitted to oviposit for 3 days and were killed thereafter." One of the two genders responded as expected to selection in each pair of selected and control lines. This shows that aging can be accelerated by forced early reproduction of laboratory stocks, although it need not *always* be so accelerated.

The second study (Mertz, 1975) used *T. castaneum* lines that had previously had overlapping generations and unlimited opportunity for late reproduction. From these initial lines, early-reproduced lines were derived: one set of four reproduced using adults no more than 10 days from eclosion, the other set of four reproduced using adults no more than 20 days from eclosion. About 11–12 generations of selection were imposed on the derived lines, although generations were not perfectly discrete. Some degree of inbreeding may have arisen in the earliest-reproduced lines. It should also be noted that longevities were assayed using perpetually virgin adults, which may have introduced a degree of genotype–environment interaction (vide Rose and Service, 1985; Clare and Luckinbill, 1985; Reznick, Perry, and Travis, 1986; Clark, 1987) in survival patterns. (Indeed, the enhancement of virgin survival that was found is indicative of this.) No statistically significant longevity difference between experimental treatments was found (Mertz, 1975), ostensibly falsifying the evolutionary theory of aging in this case. However, problems of genotype–environment interaction may have vitiated the value of the only substantial body of longevity data, that from perpetual virgins. On the other hand, it should be pointed out that the other *Tribolium* study (Sokal, 1970) also used virgins. Therefore, it is difficult to know what to conclude from this experiment.

There is a *D. melanogaster* study (Mueller, 1987) that is somewhat similar to the *Tribolium* work. In this experiment, three independent lines were reproduced using young adults and discrete generations, three others being maintained using overlapping generations allowing late adult reproduction. All six lines were derived from a common ancestral population. Aging was measured in terms of declining age-specific female fecundity. It was found that fly cultures that were reproduced at earlier ages for more than 100 generations had reduced later fecundity, a result that indicates accelerated aging. There were some inbreeding depression problems; the results were not quite as clear when $F_1$ hybrids were used. The basic pattern was sustained in both crossed and uncrossed lines, however, suggesting that the early reproduction treatment did indeed produce an evolutionary acceleration of aging, as required by the theory. While the stocks with reduced late fecundity did not undergo an initial reduction in longevity (Bierbaum, Mueller, and Ayala, 1989), just as they did not undergo an initial late fecundity reduction, longevity assays after a large number of generations have revealed some significant longevity reduction (Mueller et al., unpublished).

Taken together, the experimental findings concerning the evolutionary accelera-tion of aging are not as clear as those concerning its evolutionary postponement. This may be a result of the basic problem that inbreeding depression can readily generate false positives, in which the longevity or fecundity falls during the course of an experiment. This problem does not arise in experiments with postponed aging, providing the controls are not inbred during the experiment. Normally, tests for the evolution of postponed aging will be the experiments of choice.

## Related Experiments

Over the past century, many puzzling experiments seemingly concerning the evolu-tion of aging have been published. Most of the experiments lacked appropriate controls. Classic examples are the studies of rotifers by Lansing (1947, 1948). He found that laboratory cultures reproduced using older mothers died out in a few generations, longevity progressively falling before culture extinction. A straightfor-ward explanation of these results is that Lansing was not able to provide culture conditions of sufficient quality to maintain his experimental organisms, given the use of older, perhaps senescent, parents. In any event, it is unlikely that we will ever know what happened in those particular experiments. The results have not been reproducible (Meadow and Barrows, 1971), suggesting that they are not worthy of further consideration.

A *Drosophila* late-reproduction experiment was used to address the question of the universality of this "Lansing effect" (Comfort, 1953). An inbred *D. subobscura* stock, well established in the laboratory, was reproduced for eight generations using females that had achieved at least 30 days of adult age. The results are shown in Figure 3.8. There was no statistically detectable change in mean longevity over the eight generations, and the culture did not die out. This experiment suggests that Lansing effects are not universal. In addition, it indicates that inbred laboratory lines need not respond to natural selection's fostering later fertility and survival. This conclusion does not impinge on the evolutionary theory of aging, because any evolutionary response to selection is conditional on the presence of genetic variability.

In another historic experiment, *D. melanogaster* cultures were created in which some lines were allowed to mate immediately while others were denied mating opportunities until later in life (Glass, 1960). The results of these experiments were

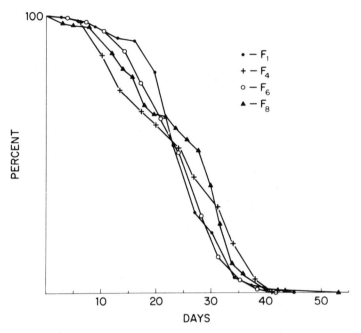

FIGURE 3.8. Sequential pattern of survivorship curve change when an inbred line of *D. subobscura* was maintained using eggs laid by adults who had achieved at least 30 days of age as imagos. Evidently, there has been no directional change. (From the data of Comfort, 1953, as displayed in Comfort, 1979, p. 157.) Reprinted by permission of the publisher from *The Biology of Senescence*, by A. Comfort, p. 157. Copyright 1979 by Elsevier Science Publishing Co., Inc.

that each line "seems to demonstrate a longer life span under those conditions of mating to which it was subjected during previous generations" (Glass, 1960). Because the *Drosophila* mating pattern has enormous effects on both female longevity (Maynard Smith, 1958) and male longevity (Partridge and Farquhar, 1981), these experiments are very difficult to interpret from the standpoint of the evolution of aging. Each mating regime will define a different environment for the expression of alleles affecting aging, and thus there will be selection to adapt to the mating regime, as the results indicate. These experiments were not, therefore, suitable tests of the evolutionary theory of aging.

Undoubtedly the most baffling recent experiments of relevance to the evolution of aging are those reported in Lints and Hoste (1974, 1977). These experiments used a hybrid laboratory population of *D. melanogaster*, created from a fourway cross of inbred "wild-type" laboratory stocks. Thus there must have been abundant genetic variation in the experimental lines, presumably including genetic variation affecting aging. Six lines were established, each reproduced at a larval density of ten per vial. Three lines were reproduced using young adults, and three were reproduced using older adults. It seems that there may have been natural selection for later reproduction. But the results did not conform to the expectations of the evolutionary theory (Lints, 1978, 1983). Mean longevities fluctuated wildly, and there was no material increase in life span. The one possible corroboration of the evolutionary theory of aging was a tendency for the day of maximal egg production to occur earlier in cultures reproduced at earlier ages, while late-reproduced cultures may have developed a somewhat later day of maximal fecundity (Lints and Hoste, 1977).

Fortunately, a penetrating analysis of the relationship between the contrasting findings of Lints and Hoste (1974, 1977) and those of Wattiaux and others has been published (Clare and Luckinbill, 1985; Luckinbill and Clare, 1985). In this experimental study, the authors duplicated the methods of Lints and Hoste (1974, 1977) with careful attention to corresponding protocols. In particular, a density of ten larvae per vial was also used, alongside populations with high rearing densities. The results of the exact repetition were in keeping with those of Lints and Hoste (1974, 1977): Erratic fluctuations in longevity occurred, with no detectable trend to increased longevity in lines reproduced at later ages with low larval densities. But populations handled at high larval densities, by contrast, did undergo evolution of increased life span. These results refuted an earlier interpretation (Rose and Charlesworth, 1981b) that the Lints results reflected a lack of selective and/or genetic equilibrium in the base population. The dependence of the evolutionary response on larval rearing density indicates that the likely explanation for the failure of response in Lints-type experiments is a genotype–environment interaction that suppresses the expression of genetic variation for aging at low larval rearing densities. The critical experimental evidence for this interpretation is that the difference in mean life span of lines that have differentiated with respect to rates of aging increases with increasing larval densities (Clare and Luckinbill, 1985). To some extent, genetic variance for longevity may be greater under more crowded, and thus stressful, conditions.

In an independent set of *D. melanogaster* experiments, it has been found that other fitness-related characters, particularly fecundity and stress resistance, did not respond to changes in the age of culture reproduction when *Drosophila* larvae were reared at low densities, while they did respond when cultures were reared at high densities (Service, Hutchinson, and Rose, 1988). As this experiment was performed with different *D. melanogaster* populations, it indicates the generality of the conclusions of Luckinbill and Clare (1985).

Lints et al. (1979) report another failure of selection to increase longevity in *D. melanogaster,* in this case direct selection. However, the larval rearing density used in this experiment was again ten per vial. Thus this experiment was also performed using an environment in which genetic variation in life span is known to be largely suppressed (Clare and Luckinbill, 1985). The conclusion of Lints et al. (1979) that life span is not normally genetically controlled is thus unwarranted.

There are some relevant studies of life-history differentiation among populations of *Poa annua,* a meadow grass species. Individuals derived from populations in frequently disturbed meadows, and thus called "opportunist," had shorter lives than individuals from less disturbed habitats. Presumably the disturbed meadows had imposed higher grass mortalities and so afforded fewer opportunities for reproduction at later ages, for the simple reason that the grass was likely to survive to those later ages. If this is in fact the case, then the shorter life span of opportunist grass is in keeping with the evolutionary theory of senescence. However, this is a somewhat weak inference, in that the meadows could have been different with respect to several variables that could have given rise to selection on life history.

A more directly relevant study involved *D. pseudoobscura* populations maintained according to two distinct culture regimes: discrete generations, in which flies were allowed to oviposit for just two days after emergence, and continuous culture, in which adult flies were not discarded, but instead preserved in continuous culture (Taylor and Condra, 1980). Evidently, among other selective factors, the continuous-culture populations were selected for late reproduction relative to the discrete-generations populations. Females from the continuous-culture populations indeed exhibited significantly greater mean longevities, compared with discrete-generations females, while males did not (Taylor and Condra, 1980). The absence of male differentiation was subsequently explained in terms of the greater mating success of young virgin males over older nonvirgin males (Taylor et al., 1981). The idea is that continued survival of nonvirgin males may enhance their total reproductive output much less than continued survival may enhance the total reproductive output of females (Taylor et al., 1981), because the older males will not be able to reproduce anyway, while the older females will, *Drosophila* males being willing to mate with any type of female. While this type of phenomenon might also seem to be a problem in late-reproduction experiments, it should be borne in mind that in those experiments the entire population ages as a single cohort, so that there is no competition between older and younger males.

One could continue to describe experiments in which selection on aging might have been engendered by changes of reproductive schedule, depending on unknown aspects of the experimental conditions. However, further multiplication of instances of this kind will only add to the accumulation of ambiguous results needing analysis. The pains that have been taken (Comfort, 1953; Meadow and Barrows, 1971; Luckinbill and Clare, 1985) to sort out the findings of Lansing (1947, 1948) or Lints and Hoste (1974, 1977) should hardly be taken for each and every puzzling experiment of possible relevance to the evolution of aging. Thus there may always be some undigested residue of elusive results where selection on senescence is concerned.

## Conclusion

Both the genetics of aging and laboratory selection on aging indicate that aging is genetically and evolutionarily distinct from fitness.

It is an absolute requirement for the evolution of any attribute that there be heritable genetic variation for it. This is certainly the case for the life-history characters that jointly comprise the aging phenotype, although they are not special in having this genetic variation. Almost all measurable phenotypes have heritable genetic variation.

The evolution of aging as a process separate from the evolution of fitness depends critically on the degree to which early and late life-history characters are positively correlated genetically. While there is abundant evidence indicating positive genetic correlations between fitness and aging, this evidence is plagued by three problems: invalid inference of genetic correlations from phenotypic correlations, inbreeding depression, and genotype–environment interaction. The last two, in particular, tend to bias estimates of genetic correlation toward positive values. Estimates of genetic correlation obtained using outbred populations in their normal environments, which are free of these three problems, generally do not indicate tight, positive, genetic correlation between fitness and aging. Therefore, organisms can evolve varying rates of aging, at least in part independently of the evolution of their fitness. Thus aging is not simply a reflection of limits to the improvement of fitness itself. It has the potential to evolve on its own, in principle.

Laboratory experiments that vary the force of natural selection acting at later ages allow critical tests of the degree to which aging does in fact evolve along the lines predicted by the evolutionary theory of aging. Specifically in experiments with *Drosophila,* it has been found that aging can evolve rapidly in the laboratory, when the force of natural selection at later ages is changed by the experimenter and there is enough genetic variability in the population employed. In particular, stocks reproduced at later ages tend to evolve postponed aging, due to the strengthening of the force of natural selection at later ages, in conformity with the evolutionary theory of aging. There is also some evidence for the acceleration of aging in stocks reproduced at earlier ages, again as the theory requires.

At the experimental level, then, the evolutionary theory of aging has been sufficiently corroborated to warrant further examination. Among the issues that are worth considering in light of the empirical success of the evolutionary theory of aging are: (1) the genetic basis of the evolution of aging, taken up in Chapter 4; (2) the degree to which comparative patterns of aging match those implied by the evolutionary theory, considered in Chapter 5; and (3) how well the evolutionary theory fares when compared with other fundamental theories for the biology of aging, a major theme of Chapters 6 to 8.

# 4

# Genetic Mechanisms for the
# Evolution of Aging

Several different genetic mechanisms could be involved in the evolution of aging. This diversity of genetic mechanisms does not, however, place the general evolutionary theory of aging in any difficulty. Any one of them would be sufficient, just as jointly they are sufficient to give rise to the evolution of aging. Thus theoretical evaluation or experimental tests of these alternative genetic mechanisms are not tests of the general theory.

This relationship between the general evolutionary theory and the particular genetic mechanisms that might subserve it is largely analogous to the problem of the population genetics of adaptation. The evolution of adaptations can be explained in terms of several hypotheses about genetic mechanisms: (1) natural selection acting on a few loci of major effects confined to the character undergoing selection, (2) natural selection acting on many loci of minor effects confined to the character undergoing selection, or (3) natural selection acting on loci of diverse effects impinging on a number of characters simultaneously (Wright, 1980). All these genetic mechanisms are perfectly compatible with fundamental neo-Darwinian theory, so that tests of its general validity do not bear on these subsidiary mechanisms individually. Conversely, one of these particular hypotheses could be erroneous without placing the general theory of adaptation at risk of falsification. Similarly, there are alternative population genetic hypotheses for the evolution of aging, hypotheses that are theoretically and empirically independent of the general theory for the evolution of aging.

The two major alternative population genetic mechanisms are: (1) *antagonistic pleiotropy,* in which alleles that have beneficial effects at early ages have antagonistic deleterious effects at later ages, and (2) *age specificity of gene action,* in which alleles having deleterious effects at later ages are essentially neutral, because of a lack of effects at earlier ages and weak selection at later ages due to the declining force of selection with age. With the first mechanism, natural selection actively engenders aging in the course of increasing mean fitness. With the second mechanism, mutation is the primary force establishing aging, and for that reason it has sometimes been referred to as the *mutation-accumulation* mechanism for the evolution of senescence. (Note that this is not a *somatic* mutation hypothesis, in that the mutations are accumulating evolutionarily in the germ lines of successive generations, not in the cells of the soma.) These two mechanisms differ with respect to the extent of pleiotropy between early and late life-history characters. It should be noted that one set of loci may mold aging according to one mechanism, while another set of loci in the same species may conform to the other mechanism. Thus *both* mechanisms could, in principle, operate in the evolution of aging in a particular species.

## Antagonistic Pleiotropy

### *Development of the Theory*

Antagonistic pleiotropy is the population-genetic formulation of the broadly conceived idea of evolutionary tradeoffs or constraints. As such, it dates back to Charles Darwin, at least in its generally conceived form. In the context of aging, Wallace and Weismann both seemed to have had some notion of immortality being sacrificed for the sake of increased reproduction, as discussed in Chapter 1. Naturally, their formulations of this mechanism were somewhat obscure, particularly as they had no understanding of Mendelian inheritance when most of their comments on aging were prepared.

The first unambiguous discussion of antagonistic pleiotropy in the context of the evolution of aging is that of Medawar (1946):

> It is by no means difficult to imagine a genetic endowment which can favour young animals only at the expense of their elders; or rather, at their own expense when they themselves grow old. A gene or combination of genes that promotes this state of affairs will under certain numerically definable conditions spread through a population simply because the younger animals it favours have, as a group, a relatively large contribution to make to the ancestry of the future population.

Similarly, Medawar (1952) proposed, "A relatively small advantage conferred early in the life of an individual may outweigh a catastrophic disadvantage withheld until later."

George C. Williams (1957, 1960), a leading American evolutionary biologist, has been the most forceful proponent of the antagonistic pleiotropy mechanism for the evolution of aging. Williams (1957) argued that, "Natural selection may be said to be biased in favor of youth over old age whenever a conflict of interests arises." This conflict arises from "pleiotropic genes . . . that have opposite effects on fitness at different ages." And thus we have the following capsule argument:

> Selection of a gene that confers an advantage at one age and a disadvantage at another will depend not only on the magnitudes of the effects themselves, but also on the times of the effects. An advantage during the period of maximum reproductive probability would increase the total reproductive probability more than a proportionately similar disadvantage later on would decrease it. So natural selection will frequently maximize vigor in youth at the expense of vigor later on and thereby produce a declining vigor (aging) during adult life. (Williams, 1957)

One of the first mathematical discussions of antagonistic pleiotropy in the evolution of aging was that of Charlesworth (1980, pp. 206–217), whose results can be rendered fairly simply. Consider the case of an allele having effects on age-specific survival probabilities. Turning to notation, let the intensity of selection on age-specific survival probability be represented by $s_{ij}(x)$ for genotype $A_i A_j$ at age $x$:

$$s_{ij}(x) = \sum_{x=a+1} e^{-r_{ij}x} \, l_{ij}(x) m_{ij}(x)$$

from Eq. (1.6). Let the denominator of Eq. (1.6) be represented by $T_{ij}$ for genotype $A_i A_j$:

$$T_{ij} = \sum_{x=1} x e^{-r_{ij}x} \, l_{ij}(x) m_{ij}(x).$$

The $s(x)$ function represents the age-specific intensity of natural selection on survival probability, scaled relative to the survival probability at the affected age. The $T$ function is a measure of generation length, for the indicated genotype.

To estimate the effects of selection acting on a genotype with effects on fitness characters spread out over a number of ages, we need some expression for the effect of substituting a copy of each allele making up a diploid genotype. This can be obtained by considering the differences between $P_{ij}$ values when alleles are changed, providing these differences are weighted by the frequencies of these alternative alleles (vide Falconer, 1981). Thus, in the present case, allele $A_2$ has an "average effect of gene substitution" at age $x_k$ given by

$$\alpha_{kP} = p_1 \ln P_{12}(x_k) + p_2 \ln P_{22}(x_k)$$
$$- p_1 \ln P_{11}(x_k) - p_2 \ln P_{12}(x_k),$$

where the $p_i$ are the gene frequencies of the $A_i$ alleles and the $P_{ij}$ are the age-specific survival probabilities associated with genotype $A_i A_j$. The $kP$ subscript of $\alpha$ indicates that the effect is at age $x_k$ and that the effect is on age-specific survival probability $P$. Using these $\alpha_{kP}$ variables, the equation for gene-frequency change can be written as

$$T_{11} \, \Delta p_2 \approx p_2(1-p_1)[\alpha_{1P} s_{11}(x_1) + \alpha_{2P} s_{11}(x_2)]$$

[Charlesworth, 1980, p. 209, Eq. (5.10)]. If $\alpha_{1P} > 0$ and $\alpha_{2P} < 0$, but $x_2 >> x_1$, then $\Delta p_2$ is likely to be positive, because $s_{11}(x_2)$ will be small. In English, when the beneficial effects of an allelic substitution occur sufficiently early, relative to deleterious effects, then selection is likely to favor the substitution, all other things being equal. Similar equations apply for genes affecting fecundity, with similar conclusions. Again, alleles that have early beneficial effects and sufficiently later deleterious effects are likely to spread due to selection. These mathematical results show that the verbal suggestions of Medawar and Williams concerning antagonistic pleiotropy were in fact well founded in terms of population genetics theory.

A different line of analysis focuses on the question of whether or not antagonistic pleiotropy could maintain genetic polymorphism (Rose, 1982, 1983, 1985). The results in the simpler discrete-generation models are easiest to understand. Suppose that there are two fitness components, $W_1$ and $W_2$, and two alleles, $A_1$ and $A_2$, with opposed effects on these fitness components. Let $W_1$ and $W_2$ be multiplicative in their contribution to fitness, so that net fitness $W$ is given by their product. For purposes of standardization, we will take

$$W_1(A_1A_2) = V$$

and

$$W_2(A_1A_2) = F,$$

where $V$ and $F$ are positive constants. The deviations of the homozygote fitness components from those of the heterozygote will be represented by Greek symbols, $\epsilon$ giving the reduction in $W_1$ associated with homozygosity for allele $A_1$ and $\delta$ giving the reduction in $W_2$ associated with homozygosity for allele $A_2$. The corresponding beneficial effects of homozygosity for these alleles are given by $h_2\delta$ and $h_1\epsilon$ for fitness components $W_2$ and $W_1$, respectively. All of these parameters are taken to be positive. The main effect of this type of parametrization is to preclude overdominance for individual fitness components, in which heterozygotes are superior. It does not preclude overdominance for net fitness itself. Note that, if each individual fitness component is subject to overdominant genetic effects, then genetic polymorphism can be maintained without pleiotropy. Therefore, it is important to consider those cases in which such fitness-component overdominance is precluded.

With all these specifications, the resulting fitnesses are given as follows:

|       | $A_1A_1$ | $A_1A_2$ | $A_2A_2$ |
|-------|----------|----------|----------|
| $W_1$ | $V - \epsilon$ | $V$ | $V + h_1\epsilon$ |
| $W_2$ | $F + h_2\delta$ | $F$ | $F - \delta$ |
| $W$   | $VF - F\epsilon + h_2\delta(V - \epsilon)$ | $VF$ | $VF - V\delta + h_1\epsilon(F - \delta)$ |

It has been proved for a variety of population genetic models with discrete generations that if the $h_i$ dominance parameters are sufficiently small, then protected polymorphism due to heterozygote superiority with two alleles, or similar genotypic fitness patterns with more alleles or loci, is assured (Rose, 1982, 1983). This is easily seen in the present example. If $h_1 = h_2 = 0$, corresponding to fully recessive deleterious effects, then the homozygote fitnesses are $VF - F\epsilon$ and $VF - V\delta$, while the heterozygote has fitness $VF$. Since $F\epsilon$ and $V\delta$ are both positive, both homozygote fitnesses are less than that of the heterozygote, ensuring overdominance and thus stable genetic polymorphism.

The results with age structure are analogous (Rose, 1985). The complete model for an arbitrary number of small effects on mortality and fecundity characters has been analyzed, but discussion of the case of antagonistic pleiotropic effects on two age-specific fecundities will suffice here. Again, take one locus with two alleles, with effects on age-specific fecundity $m(x)$ at ages $x_a$ and $x_b$ given by $f_a$ and $f_b$, respectively, in the case of the homozygous deleterious effect, and $h_a f_a$ and $h_b f_b$, respectively, in the case of the homozygous beneficial effects. The idea is that these effects would have the same constraints as in the multiplicative fitness-component model above, with no heterozygote superiority for individual fitness components. With these assumptions, the resulting fecundities are as follows:

|            | $A_1 A_1$         | $A_1 A_2$ | $A_2 A_2$         |
| ---------- | ----------------- | --------- | ----------------- |
| $m_{ij}(x_a)$ | $m(x_a) - f_a$   | $m(x_a)$  | $m(x_a) + h_a f_a$ |
| $m_{ij}(x_b)$ | $m(x_b) + h_b f_b$ | $m(x_b)$  | $m(x_b) - f_b$    |

With these genetic effects, maintenance of genetic polymorphism requires that

$$e^{-r_{11}x_a}\, l(x_a)f_a - e^{-r_{11}x_b}l(x_b)h_b f_b$$

and

$$e^{-r_{22}x_b}\, l(x_b)f_b - e^{-r_{22}x_a}\, l(x_a)h_a f_a$$

be sufficiently large, where the $l(x)$ functions give the age-specific survivorship, as in Chapter 1. There are two things to be noted about these expressions. First, the dominance parameters $h_a$ and $h_b$ play the same role as they did in the discrete-generation models; the smaller their value, the more likely protected polymorphism becomes. This can be seen from the position of the $h$ parameters; they follow the minus sign. Since all the terms in each of these expressions are positive, reducing the magnitude of the $h$ parameters reduces the magnitude of its associated term. This then makes the value of the complete expression larger, in turn, making it easier to satisfy the parametric conditions for overdominance with respect to fitness. Second, the weighting of the genetic effects in these expressions is the same as that of the numerator of Eq. (1.7), $e^{-rx}\, l(x)$, so that genetic effects expressed at later ages will normally be less important in determining the outcome of selection, providing the population size is not rapidly declining, since $l(x)$ declines with age.

These essential findings are general to mortality and fecundity effects, separate or joint, although they become quite cumbersome in cases in which there are multiple effects on survival probabilities (Rose, 1985). In any case, it remains true that antagonistic pleiotropy can, in theory, maintain abundant genetic variability for age-specific fitness characters, in the absence of overdominant effects on specific life-history characters.

The significance of these theoretical results is that it should be possible to detect antagonistic pleiotropy among segregating alleles at some loci, if alleles exhibiting antagonistic pleiotropy have often arisen in the evolutionary history of a population. This is because at least some of the resulting combinations of allelic effects should maintain genetic polymorphism. Thus the present state of populations can provide some information as to the importance of antagonistic pleiotropy in the evolution of aging, both in the present and in the past. This will be true even if many alleles exhibiting antagonistic pleiotropy have gone to fixation due to natural selection.

## Experimental Evidence

There are two types of experimental evidence that indicate the action of the antagonistic pleiotropy mechanism: (1) negative genetic correlations between early and late life-history characters, and (2) antagonistic correlated responses of life-history characters to selection on other life-history characters.

### GENETIC CORRELATIONS

As has already been discussed in Chapter 3, there has been some controversy about genetic correlations between age-specific components of fitness. Some authors have generally detected positive genetic correlations or their equivalent (e.g., Giesel, 1979; Bell, 1984a). These experiments have been subjected to stringent criticism (e.g., Rose and Service, 1985; Reznick, Perry, and Travis, 1986; Clark, 1987) as well as experimental attacks in which artifacts have been shown to arise from the procedures employed (Rose, 1984a; Service and Rose, 1985). This was described in detail in Chapter 3; those experiments will not be discussed further here.

Of greater interest here is the fact that the two most important sources of artifact in experiments on genetic correlations between fitness characters, inbreeding depression and genotype–environment interaction, both bias the results toward *positive* genetic correlations (Rose and Service, 1985). Therefore, studies that have suffered from these problems, but that nonetheless find some evidence for negative genetic correlations, still constitute evidence for the existence of negative genetic correlations, and thus antagonistic pleiotropy.

As before, the evidence divides into studies of *Drosophila* and studies of other species. Some *Drosophila* experiments in which inbreeding depression may have arisen nevertheless gave evidence for negative genetic correlations between early reproduction and longevity (Gowen and Johnson, 1946; Hiraizumi, 1985). Studies using stocks recently derived from the wild, and thus biased towards positive genetic correlations as discussed in Chapter 3, still yielded results indicating negative genetic correlations (Tucić, Cvetković, and Milanović, 1988; Hughes and Clark, 1988; Scheiner, Caplan, and Lyman, 1989). A *Drosophila* study free of either artifact found a negative additive genetic correlation between early fecundity and longevity in *D. melanogaster* (Rose and Charlesworth, 1981a), although there is no confidence interval about the result. A noteworthy feature of the range of *Drosophila* experiments indicating negative genetic correlations is that they involved a number of different methodologies: between-line correlations over laboratory stocks (Gowen and Johnson, 1946), quantitative genetic sib analysis (Rose and Charlesworth, 1981a; Tucić, Cvetković, and Milanović, 1988; Scheiner, Caplan, and Lyman, 1989), and chromosomal extraction (Hiraizumi, 1985; Hughes and Clark, 1988). The concordance of results using these diverse methods indicates that, in at least some *Drosophila* populations, negative genetic correlations between early reproduction and longevity may occur.

Worthy of special mention is the *abnormal abdomen* allele in *Drosophila mercatorum*. This allele greatly increases early fecundity, but pleiotropically reduces longevity (Templeton and Rankin, 1978; Templeton, Crease, and Shah, 1985). As such, it is a type specimen of the kind of allele that natural selection might actively favor, in spite of the acceleration in aging that it produces.

Turning to other genera, high early reproduction was correlated with reduced later survival and reproduction in *Poa annua* lineages (Law, 1979). Antagonistic covariation occurred among inversions of the seaweed fly, *Coelopa frigida,* such that one karyotype increased total fertility and longevity while increasing the age at first reproduction, thereby reducing early reproductive output (Butlin and Day, 1985). One of the most dramatic demonstrations of antagonistic pleiotropy to this point is the discovery of a *Caenorhabditis elegans* mutant, *age-1,* that confers increased life span in association with a considerable reduction in fertility (Friedman and Johnson, 1988). [This is somewhat analogous to *grandchildless* in *D. subobscura,* which produces progeny with increased longevity in conjunction with a lack of ovaries (Maynard Smith, 1958).] However, the range and quality of the *Drosophila* data far exceed those available for any other genus.

Of some interest is the argument that Albin (1988) has put forward for Huntington's chorea being an instance of antagonistic pleiotropy. This genetic disease is caused by a single autosomal dominant and clearly shortens life span. The question of interest is the evidence for an enhancement in early fertility. The average relative fertility of Huntington's chorea victims over the studies reviewed by Albin was 1.09, an increase of nine percent above normal fertility. Since the deleterious impact of Huntington's chorea is late enough in life that it would be unlikely to play much of a role in natural selection, it must be asked whether the allele is spreading through human populations. Albin finds a little evidence for such a spread, which is epidemiologically alarming, to say the least.

CORRELATED RESPONSES TO SELECTION

The best evidence in favor of antagonistic pleiotropy comes from the response of early reproduction to selection for postponed aging and vice versa. Reduced early male mating success was found in a *D. subobscura* population that had evolved greater longevity in the laboratory (Wattiaux, 1968a). Substantially reduced early female fecundity was observed in *D. melanogaster* populations that had been successfully selected for increased longevity (Rose and Charlesworth, 1980, 1981b; Luckinbill et al., 1984, 1987; Rose, 1984b; Hutchinson and Rose, 1990). Illustrative results are shown in Figure 4.1. In the opposite type of experiment, in which selection is on increased early fertility, longevity was reduced in the amphipod *Gammarus lawrencianus* as a result of selection for increased early reproduction (Doyle and Hunte, 1981). *Poa annua* inhabiting a stable habitat that appeared to select for longer life span have reduced early reproductive output (Law, Bradshaw, and Putwain, 1977). All these selection results appear to support antagonistic pleiotropy in a quite straightforward manner.

A major cause for caution in accepting this conclusion is the possibility of inbreeding depression, which can arise quite readily among laboratory populations undergoing selection (Wright, 1977), particularly affecting fitness components like early fecundity. This has been tested for in some of the *Drosophila* selection experiments (Clare and Luckinbill, 1985; Hutchinson and Rose, 1990). If inbreeding depression were the cause of reduced early female fecundity in these experiments,

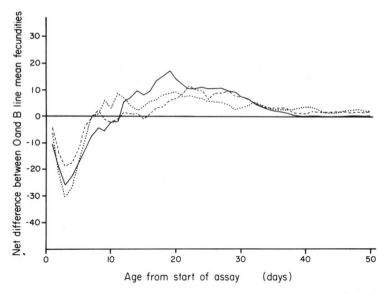

FIGURE 4.1. Net difference between the fecundities of pairs of lines of *D. melanogaster*, the O line having been reproduced at later ages, the B line having been reproduced at early ages. At early ages the O lines have relatively depressed fecundity. At later ages the O lines have relatively enhanced fecundity. (From Rose, 1984b.)

then crosses of control and selected lines should yield $F_1$s that are significantly superior to the mean of the parental lines, as in Clarke and Maynard Smith's (1955) study of longevity in hybrid *D. subobscura*. Instead, the results of such crosses using the selected lines of *Drosophila* indicate rough additivity for these characters, under appropriate assay conditions, and therefore the selected lines were probably free of inbreeding depression.

One further point that should be made is that some of the studies using *D. melanogaster* (Rose and Charlesworth, 1980, 1981a,b; Rose, 1984b; Hutchinson and Rose, 1990) examined *both* genetic correlations and selection responses, in both cases yielding results that supported the presence of antagonistic pleiotropy among segregating alleles. Genetic correlation studies and selection experiments are normally affected by quite different sorts of artifacts (Rose and Service, 1985; Clark, 1987). The concordance of results from two distinct lines of evidence lends credence to the conclusions drawn from them separately.

At this time it seems fair to conclude that the existence of alleles exhibiting antagonistic pleiotropy affecting aging has been established in a few experimental systems. This in turn suggests the general importance of antagonistic pleiotropy in the evolution of aging in these organisms, since the class of loci exhibiting polymorphism for such alleles must be only a subset of those loci that have alleles exhibiting antagonistic pleiotropy, as discussed earlier. Similarly, species that have such polymorphic loci may be only a subset of all the species that have been subject to the evolution of aging due, at least in part, to antagonistic pleiotropy.

Thus there seems little cause to doubt that antagonistic pleiotropy has often been important in the evolution of aging, as Williams (1957) so forcefully argued. However, this in no way implies that alternative population genetic mechanisms, such as mutation accumulation, have not also played a role. Exclusive importance cannot be claimed for the antagonistic pleiotropy mechanism for the evolution of aging, only that it appears to have made some contribution in an indeterminate number of species.

## Age Specificity of Gene Action

There are three alternative modes of age-dependent gene action: (1) qualitatively *uniform* effects over all ages, either beneficial or deleterious; (2) *varying* effects, both beneficial and deleterious, over a range of ages; and (3) strictly *age-specific* effects, either beneficial or deleterious. With uniform gene action the evolution of aging is directly coupled to the evolution of fitness, as discussed in Chapter 3. With varying gene action, antagonistic pleiotropy arises, with the consequences discussed earlier in this chapter. Here our concern is with the third alternative, age specificity of gene action.

### Stasis of Later Adaptation

The simplest population-genetic mechanism for the evolution of aging based on age-specific gene action is that proposed by W. D. Hamilton (1966). His suggestion was that, since selection would be powerful at earlier ages compared with later ages, early fitness characters would be more improved over evolutionary time, relative to later fitness characters. Since later characters would not improve at the same rate, older individuals would find themselves "failing to keep up" in the evolutionary struggle with other species, and perhaps conspecifics as well. This mechanism engenders aging of a "relative" kind, the characters expressed at later ages representing an unimproved ancestral condition.

There is a major theoretical problem with this mechanism: It ignores mutation pressure. Variants of selectively favored alleles that differ only in having deleterious effects at ages considerably greater than that of the onset of reproduction will be selectively indistinguishable from the original alleles. Mutation pressure will act to increase the frequency of such alleles to an equilibrium determined by the relative balance of mutation and selection (Charlesworth, 1980). Thus the putatively unimproved ancestral condition will not simply be left intact in the course of evolution. Rather it will degenerate under the pressure of mutations that are deleterious at later ages, but of little effect upon fitness, on Hamilton's assumption of alleles having strictly age-specific effects.

Indeed, as Hamilton (1966) himself realized, stasis of later adaptation does not adequately explain the extreme debility of older organisms kept free of disease, predation, and competition in the laboratory: "The implication of this view that rising late mortality is due to severity of the environment in conditions of over-population rather than to intrinsic senescent changes does not square well with the fact that when the environment is made as favorable as possible deterioration is still observed." Accordingly, Hamilton (1966) falls back on antagonistic pleiotropy to explain such later intrinsic deterioration, although this is unnecessary, *a priori,* as will be discussed. In any case, this population genetic mechanism for the evolution of aging can be regarded as irrelevant. It is both theoretically misconceived and empirically falsified.

## Postponement of Genetic Diseases

Haldane (1941, pp. 192–94) and Medawar (1946, 1952) proposed that aging arises because of the spread of alleles at modifier loci that postpone the age of onset of severe genetic diseases engendered by other loci. This was essentially an adaptation of Fisher's (e.g., 1928a,b) theory for the evolution of dominance, in which it was supposed that dominance evolves to protect the organism from the impact of deleterious alleles by making them recessive. Because effects expressed late in life are also largely suppressed in terms of their impact on fitness, like recessive effects when homozygosity is unlikely, modifier loci that postpone deleterious effects shield the organism from the pressure of repeated mutations, at least in theory.

> If hereditary factors achieve their overt expression at some intermediate age of life; if the age of onset of overt expression is variable; and if these variations are themselves inheritable; then natural selection will act so as to enforce the postponement of the age of the expression of those factors that are unfavourable, and, correspondingly, to expedite the effects of those that are favourable—a recession and a precession, respectively, of the variable age-effects of genes. (Medawar, 1952)

Again there are both theoretical and empirical problems with this hypothesized mechanism. As Wright (e.g., 1929a,b) pointed out long ago, in the context of Fisher's theory for the evolution of dominance, the intensity of selection for a modifier allele acting on another locus at equilibrium between the opposed forces of mutation and selection will be on the order of the mutation rate at the second locus. This occurs because severe genetic disorders, which would be most advantageous to postpone, will be at low frequencies, while milder genetic disorders, which are likely to be present at higher frequencies, lead to reduced advantageousness for modifier alleles that postpone them. Thus the fitness effects of the genetic disease factor out of the selection equation for the modifier allele, leaving a selection differential favoring modifier alleles on the order of the mutation rate of such alleles (Ewens, 1979, pp. 195–98; Charlesworth, 1980, p. 219). Therefore, theory suggests that selection for modifier alleles should be too weak to postpone the age at which genetic disease strikes.

The empirical evidence against postponement of genetic disease is that, if this theory is correct, there should be a plethora of well-defined genetic disorders associated with aging, and a dearth of such disorders expressed at early ages. (Note that the diseases in question must be genetic in etiology and age specific, not merely diseases associated with aging.) The best species with which to test this idea are *Homo sapiens* and *D. melanogaster,* since there is such extensive knowledge of mutations in these species. Certainly, genetic disorders afflicting the early ages are well known for both species and are apparently abundant. There is no apparent trend to increasingly common genetic disorders with age. Indeed, while there are quite a number of well-characterized human genetic pathologies that arise congenitally or by early adulthood (phenylketonuria, hemophilia, progeria, Tay–Sachs, etc.), there are only a few that are known to have late ages of onset, Huntington's chorea and idiopathic hemochromatosis being notable examples (Martin, 1978; Albin, 1988). In *Drosophila*, there is a vast array of well-known mutant syndromes affecting development, but few that affect aging specifically (e.g., Leffelaar and Grigliatti, 1984). Moreover, it is not as if *Drosophila* workers have not sought such mutations; research that could have picked up such mutations has been ongoing since the 1920s (e.g., Pearl, 1922; Gonzales, 1923). While none of this work has been specifically focused on the evolutionary genetic mechanism at issue here, the relevant experimental evidence speaks against this mechanism for the evolution of aging, suggesting that the *a priori* criticisms of Charlesworth (1980, p. 219) are indeed just. The postponement of genetic diseases does not appear to have been important in the evolution of aging.

## Mutation Accumulation

### THEORY

Up to this point, age-specific genetic mechanisms for the evolution of aging seem to be neither cogent nor empirically supportable. However, there is a mechanism that is at least cogent.

> There is a constant feeble pressure to introduce new variants of hereditary factors into a natural population, for "mutation," as it is called, is a recurrent process. Very often such factors lower the fertility or viability of the organisms in which they make their effects apparent; but it is arguable that if only they make them apparent late enough, the force of selection will be too attenuated to oppose their establishment and spread. (Medawar, 1952)

Aging might thereby arise from a process of accumulation of exclusively late-acting deleterious mutations, where such mutations are allelic variants that preserve all early functions of the locus. Edney and Gill (1968) proposed that this would be the major genetic mechanism in the evolution of aging: "late acting harmful mutations are allowed to accumulate, so that aging develops."

Charlesworth (1980, pp. 140–42, 217, 218) has mathematically analyzed the balance between mutation and selection for deleterious alleles having effects confined to the survival probability at a specific age. Consider the case of a mutant allele that is not fully recessive, with effects at age $x$. The magnitude of the frequency of heterozygotes carrying the mutant allele (most of the individuals affected by the allele will be heterozygotes) is given by

$$-2u/\{[\ln P_{12}(x) - \ln P_{11}(x)]s_{11}(x)\},$$

where $u$ is the rate of recurrent mutation, the $P_{ij}$ are age-specific survival probabilities as before, and $s_{11}(x)$ is the numerator of the intensity of selection expression given by Eq. (1.6). Recall from Chapter 1 that $s_{11}(x)$ decreases with age after the onset of reproduction, eventually reaching zero. Since $s_{11}(x)$ is in the denominator, its decline to zero will cause the frequency of heterozygotes of reduced fitness to increase radically in magnitude. Thus, as the force of natural selection falls with age, mutation accumulation of age-specific deleterious gene effects can have progressively more severe effects. Mutation accumulation thus appears to be a perfectly plausible population-genetic mechanism for the evolution of aging.

EXPERIMENTAL EVIDENCE

According to the theory just outlined, the mutation-accumulation mechanism makes the later part of the life cycle a genetic "garbage can," in which alleles with deleterious effects accumulate. At early ages selection keeps the frequency of deleterious alleles low. At later ages selection fades out, and mutation comes to dominate in the determination of gene frequencies. [This assumes that natural selection is only provided with loci having age-specific frequency-independent effects on single life-history characters, effects that are not themselves overdominant (cf. Rose, 1985).] The additive genetic variation affecting age-specific life-history characters should then reflect mutation-selection balance solely. Charlesworth (1987) has argued that the available genetic evidence (e.g., Mousseau and Roff, 1987; Roff and Mousseau, 1987) indicates the general importance of mutation-selection balance in maintaining genetic variation for fitness components. In age-structured populations, mutation-selection equilibria would move from near fixation of beneficial alleles at early ages to higher frequencies of deleterious alleles at later ages. Accordingly, the additive genetic variance of age-specific life-history characters should increase with age. (The "additive" part of the genetic variance is that part of the genetic variance that, at selective equilibrium, is not increased by genetic polymorphisms arising from overdominance. Such genetic polymorphisms contribute to the "dominance" part of the genetic variance at selective equilibrium.) So far, this prediction of increasing additive genetic variance has been tested directly only once, in a *D. melanogaster* experiment using daily female fecundity as the age-specific character (Rose and Charlesworth, 1980, 1981a). The results of this test are shown in Figure 4.2. As may be seen, the additive genetic variance did not increase with age, contrary to the hypothesis.

A related experiment used chromosomal manipulation to produce a set of *D. melanogaster* lines, each of which was homozygous or heterozygous for one of a defined set of chromosomes (Kosuda, 1985). These lines were studied for age dependence in the effect of chromosomal variation on male mating success. There was more of an effect of chromosomal variation at later ages than earlier ages. This suggests that there might have been some accumulation of genetic variation affecting later male fertility, as expected on the hypothesis of mutation accumulation. Thus there are two experiments focusing on standing genetic variation that differ in technique and give opposite results concerning the occurrence of mutation accumulation.

Before turning to experiments of completely different design that might resolve this disparity, a couple of problems with experiments on standing genetic variation should be mentioned. First, there is that of scale effects, in which a reduction in phenotypic variance as a whole arises from the reduction in the mean value of age-

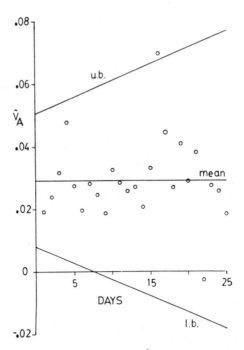

FIGURE 4.2. Additive genetic variance estimates ($\hat{V}_A$) for age-specific female fecundity in *D. melanogaster*, plotted against day of assay, from the start of peak reproductive output. [U.b. and l.b. indicate upper and lower bounds of a confidence interval for each day, respectively.] There was no statistically significant tendency for the additive genetic variance to increase with age. The slope of the linear regression through the data was negative. (From Rose and Charlesworth, 1981a.)

specific life-history characters that is due to aging itself. This can be corrected by transforming the data to remove the dependence of the standard deviation on the mean at each age (vide Wright, 1968; Rose and Charlesworth, 1981a).

Second, there may be antagonistic pleiotropy confined to earlier ages, having no effect on later characters and thus the evolution of aging, but nonetheless maintaining abundant additive genetic variability for early fitness components (Rose, 1982, 1985). This will tend to obscure any rise in additive genetic variance at later ages, because of the inflation of the additive genetic variance for early life-history characters. This problem is particularly important in view of the evidence that antagonistic pleiotropy does in fact affect some life-history characters. Tests of mutation accumulation that concern age-dependent trends of additive genetic variances are therefore reliable only if antagonistic pleiotropy plays little or no role in the life-history variation of the species under investigation. Therefore, these tests are not suitable for tests of the joint occurrence of the two population-genetic mechanisms for the evolution of aging.

Selection experiments can be used to test for the possibility of mutation accumulation in a way that is not dependent on the virtual absence of antagonistic pleiotropy. The experiments in which *Drosophila* populations were cultured at later ages have shown that laboratory populations with postponed senescence are readily obtained by increasing the force of selection at later ages, as discussed in Chapter 3. If *all* these gains in later life-history characters have been at the expense of earlier life-history characters, then resuming laboratory culture reproduction at early ages should lead to the fairly rapid eradication of postponed aging. (This assumes that the selected populations have not undergone fixation of the alleles involved in the selection response.) If *none* of these gains in later life-history characters has been at the expense of earlier life-history characters, then early culture reproduction should have no initially detectable effect on the postponed aging.

There are further possible variations on experiments of this kind. One is to consider a number of different characters that have responded to selection for postponed aging. A variety of physiological characters are associated with prolonged life in *D. melanogaster* stocks, among them resistance to starvation, resistance to desiccation, and resistance to low levels of ambient ethanol (Service et al., 1985). While all three of these characters could depend on a single underlying physiological mechanism, in principle, there is also the possibility that they reflect physiological changes that have occurred as a result of gene frequency changes at disjoint loci. If the latter is the case, then some of these loci may be subject to antagonistic pleiotropy, while others may not. One interesting possibility would be to have one character molded by loci subject to antagonistic pleiotropy, while another character might be subject to loci with allelic variants free of antagonistic pleiotropy. In this case, one character would rapidly revert to its mean value before selection for postponed aging, while the other would remain at the level achieved during such selection.

The first type of experiment has been performed using age-specific fecundity in *D. melanogaster* as the test character (Mueller, 1987), as discussed in Chapter 3. Populations reproduced at early ages exhibited no enhancement in early reproduction, and initially there was no decrement in later fecundity (Bierbaum, Mueller, and Ayala, 1989). But after more than 100 generations of strictly early reproduction of cultures, and thus time for some mutation accumulation, the late fecundity of such cultures began to fall. Early fecundity remained unaltered. This is evidence for the gradual accumulation of age-specific deleterious alleles affecting later fecundity.

The second type of experiment has been performed in *D. melanogaster* using the three characters discussed above: starvation resistance, desiccation resistance, and ethanol vapor resistance, together with early fecundity (Service, Hutchinson, and Rose, 1988). The results are shown in Figures 4.3–6. Fecundity recovered its former level, while starvation resistance fell significantly. This fits with other evidence of antagonistic pleiotropy between starvation resistance and early fecundity, such as negative genetic correlation between them (Service and Rose, 1985). Desiccation resistance and ethanol resistance, on the other hand, did not fall statistically over 22 generations of relaxed selection, suggesting either a general absence of antagonistic pleiotropy between these characters and early fitness components or near-fixation of the alleles affecting these characters. Assuming that the latter possibility did not arise, these results indicate the presence of loci affecting aging that are subject to mutation accumulation. Such loci warrant greater study.

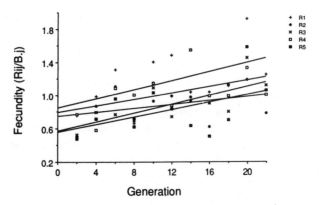

FIGURE 4.3. Response of late-reproduced *D. melanogaster* stocks to reimposition of an early-reproduction cultural regime. The data are plotted as the ratios, per generation, of the mean of a relaxed late-reproduced (R) stock over the mean of a control early-reproduced (B) stock. These data are for the character of early fecundity. (From Service, Hutchinson, and Rose, 1988.)

## Conclusion

There is evidence for the action of both antagonistic pleiotropy and mutation accumulation in the evolution of aging. The evidence for antagonistic pleiotropy takes three forms. First, a number of negative estimates for the genetic correlation between early reproduction and longevity, or their equivalents, have been found. Those experimental results indicating predominantly positive genetic correlations between early reproduction and longevity are subject to demonstrable artifact. Sec-

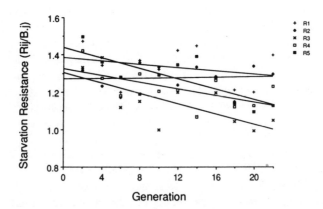

FIGURE 4.4. Response of late-reproduced *D. melanogaster* stocks to reimposition of an early-reproduction cultural regime. The data are plotted as the ratios, per generation, of the mean of a relaxed late-reproduced (R) stock over the mean of a control early-reproduced (B) stock. These data are for the character of starvation resistance. (From Service, Hutchinson, and Rose, 1988.)

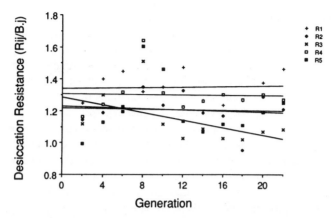

FIGURE 4.5. Response of late-reproduced *D. melanogaster* stocks to reimposition of an early-reproduction cultural regime. The data are plotted as the ratios, per generation, of the mean of a relaxed late-reproduced (R) stock over the mean of a control early-reproduced (B) stock. These data are for the character of desiccation resistance. (From Service, Hutchinson, and Rose, 1988.)

ond, *Drosophila* laboratory populations that have evolved postponed aging typically have reduced early reproductive output. Third, there are known alleles in *Drosophila* and *C. elegans* that enhance early reproduction jointly with reducing longevity or that depress early reproduction jointly with increasing longevity. These combinations of effects are excellent examples of antagonistic pleiotropy.

The best evidence in favor of mutation accumulation comes from *Drosophila* selection experiments in which alleles with deleterious effects confined to later ages

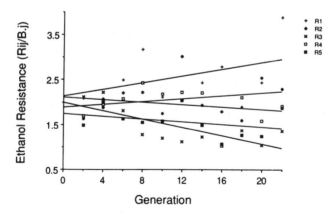

FIGURE 4.6. Response of late-reproduced *D. melanogaster* stocks to reimposition of an early-reproduction cultural regime. The data are plotted as the ratios, per generation, of the mean of a relaxed late-reproduced (R) stock over the mean of a control early-reproduced (B) stock. These data are for the character of ethanol resistance. (From Service, Hutchinson, and Rose, 1988.)

are allowed to accumulate. In such experiments, fitness components have been found to be subject to the accumulation of deleterious age-specific alleles, with an absence of antagonistic pleiotropy. There is also some evidence against the action of antagonistic pleiotropy in the evolution of some of the characters associated with postponed aging, indicating age specificity in allelic effects and the possibility of the evolution of these characters by mutation accumulation.

Overall, the best of the population-genetic evidence comes from the genus *Drosophila*, but there is also some pertinent evidence available from other taxonomic groups. Both antagonistic pleiotropy and mutation accumulation appear to be genetic mechanisms involved in the evolution of aging, the evidence for the former being particularly good. However, there is as yet no evidence bearing on the relative importance of the two mechanisms. This may, indeed, not be a particularly profitable problem to investigate, since the likely answer would have a "more or less" quality.

# 5

# Comparative Biology of Aging

The comparative method is the classical basis for testing evolutionary hypotheses concerning natural selection. One need look no farther than Darwin's (1859) *Origin of Species* for ample illustration of this point. And the comparative method continues to be used by evolutionary biologists in the present day, although now with a profound increase in sophistication (e.g., Clutton-Brock and Harvey, 1979; Huey, 1987). Nonetheless, comparative biological reasoning has come under considerable attack (e.g., Gould and Lewontin, 1979), especially its frequent, blithe assumption of adaptive excellence, if not perfection. On the other hand, it would be inconceivable for biologists, particularly evolutionary biologists, to treat all patterns of interspecific differentiation as if natural selection need not have played any material role. Terrestrial vertebrates acquire oxygen and dispose of carbon dioxide using lungs, while fish use gills to this same end. This is clearly not coincidental. The obvious hypothesis is that natural selection molded the respiratory apparatus of some vertebrates to adapt them to terrestrial life. That natural selection is not omnipotent is demonstrated by the continued use of air breathing by cetaceans, rather than aqueous gas exchange. However, it should be possible for all modern biologists without theological or ideological inhibitions to agree that, on occasion, natural selection has acted in ways that can be reflected at the level of interspecific comparisons.

The concern of this chapter is with the extent to which the evolutionary theory of aging, and its ancillary population-genetic mechanisms, can *either* be used to explain the comparative patterns of senescence over species *or* be tested using such patterns. It should be noted that a failure in the former respect does not constitute one in the latter. It could simply be a lack of appropriate information that precludes successful explanation, a characteristic problem in biology, particularly evolutionary biology.

Perhaps this point needs more elaboration. The failure of a scientific theory to predict the particular patterns exhibited by a specific case within its ambit is not evidence of falsehood. Most scientific theories make practically testable predictions about only a small set of the phenomena under their purview. Of the three possible meanings of a piece of scientific information bearing on a theory, corroborative, falsifying, or ambiguous, only a small fraction will fall in the first or second categories, on first inspection, unless the theory is grossly unreasonable. Further inspection is likely to shift many of the cases in this small fraction also into the third category. This is easily illustrated in the context of experimental work on the evolution of aging, as has already been discussed in Chapter 3. Toward the end of that chapter, a number of experiments that are of only ambiguous status with respect to the evolutionary theory of aging were mentioned. This is far from unique, in science generally or in evolutionary biology specifically (e.g., Lewontin, 1974). The problem is fundamentally one of a lack of information. Proponents of alternative theories can argue that unmeasured parameters took on values that make the empirical result fully compatible with their favored theory. This is not a rare occurrence in scientific discussion, but a common feature of theory defense (Lakatos, 1970).

This is not to say that the evolutionary theory of aging cannot be falsified. Particularly in the comparative context, it is readily falsifiable. However, one of the uses of the evolutionary theory of aging is as a device for explaining comparative patterns of aging. Such explanations do not put the evolutionary theory at risk, since in virtually all cases too little is now known for the purposes of strong inference. (This is why laboratory experiments are so important, because there, if too little is known, more can often be found out.) The value of the comparative analyses to be offered may lie instead in their potential for provisionally testing ideas that could be more incisively tested in experimental contexts or in intensive studies of interspecific differences of exceptional clarity and practical tractability (vide Huey, 1987, for appropriate comparative methods). Such applications must await the attention of future investigations.

## The Comparative Data

### Practical and Fundamental Problems

The quantity and quality of data concerning the pattern of aging, to say nothing of data concerning its causes, have been a subject of enduring complaint since Sir Francis Bacon in the seventeenth century. The reasons for this are not hard to find. Aging is primarily a phenomenon occurring among organisms that have been kept in artificially protective conditions for some time. Accurate estimation of patterns of decline in age-specific survival and fecundity requires that many organisms be kept. In large organisms the resources required to perform such feats of husbandry are often prohibitive. Space of course is only the most obvious limiting variable. Provision of air, food, water, and adequate opportunity for movement, in the case of animals, or insolation, in the case of plants, all may require enormous expense. Small organisms will normally entail fewer problems with space or resources, but for the extremely small organism, adequate monitoring becomes problematic, particularly if records of individuals are to be kept. Long-lived organisms may still be alive after the death of the observer's body, brain, or interest. Rapidly developing organisms may be difficult to age in well-defined cohorts because of frequent production of newborn individuals who then become indistinguishable from adults before they can be discarded. And so on.

Even if an investigator is able to obtain actuarial measurements, material problems may arise with respect to the quality of such measurements. Measuring aging can give rise to artifactual distortions of the data. In particular, the environmental conditions under which the population is kept by the experimenter may be highly unusual, relative to the population's evolutionary history. Yet the environmental sensitivity of a species' pattern of aging may be profound. For example, the notion of "the life span of *Drosophila melanogaster*" is virtually meaningless, since it can vary severalfold within the range of temperatures and nutrient conditions capable of sustaining a laboratory culture of the species. Thus in one laboratory the mean life span observed may be 65.2 days, while in another it may be only 37.3 days. These differences can have recondite causes, rather than being a result of a known environmental variable, greatly aggravating the problem of comparative inference using data from different laboratories or experiments. Indeed, the whole notion of "a life span" for a species is clearly typological, and very much out of keeping with the whole thrust of evolutionary or genetic research (Mayr, 1982). Its strict validity is probably confined to species that die shortly after a single bout of reproduction, such as monocarpic plants and Pacific salmon.

Finally, there are the problems associated with the genetic structure of the samples observed, discussed in Chapters 2 to 4. The mean longevity of inbred organisms can be greatly reduced from that of hybrids (e.g., Clarke and Maynard Smith, 1955) when the organism is normally outbreeding (cf. Johnson and Wood, 1982). Aging data are normally obtained from laboratory, zoo, or domesticated populations, precisely those that are most likely to be artificially inbred.

## Maximum Recorded Longevity

The gerontological community is well aware of many of the diverse problems with "measuring aging," since they are the ones who have most often collected, or attempted to collect, such data. The commonly accepted solution to this problem is to use maximum longevities, the maximum being over the entire range of data collected for the species. Comfort (1979, p. 59), the most unsparing critic of poorly collected data in gerontology, allows that "Maximum longevity records of animal species have a definite, but limited, use in giving a comparative picture of the possible longevity in different forms." Certainly there is little reason to place great weight on maximum longevity differences of 10–30 percent, where comparisons of a single pair of species are concerned, unless these estimates have been collected from well-studied species under conditions that are well understood.

In comparisons of a large number of species from different taxa, a more reliable picture may emerge, simply because the sources of error may tend to average out, giving rise to "white noise," as opposed to confounding biases. For example, the comparison of the maximum longevities of small birds with those of small mammals should have a fair degree of reliability, because large numbers of species of both groups have been reared in captivity and kept alive until what appear to be natural deaths. On the other hand, problems of artifactual bias may arise in such comparisons when the species of one group are more readily observed or maintained than those of other groups. For example, one of the major issues in the comparative biology of vertebrate aging is whether or not all fish senesce. There is no evidence indicating the existence of mammals that do not senesce, despite the large numbers of mammalian species that have been observed. Few fish species have been studied systematically from a gerontological standpoint, although there have been some studies of fish longevities in the wild (Beverton, 1987), which is a very different kind of problem. Those that have been studied in the laboratory seem to senesce (e.g., *Poecilia reticulata,* Comfort, 1960, 1961), but it is too early to propose as an inductive generalization that "all fish senesce." Yet this is not sufficient reason to suppose that there are some that do not. The lack of evidence for aging in this case arises from technical factors, so far as can be told. Thus the ease of observation of aging in the taxa being compared should always be borne in mind, along with the actual degree to which the taxa have been studied.

## VERTEBRATE DATA

The best-known phylum from the standpoint of the comparative biology of aging is Chordata, the Class Mammalia in particular. A primary reason for this is of course the anthropocentrism of such a medically relevant discipline as gerontology. But there are other major reasons. Vertebrates are large and have a well-defined life cycle. Vegetative forms of reproduction, in which large somatic fragments break off and grow into new individuals, have never been found, and the life cycle, from birth to sexual maturity, is never so short as to create any problems with maintaining well-defined cohorts. Methods of keeping terrestrial vertebrates, particularly mammals, alive and healthy are generally well known. Finally, vertebrate diseases are relatively easy for us to detect, thanks in part to medical research, so that the experimenter should be able either to discount deaths and infertility due to such causes or to abort an experiment on aging in a diseased population. Thus, from the standpoint of testing hypotheses concerning the comparative biology of aging, the terrestrial vertebrate data, and those from mammals and birds in particular, are the best available.

A wide array of maximum longevities for mammals, birds, reptiles, and amphibians has been published (Altman and Dittmer, 1972; Comfort, 1979). Even though these data are much more reliable than any other comparable body of data for other taxa, they still lack uniform reliability. Within the mammals the longevity of *Felis catus,* the domestic cat, is indubitably better known than that of *Gorilla gorilla.* And there cannot be much confidence in our knowledge of amphibian longevities compared with our knowledge of mammalian longevities.

## INVERTEBRATE DATA

In proceeding from terrestrial vertebrate to invertebrate data, one is trading moderately reliable knowledge for oceanic ignorance. Not only is there far less information available for invertebrates, relative to the total number of species, it is of necessity less reliable than that for vertebrates because the basic biology is often not known. Cultures may be difficult to maintain, because of unknown nutritional deficiencies, disease, or environmental sensitivities. Vertebrates are inherently easier to deal with because of their many homeostatic physiological adaptations, home-othermy in mammals and birds being the most obvious of these, together with the great capacity for disease resistance conferred by their elaborate immune systems. And there is the vast increase in the extent to which the entire invertebrate life history responds to environmental variables, such as temperature, which has already been discussed in Chapter 2.

There is a still more radical problem with the invertebrate maximum longevity data. At least some invertebrates, such as some sea anemones, do not appear to senesce. The irony in the invertebrate maximum longevity data is that species that do not senesce, but have been studied rarely or are difficult to maintain in the laboratory, may have a low or moderate reported maximum longevity. Thus a published invertebrate "maximum longevity" datum does not constitute evidence for the existence of aging in a species. This is especially important for data collected from wild specimens, with indirect inference of age, in that the death of these specimens may have had little or nothing to do with endogenous aging. In no sense should maximum longevity data for invertebrates be interpreted in the same fashion as those for terrestrial vertebrates. Invertebrate maximum longevities often may not be a reflection of aging, while maximum longevities for terrestrial vertebrates will often reflect aging.

Comfort (1979, pp. 71–80) has provided extensive tables of maximum recorded longevities for a wide range of invertebrates. Many of these are based on wild specimens, rather than laboratory studies. An obvious feature of these data is the wide range of longevities, from 90 years in *Cereus pedunculatus,* a sea anemone, to 4 weeks in *Cloeon dipterum,* an insect from the Order Ephemeroptera. The circumstances surrounding the collection of sea anemone figures illustrate the ambiguities of interpretation where the invertebrate data are concerned. A group of sea anemones was kept alive, healthy, and apparently reproducing for 80 years in an aquarium at Edinburgh University. One day they all were found dead, presumably as a result of some failure of culture, such as lack of aeration or an extreme temperature (Comfort, 1979, p. 110). Thus the maximum longevity report for this species has no apparent relevance to aging. At the other extreme, many adult lepidopterans wholly lack mouth parts, death being a matter of time until depletion of caloric reserves. The task of sorting out this vast array of information is formidable.

## PLANT DATA

Comparative data on plant aging suffer from both extreme practical difficulties and the lack of interest of gerontologists. There is also a pronounced problem involved in delimiting the organism in studies of plant aging (vide Harper, 1977; Buss, 1987), a problem that does not normally arise in studies of animals, excepting colonial forms. (This problem will be addressed in more detail a bit later in this chapter.) In any case, the compilation of plant aging data has not yet achieved a level comparable to that of the animal data. Tables of estimated maximum longevities for tree species (Noodén, 1988) indicate that they can live an order of magnitude longer than vertebrates, common conifer species having maximum longevities of thousands of years.

## Presence and Absence of Aging

### A Comparative Prediction Critical to the Theory

In spite of all the problems with comparative data, one of the most critical falsifiable predictions of the evolutionary theory concerns the comparative pattern of aging. This prediction was stated with clarity by Williams (1957):

> There are organisms in which the distinction between soma and germ-plasm may not exist, but the other assumptions of the theory would seem to be inevitable for any organism, at least for any that has a clear distinction between soma and germ-plasm. The theory regards aging as an evolved characteristic of the soma. We should find it wherever a soma has been evolved, but not elsewhere.

In terms of the mathematical theory for the evolution of aging given in Chapter 1, the point of Williams' prediction is that, in species that do not have a soma, age-structured population genetics is not applicable. Bacterial species, for example, do not have adult age classes that might vary in the intensity of selection acting upon them. Once the bacterium divides, a new generation begins. For such species, there is only selection among clonal lineages; there is no adult. If there were some type of cumulative "aging" among clonal lineages, then such lineages would be eliminated by selection. Thus, in cases of strictly vegetative reproduction, selection does not allow the evolution of aging. Only when there is an adult that produces a delimitable offspring, as opposed to splitting in two, can aging evolve, and then it must always evolve. This is one of the strongest theoretical predictions in all of evolutionary biology.

All known vertebrates have a clear distinction between somatic and germ-line cells. Therefore, a critical falsifiable prediction of the evolutionary theory is that *all vertebrates should exhibit aging*. If there were a vertebrate discovered that exhibited no increase in age-specific death rates after the onset of reproduction, then there would be something fundamentally wrong with the evolutionary theory. At the other extreme, all prokaryotes should be free of aging, since they are strictly unicellular, without any soma or germ-plasm distinction. Indeed, at present no senescing prokaryotes are known.

The only problem with this strikingly clear prediction of senescence evolving only when there is a distinction between soma and germ line is that there is some degree of ambiguity in this distinction among some organisms. Unicellularity is not the only fashion in which an organism may lack a somatic–germ-plasm distinction. Multicellular organisms that reproduce by vegetative fission (sometimes termed *paratomical reproduction*), without *either* specified cell lineages responsible for the reproductive functions *or* marked heterogeneity between the two products of "fission," may be equivalent to an asexual single-celled organism (vide Bell, 1984c). Conversely, ciliates, with their multiple nuclei, have macronuclear lineages with strictly somatic roles and micronuclear lineages that are apparently confined to sexual recombination and gene transmission (Sonneborn, 1957). Some ciliates that have lost their micronuclei are sometimes able to continue dividing indefinitely, but ciliates with micronuclei sometimes deteriorate over repeated cycles of asexual fission without sexual recombination, autogamous or syngamous (Bell, 1988). There are many problems with sorting out the situation in ciliates (Smith-Sonneborn, 1983; Bell, 1988), some of which will be discussed in the following, but for now it is enough to point out that protozoa are not all simply uninucleate and immortal. Thus the existence of a soma distinct from a germ line is not an obvious phenomenon, as Child (1915) argued some time ago in the context of aging. [See Buss (1987) for a contemporary discussion of the problem of the evolution of the soma.]

A further problem that should be pointed out is that low phenotypic fitness does not imply senescence. If a culture of asexual, potentially immortal, unicellular organisms is being maintained in the laboratory, some of them may die in spite of a lack of disease, provision of adequate nutrition, and so on. Among the causes of such deaths could be the accumulation of deleterious mutations (Bell, 1988). Aging is not the only endogenous cause of death, so that endogenous deaths do not necessarily indicate its presence. Rather, aging is to be detected as a progressive deterioration in age-specific fitness components (Bell, 1984c).

In addition to the question-begging term *soma,* another problematic term in Williams' (1957) prediction is the seemingly innocuous "organism." Again, there are cases for which no problem arises. Individual mice are organisms; their constituent cells are not. Individual amoebae are organisms; groups of them are not. But what of the polyps of a coralline coelenterate? The amoeboid cells of a slime mold? Vegetative extensions of a plant, connected to the parent plant's root system? These cases are not as clear (cf. Child, 1915). To some extent, this should not be surprising in an evolutionary discussion, since the Darwinian presumption must be one of some degree of continuity in the evolution of integrated multicellular organisms. Particularly among simple multicellular organisms, such as the green alga *Volvox,* there can be considerable difficulties of interpretation. Thus continuity from unicellular organisms to multicellular organisms to colonial forms greatly obscures the meaning of the term *organism,* both in principle and in concrete cases (vide Buss, 1987).

Finally, there is the complication of life cycles that involve both asexual and sexual reproduction, particularly when the alternation between these modes is indispensable but flexible in the number of reproductive passages of either type. Thus an organism that must undergo sexual reproduction after 50–60 rounds of asexual reproduction, but is denied the opportunity to do so, might continue reproducing asexually with progressive loss of vigor, all descendant cells eventually dying. This is a failure of reproduction, rather than aging, and may be a large part of that which is considered aging among the ciliates (cf. Bell, 1988).

## Vertebrates

While it is widely accepted that all terrestrial vertebrates senesce, with life inevitably terminated by endogenous deterioration when not ended sooner (e.g., Lamb, 1977, p. 54), the situation among fish and aquatic amphibians is still held to be ambiguous, with some claiming that there are species from these groups that do not senesce (e.g., Moment, 1982). This notion of vertebrates that do not age has been around since ancient times. Francis Bacon discussed it in the seventeenth century, suggesting then that too little was known to test the idea. Its major twentieth century proponent was Bidder (1925, 1932), who regarded terrestrial aging as a byproduct of growth termination for the purpose of mechanical efficiency. Indeed, he regarded aging as "negative growth." Some fish, such as female plaice, are known to continue to grow after reproductive maturity, and indeed reproductive output can increase for some time after the onset of reproduction in such species (Comfort, 1979, pp. 91–105). Unfortunately for Bidder's hypothesis, Comfort (1960, 1961) has shown definitively that growth and aging, both actuarial and pathological (e.g., Woodhead and Ellett, 1969a,b), can occur simultaneously in guppies (*Poecilia reticulata*). There can be no doubt that many fish senesce, and this has been shown directly in a number of short-lived fish (Comfort, 1979, p. 102). There are no apparent reasons for supposing that larger fish are fundamentally different, given the refutation of Bidder's hypothesis. Similarly, there has been no demonstration of unlimited life span in an amphibian. No one has yet found a vertebrate that does not senesce under laboratory conditions when the relevant demographic parameters are measured. Since all vertebrates conform to the stipulations of the evolutionary theory for the presence of aging, our knowledge of vertebrate aging can be regarded as corroborating the theory.

## Invertebrate Metazoa

The term *invertebrate* is normally an absurdity, but in the context of the comparative biology of aging it serves to demarcate the boundary of relatively satisfactory knowledge, as has already been discussed in this chapter. While the invertebrates are of course a vast group of disparate species compared with vertebrates, so little is known of their aging in most cases that they can be handily reviewed together.

Most gerontological research on invertebrates has used insects, particularly *Drosophila, Musca,* and *Tribolium.* In a rare synoptic statement, Comfort (1979, p. 120) suggests that "Senescence in arthropods is widespread and probably universal." With respect to the distinction between soma and germ line, arthropods are if anything better defined than vertebrates; cell division is rare among somatic cells in the adult (Bozcuk, 1972). The data indicating a decline in adult age-specific survival and fecundity in laboratory insects are excellent (e.g., Pearl and Parker, 1924; Pearl, Park, and Miner, 1941; Rockstein and Lieberman, 1958; David et al., 1975). Certainly insects can be claimed as another corroborative case for the evolutionary theory, although the comparative data on other arthropods are pretty scarce.

The other major invertebrate group traditionally studied by gerontologists is the phylum Rotifera. Rotifers are among the smallest metazoa, primarily solitary and motile, but occasionally sessile and colonial. In spite of their small size, the reproductive organs are well defined, with an extremely limited number of female germ-line cells that will develop into eggs, often only 10–20. The pathology of aging in rotifers has been studied extensively over the past century, and there is little doubt that the aging observed is endogenous (Comfort, 1979, pp. 114–20). Every characterized species exhibits well-defined aging, and there is a fair amount of useful data (e.g., Meadow and Barrows, 1971; King and Miracle, 1980; Bell, 1984c). Once again, a taxonomic group that must exhibit aging, if the theory is valid, does so to the best of our knowledge.

Mollusc life histories have most often been studied using the growth patterns of the shells of wild-caught specimens, although there are a few life-table studies on laboratory cohorts (e.g., De Witt, 1954). This body of data indicates senescent decline in survival rates. There are species that die shortly after a single bout of reproduction, such as some nudibranchs and octopuses. Many other molluscs, such as bivalves, exhibit growth after the onset of reproduction, with wild specimens showing few signs of aging. Some wild-caught specimens have had quite great ages attributed to them (Comfort, 1979, pp. 131–35). The gonad is well defined, and there are no known cases of paratomical or fissile reproduction. In sum, the situation among molluscs is rather like that in fish. Their reproductive biology requires universal aging, according to the evolutionary theory. But while there is no evidence of potential immortality among molluscs, the documentation of aging in the phylum is rather limited.

The invertebrates discussed up to this point all have well-defined germ lines, like vertebrates, and the available evidence suggests that aging in fact occurs in all members of these phyla. There are not well-established instances of unlimited life span free from endogenous deterioration, again like the situation among vertebrates. Further proliferation of such instances is hardly informative. The converse type of case now deserves more attention: absence of aging when there is no distinction between soma and germ line.

This task was explicitly taken up by Bell (1984c), who studied the relationship between survival rate and cohort age in laboratory cultures of six asexual freshwater invertebrates: two rotifers, two arthropods, and two annelids. The rotifers and arthropods reproduce by laying eggs, with preservation of germ-line integrity. The two annelids, the oligochaetes *Aelosoma tenebrarum* and *Pristina aequiseta,* reproduce by transverse fission. Therefore, the first four species should senesce, while the last two should not. There were statistically detectable decreases in age-specific adult survival rates among the rotifers and arthropods, but none among the fissile annelids. This directly matches the expectations of the evolutionary theory of aging.

There are no other studies as directly posed to test for the absence of aging among fissile metazoa as that of Bell (1984c), but there is some suggestive comparative evidence. Among chordates, some tunicates with fissile reproduction apparently do not senesce (Berrill, 1951; Sabbadin, 1979). Most important, three phyla that are known to exhibit fissile and other forms of paratomical reproduction, Coelenterata, Annelida, and Platyhelminthes, have species in which there is fairly respectable evidence of endogenously unlimited life span. The best documented case of unlimited life span is that of the sea anemones kept at Edinburgh University, already discussed. Sea anemones commonly reproduce in a strictly fissile fashion, with longitudinal division and symmetry of fission products, although some sea anemones reproduce sexually. The chief proponent of unlimited life span among planarians is Child (e.g., 1915). While some cases of nonaging in the Platyhelminthes are controversial, there are other cases that are considered likely (Bell,

1988, pp. 84–93). At present, Bell's (1984c) study provides the best evidence for aging-free annelid species. There remains a need for more studies of this kind, particularly within classes of the Coelenterata, Platyhelminthes, and Annelida, so that the comparative contrasts can be made in as straightforward a manner as possible. In any case, the extant evidence provides some indication that those metazoa that lack any distinction between soma and germ line do not senesce, as Williams (1957) predicted.

## Protozoa

As discussed at the outset of this section, while it might be imagined that unicellular species should not senesce, this need not be the case when there are multiple nuclei. A further case in which aging is possible is that of asymmetrical fission, as in *Tokophyra,* where a large "mother" cell produces much smaller "daughter" cells repeatedly (Rudzinska, 1961). [The yeast *Saccharomyces cerevisiae* also buds, and also undergoes aging (Mortimer and Johnston, 1959; Egilmez and Jazwinski, 1989), unlike the fissile yeast *Schizosaccharomyces pombe.*] Nonetheless, there are protozoa with the simplest possible life cycle: reproduction by fission of a cell possessing a single nucleus that combines somatic and germ-line functions. On the evolutionary theory of aging, such cells should never senesce. The classic instances of such species are *Amoeba proteus* and *Amoeba discoides.* Danielli and Muggleton (1959) have shown that, when such amoebae are given good culture conditions, they appear to be able to undergo indefinite rounds of growth and division, with no apparent deterioration. (The death and limited replicative capacity of cells kept under deficient conditions, in these experiments, are not relevant in the present context.) There are of course other cases of protozoan laboratory cultures that apparently do not undergo aging (Comfort, 1979, p. 149; Bell, 1988).

The protozoa are not entirely straightforward in the comparative biology of their aging, however. Indeed, few groups of organisms have more confusing life cycles than ciliates, particularly *Paramecium* (Sonneborn, 1957, 1960; Smith-Sonneborn, 1983; Anderson, 1988; Bell, 1988). There is no clear distinction between soma and germ line, yet the multiple nuclei that are present in each cell differentiate into somatic and gene-transmission roles. They may "self-fertilize," undergo exogamy, or reproduce vegetatively. During vegetative reproduction, macronuclear chromosomal transmission may fail in part, resulting in phenotypic deficiencies. Such macronuclear deficiencies are readily made up after sexual reproduction, at which time all or some of the macronuclear complement may be regenerated. After some cycles of asexual division, many ciliate cultures die or lose their ability to reproduce. Indeed, it was discovered that mortality among sexual progeny is positively correlated with the period of asexual culture (Pierson, 1938). Bell's (1988) extensive review of this literature has shown that this is a general pattern. The problem is how to reconcile this phenomenon with the evolutionary theory of aging. There are at least two ways to do so. One is to assert that the deterioration of these cultures occurs evolutionarily, due to "Muller's Ratchet": the accumulation of deleterious mutations in asexual populations because recombination cannot remove them (Maynard Smith, 1978; Bell, 1988). Another is to suppose that ciliates have a distinction between germ line and soma that is not founded on differentiated cells, but that may nonetheless give rise to aging of some cell lineages, depending on the partitioning of the different types of nuclei. Muller's Ratchet may be involved in selection for the complicated ciliate life cycle, the period of "sexual immaturity" reflecting a balance between selection for efficient asexual reproduction and selection for sex to avoid Muller's Ratchet (Bell, 1988, pp. 131–34). It has been argued that the deterioration of ciliate cultures is irrelevant to metazoan aging (e.g., Comfort, 1979, pp. 151–52; Bell, 1988, pp. 118–34). It has also been argued that these cultures are highly relevant (e.g., Smith-Sonneborn, 1983). Whichever is more correct, it seems apparent that the ciliates are not a good testing ground for evolutionary hypotheses concerning the relationship between soma–germ-line distinctions and the evolution of aging, given the obscurities generated by their nuclear differentiation.

## Plants

Any discussion of aging or senescence in plants is made difficult by the use of these terms in any of three senses by botanists: (1) as defined here; (2) the deterioration of specific structures, such as leaves and fruit, at the end of the growing or flowering seasons, usually called *senescence;* and (3) the complete collapse of monocarpic (semelparous) plants after reproduction (e.g., Leopold, 1961; Thimann, 1980). While it has been argued that there should be a distinction made between monocarpic plant aging and that of iteroparous plants (Leopold, 1961), there is no substantive reason to do so. Precipitate aging after a single round of reproduction is just an extreme form of the onset of aging after the onset of reproduction. *Organ senescence,* which features so largely in discussions of plant aging (e.g., Thimann, 1980; Noodén and Leopold, 1988), will not be discussed here. It is strictly analogous to the deterioration of erythrocytes in mammals: the cycling of a specialized body part that is more efficiently discarded than repaired. Thus the discussion here will not distinguish between the first and last types of botanical aging, while neglecting the second entirely.

As defined here, aging indisputably occurs among plants. Indeed, the disintegration of monocarpic plants after reproduction is perhaps the most dramatic illustration of aging in the living world, with entire fields of monocarpic crops being known to die "essentially simultaneously" (Noodén, 1980). While individual trees are the oldest known living organisms, even extremely long-lived tree species are thought to suffer loss of function over time (Heath, 1957; Noodén, 1988).

On the other hand, it is possible to argue that there are plant species that are effectively immortal. It is thought that some grass clones have survived more than 15,000 years (Leopold, 1980). In such species, a given clonal genotype, called a *genet,* may be represented by numerous interconnected plants, each called a *ramet.* The ramets may die and be replaced, but the genet survives indefinitely. This form of life is like that of coralline coelenterates, in which coral aging is very difficult to establish, even though the zooids may exhibit obvious signs of aging (Palumbi and Jackson, 1983; Buss, 1987). The problem is first that it is difficult to establish what "the organism" is, as discussed above, and second that the extensive vegetative expansion of the collectivity may make a definite specification of germ-line tissue impossible. In a sense, one can regard some plants, and grasses in particular, as intermediate between what zoologists would consider organisms and what they would consider populations (Harper, 1977). Thus the evolutionary theory of aging can offer no clear prediction about the presence of aging in such cases.

A problem fraught with considerable ambiguity is the extensive asexual propagation of plants by means of cuttings (Noodén, 1988). In some cases, these clonal derivatives last indefinitely, as do some apple cuttings, while others die out, as does sugar cane, although disease has been implicated in some of these cases (Noodén, 1980). A complication in interpreting such agricultural practices is doubt about the extent to which such clones have been subject to inadvertent selection for indefinite propagation.

## The Comparative Data Support the Evolutionary Theory

The preceding survey of comparative patterns in the presence and absence of aging suggests three general conclusions.

First, there are a great many taxa for which information is largely lacking. There is great potential for experiments of the type performed by Bell (1984c), in which age-specific mortality rates are regressed against age. In particular, the contrasting expectations for aging in organisms that do and do not reproduce by fission deserve repeated testing in coelenterates, platyhelminthes, and oligochaetes. No doubt there are other groups in which such studies could, and should, be performed. While the call for more research is in many ways platitudinous, it should be said that comparative tests of the evolutionary theory of aging are in many ways easier to perform than the laboratory tests discussed in Chapter 3. Such comparative tests would also help mitigate the criticism that most of the evidence supporting the theory comes from the genus *Drosophila,* a familiar problem in evolutionary genetics.

Second, the simple contrast between species with a soma distinct from a germ line and those species without a soma often fails. Ciliates, colonial coelenterates, and some plants are among the cases in which the ambiguities become grievous. In a sense, what is lacking is a background theoretical framework accounting for the evolution of the multicellular/multinucleate organism itself, as has been pointed out before (Buss, 1987). The domination of whole-organism biology by vertebrate and arthropod zoology, on one hand, and microbiology, on the other, may explain the lack of attention that has been given to the many species that conform to neither type of life cycle. Until our understanding of these other cases becomes much more profound, they do not provide suitable material for comparative tests of the evolutionary theory of aging.

Third, there do not seem to be any clear refutations of the evolutionary theory of aging to be found in the comparative data. All species from groups with a well-defined soma separate from the germ line do senesce when observed under good laboratory conditions. Conversely, species that unequivocally lack such a separation of the soma, such as some sea anemones, some protozoa, and all known pro-karyotes, appear to lack aging. This body of comparative evidence provides a respectable degree of corroboration for the evolutionary theory, complementing the taxonomically limited experimental corroborations that were discussed in Chapter 3. While this degree of corroboration is not outstanding by the standards of transmission genetics or molecular biology, compared with other evolutionary theories it is respectable. Compared with other gerontological theories, it is remarkable, as the next three chapters will discuss.

## Comparative Patterns of Aging

### *Corollaries of the Evolutionary Theory*

While patterns of presence and absence provide the only comparative patterns that expose the evolutionary theory to direct falsification, there are many other corollaries of the theory that help to introduce some sense into the comparative biology of aging. It should be borne in mind that none of these corollaries afford good opportunities for falsification of the overall theory, because they are so laden with *ceteris paribus* clauses. Williams (1957) has provided a good list of predictions:

> 1. Low adult death rates should be associated with low rates of aging, and high adult death rates with high rates of aging.
> 2. Aging should be more rapid in those organisms that do not increase markedly in fecundity after maturity than those that do show such an increase.
> 3. Where there is a sex difference, the sex with the higher mortality rate and lesser rate of increase in fecundity should undergo the more rapid aging. (Williams, 1957, renumbered from the original)

These predictions are ostensibly direct corollaries of Eqs. (1.6) and (1.7). Equation (1.6) is easily used to illustrate this. [Similar arguments apply when Eq. (1.7) is used, with the exception of prediction (2).] As the age at which selection acts, represented by $a$, increases, Eq. (1.6) undergoes a series of fractional diminutions of the sum $\Sigma_{x=a+1}e^{-rx}$ $l(x)m(x)$, which is $s(a)$ in the notation of Chapter 4. Equation (1.6) is equal to $s(a)/T$, where $T = \Sigma_{x=1}e^{-rx}$ $l(x)m(x)$, again in the notation of Chapter 4. This occurs because, as $a$ increases, terms from the start of the sum defining $s(a)$ are dropped. Thus, for $a = 0$, Eq. (1.6) gives a value of 1, because $s(0) = T$. Both predictions (1) and (2) can be derived from the fact that, the larger the later values of $l(x)$ and $m(x)$ are, the less effect the loss of relatively smaller early terms from the series has. This lets $s(x)/T$ remain close to one. Prediction (3) implicitly assumes sex-specific gene expression and thus the evolutionary independence of the sexes. The prediction is then simply a restatement of predictions (1) and (2).

The intellectual sleight-of-hand in deriving these predictions from Eq. (1.6) lies in skipping over a large body of ceteris paribus assumptions. A partial listing of these assumptions includes achievement of stable age distributions, relatively weak selection, and similar genetic variation for selection to act upon. (See Chapter 1.) The third of these assumptions is most likely to be violated in comparisons of disparate taxa, since "similar genetic variation" in fact implies selectively analogous phenotypic capacities for allelic variants to mold. Yet most taxonomic contrasts rest directly upon differences in the nature of the heritable phenotypic options available to natural selection. Birds have considerably greater evolutionary opportunities for reducing levels of predation due to terrestrial predators compared with mice. Mitigation of this problem can be achieved if appropriate species are chosen for comparison (Huey, 1987), particularly when phylogenetic information is available, but the degree of mitigation will not be known in most cases. Thus the listed predictions cannot be taken as absolute, unlike those concerning the presence and absence of senescence.

Williams (1957) offered two further comparative predictions that hinge on the involvement of antagonistic pleiotropy in the evolution of aging: "Rapid individual development should be correlated with rapid aging", and "Successful selection for increased longevity should result in decreased vigor in youth." These predictions are somewhat infelicitously formulated; they are more correctly rendered in terms of reproduction. The available evidence implicates early reproduction as the critical factor with an antagonistic relationship with longevity (e.g., Leopold, 1961; Robertson, 1961; Rose and Charlesworth, 1981a; Rose, 1984b; Luckinbill et al., 1984, 1987), and indeed much of the evidence that Williams (1957) himself discusses concerns the effects of reproduction, rather than development. Thus these predictions might be better recast as follows:

> 4. Early reproduction should be correlated with early aging, and, conversely, longer-lived organisms should exhibit lower early reproductive rates.

It should be noted that prediction (4) is a corollary of the antagonistic pleiotropy mechanism for the evolution of aging, not the general theory. Even if there were not all the *ceteris paribus* problems with such comparative tests, refutations of this prediction would not falsify the general theory for the evolution of aging.

## Tests of the Mortality-Rate Prediction

The major practical problem in testing the prediction of a correspondence between adult death rates in the wild and aging in the laboratory is the difficulty of estimating death rates in nature. Reproductive rates and patterns of aging are often readily inferable from laboratory data, at least to fair approximation, since they are largely endogenous. By contrast, death rates in the wild are obscure functions of predators, disease, weather, availability of food, and mechanical damage, all of which can only be estimated from field data collection. The solution to which Williams (1957) resorts is indirect inference of mortality rates based on intuition and a modest amount of concrete evidence, as illustrated by his discussion of the relatively greater maximum longevities of birds compared with mammals:

> Birds have lower adult mortality rates than mammals of similar size, and, as expected, greater potential longevity. The difference in senescence rate has been attributed to some fundamental difference between the physiological organizations of birds and mammals. . . . I believe it is unlikely that any single physiological

difference is responsible. The evolutionary cause of the low rate of bird senescence must be that birds can fly, are thereby less liable to predation and accidents, and therefore have lower mortality rates. (Williams, 1957, references suppressed)

As Williams discusses, these ideas can be tested using data on flightless birds, such as the ostrich, and on bats, the only efficient flying mammals. In an ordered list of 45 bird species' maximum longevities (Comfort, 1964, p. 70), the ostrich and the emu have the third and fourth lowest longevities, respectively. In mammals life span is strongly dependent on body weight (Sacher, 1959; Prothero and Jürgens, 1987), which makes comparisons between bats and horses somewhat tenuous. If bats are compared with mammals of a similar range of sizes, such as rodents, their longevities are evidently much greater, the averages for the *Biology Data Book* (Altman and Dittmer, 1972) being 9.04 ± 1.34 years (mean plus or minus the standard error) for rodents and 21.0 ± 1.67 years for bats, with maximum longevities for each species rounded to the nearest year. [Herreid's (1964) more extensive bat longevities give a mean of 13.98 ± 0.88 years.] Allowing for body weight, bats in general live longer than other mammals (Prothero and Jürgens, 1987). These findings tend to corroborate Williams' (1957) analysis. On the other hand, some bats undergo frequent torpor, unlike rodents, which tends to undermine such comparisons on those grounds. This, of course, is a good illustration of the problems with broad comparative analyses of aging.

There are many adaptations other than flight that can be approached in a similar fashion. Shells are also a plausible mortality-rate-reducing feature, most elaborately developed among the vertebrates by the chelonians. The mean maximum longevity of the chelonian species listed in Comfort (1979, p. 66) is 71.36 ± 9.57 years, while the comparable figure for other reptiles in Altman and Dittmer (1972) is 17.69 ± 4.12 years, although Comfort (1979, p. 67) suggests that many of the other reptiles are difficult to keep in captivity. Nonetheless, the pattern is dramatically in accord with expectation. Among the invertebrates, the best phylum for such a comparison is Mollusca, particularly the contrast between the thick-shelled bivalves and all other mollusc species, with their generally thinner or nonexistent shells. From Comfort's (1979, pp. 73–78) data, we find mean maximum longevities of 14.67 ± 2.18 years for bivalves and 3.96 ± 0.38 years for other molluscs. More generally, the molluscs have many more high maximum longevities than the other major invertebrate phylum that is known to senesce, Arthropoda, although there is the confounding variable of size, in that the arthropods are normally smaller. Still, generally the comparative pattern broadly fits the prediction that aging should be slower in species that have lower adult death rates in the wild.

This line of comparison could continue at some length, covering such features as venom, inaccessible habitats, and so on. It is enough for now to have illustrated the kind of approach possible.

## *Tests of the Reproductive Rate Prediction*

The prediction that species with increasing fecundity should age more slowly is in principle more reliably testable than the mortality-rate prediction, but the problem is that there are relatively few data available for such tests. Mammals, birds, insects, and rotifers all rarely exhibit increasing fecundity after full reproductive maturity, and these are the organisms for which the gerontological data are best.

The most obvious comparison that bears out the prediction is that of trees with all other organisms. Trees grow to enormous sizes compared with all extant terrestrial organisms, with great increases in their fecundity as they do so, growth continuing long after reproductive maturity. Trees also have the greatest known longevities. It could be argued that tree rings give us the best means available for estimating longevity in the wild, so that more high maximum longevities are likely to be reported for the tree species. But there are comparable age-determination methods for fish and bivalves. There seems little reason to doubt that trees indeed conform to the expected pattern, as they combine slow aging with increasing fertility. One major reservation that ought to be offered is that adult trees also have much lower mortality rates than many other organisms, and thus should live longer according to the mortality-rate prediction. Of course, this broad taxonomic comparison is also largely vitiated by the lack of evolutionary homology between trees and the other taxonomic groups to which they are being compared implicitly.

Fish provide the most extreme examples of reproductive output increasing with adult age among the vertebrates, but information about both mortality rates and patterns of aging is largely lacking, making reasonable comparisons difficult. Since fish lead such different lives from other vertebrates, it is inappropriate to compare them with other vertebrate classes. Among iteroparous fish, too little information has been compiled concerning reproductive output and aging patterns to allow a reasonable comparative test of the reproductive output prediction. This is an obvious area for work on primary data sources from a comparative standpoint. For now, it can be said that there are some fish, such as carp, female plaice, and sturgeon, that have increasing adult size, and thus reproductive output, coupled with apparently quite slow aging (Comfort, 1979, pp. 91–105).

Among invertebrate metazoa, the lack of necessary knowledge is even more severe. Crustaceans, like the lobster *Homarus,* are offered by Williams (1957) as corroborations of his prediction. *Homarus* indeed lives longer than any other arthropod is known to, perhaps up to 50 years (Comfort, 1979, p. 72), and continues to grow and, presumably, increase in fecundity. But too little is known of crustacean aging in general. Molluscs are another group that could be used to test this prediction, since many of them continue to grow after sexual maturity.

### Tests of the Gender-Differences Prediction

One of the most promising contexts for "comparative" analysis of the evolution of aging is the comparison of males with females, within a species. In this case, the assumption of *ceteris paribus* is much more reasonable, and the potential for direct field and laboratory comparison much greater, since the two genders will often be "side-by-side" in nature and can be readily kept that way in the laboratory. Useful research can proceed by direct study of one species at a time, rather than relying on compilation of a large mass of data from other sources.

Of course, little work of this kind has been done to date, and still less that has been interpreted in terms of the evolution of aging. However, one major finding is already relatively well established among metazoa: Males of a species often senesce before the females, whenever there is a difference between the genders. This is well known for mammals, man being an obvious example, and insects, the most abundant data coming from *Drosophila* (Comfort, 1979, pp. 163–67), among other taxa. There are reports of exceptions to this rule, even within such species; so the pattern cannot be regarded as a universal rule. There are no widely accepted physiological explanations for this pattern.

Williams (1957) proposed that this difference arises because males are more exposed to predation and because male body size is less important in determining male reproductive success; so males can reproduce more when young. Perhaps the source of the difference can be put more generally. Males often compete with each other for females, whether in male–male contests or by female evaluation. [Females rarely compete with each other for access to males, exceptions being confined to cases in which the male provides the greater parental investment, as in the spotted sandpiper, for example (Krebs and Davies, 1981, p. 149).] In this competition the most vigorous males will normally be more successful (cf. Partridge, 1980). Thus much older males may have little chance to reproduce, because of the *relative* advantage of younger males. This has been documented in animals as diverse as red deer (Clutton-Brock, Guiness, and Albon, 1982) and *Drosophila* (Tayior et al., 1981). Older females can often still reproduce, if they are able to produce gametes, because males are almost always willing to mate with them. Georgiadis (1985) showed that polygynous species of African ruminants with larger males exhibited lower rates of adult male survival, and these are the species in which competition for females will be most intense. Thus the force of selection will often be weaker at later ages for males, relative to females, and aging should accordingly evolve at earlier ages, whether by mutation accumulation or antagonistic pleiotropy. The critical test of this hypothesis would be a reversal of the sex difference for longevity in species in which older males had large reproductive advantages over younger males.

A note of caution for this entire line of thinking is that Prothero and Jürgens (1987) found no systematic gender difference in mammalian species' longevities, once body weight is accounted for. One possibility is that the dependence of aging on gender is actually a reflection of body-size effects. A further complication is that males in polygynous species often exhibit delayed sexual maturation and prolonged growth, in mammals and birds, a phenomenon that Charlesworth (1980, p. 261) also attributes to male–male competition that is dependent on size. This will then tend to foster the evolution of postponed aging in males, all other things being equal. This effect is also in juxtaposition to Williams' analysis of the pattern of selection on males as a function of size, compared with females. The overall situation, then, is one in which there are a number of different selective factors and some ambiguity in the data. It is doubtful that intraspecific comparisons of sexes will prove to be quite as revealing as might have been thought. This also illustrates the general tenuousness of the use of the comparative method to study aging.

## Tests of the Antagonistic Pleiotropy Prediction

The idea that there is an evolutionary "tradeoff" between adult survival and reproduction, and thus antagonistic pleiotropy, is one of the centerpieces of evolutionary ecology (Stearns, 1976, 1977; Charlesworth, 1980, Chapter 5). The best tests of this idea use quantitative genetics and selection experiments, discussed in Chapter 4. Comparative patterns of aging should conform to prediction (4), if antagonistic pleiotropy between early reproduction and later survival is sufficiently important evolutionarily so as to overcome the many other selective forces that differ between species. The only comparative data that are sufficiently complete to analyze with confidence are those for birds and mammals. For mammals, Harvey and Zammuto (1985) showed that there is a strong positive correlation between age at first reproduction and life expectancy in the wild, even when the confounding effects of adult body size, gestation length, litter size, neonatal weight, and litter weight are removed. This fits the antagonistic pleiotropy prediction, except that life expectancy in the wild may not be a good test of aging. Longevities in captivity would be necessary for that. Evidently, more work of this kind is needed.

Turning to invertebrates, Schnebel and Grossfield (1988) compared the longevities of 12 *Drosophila* species and semispecies. They were particularly concerned with correlations between early fitness components and life span, with a view to testing the antagonistic pleiotropy hypothesis. The correlations were not generally negative, ostensibly contrary to the hypothesis. The problem is that genotype–environment interaction, to which small invertebrates will be particularly sensitive (vide Service and Rose, 1985), could be obscuring the pattern of covariation due to a novel environment effect, as discussed in Chapters 3 and 4. That is, some species could have been generally better adapted to the laboratory media and conditions used in the study, compared with other species, giving rise to enhanced early reproduction and longevity. Therefore, it is difficult to evaluate the conclusions of Schnebel and Grossfield.

Most comparative work on life-history covariation has sought correlates of maximum longevity in mammals (e.g., Sacher, 1959, 1978; Western and Ssemakula, 1982; Stearns, 1983; Prothero and Jürgens, 1987). Body weight and organ weights have been consistently found to explain most of the variation in life span. Brain growth in turn is negatively correlated with speed of reproduction (Sacher and Staffeldt, 1974; Western and Ssemakula, 1982), giving what seems to be a negative relationship between reproductive rate and potential life span, in conformity with prediction (4). While it has been argued that brain weight has special importance over body weight (Sacher, 1959), extensive data analyses reveal that organ weights do not account for more of the variation in the data than total body weight (Prothero and Jürgens, 1987).

Stearns (1983) has supplied the most incisive analysis of comparative data from the standpoint of evolutionary ecology. Principal-components analysis on a large body of mammalian comparative data revealed a leading factor that explained about 70 percent of the variation in life-history characters. This leading factor separated species along an axis that had early-maturing, small, short-lived, and rapidly reproducing species at one end, and late-maturing, large, long-lived, and slowly reproducing species at the other. That is, mice were at one end and elephants were at the other. Stearns's (1983) analysis also reveals a negative correlation of reproductive rate with size and a positive correlation of longevity with size. Reproductive maturity is also later among larger animals. Interestingly, when the effects of size are removed from the analysis, the antagonistic relationship between early reproduction and longevity remains. In general, then, the analysis of Stearns (1983) appears to corroborate the prediction of an evolutionary antagonism between early reproduction and longevity.

It is only fair to note that most of the authors who have applied multivariate data analysis to comparative patterns of vertebrate life history do not reason along the lines sketched by Williams (1957) and discussed extensively in this book (e.g., Sacher, 1968, 1978). Instead, they propose that there exist fundamental "allometric" relationships involving size and physiological rate constants that determine the direction of evolution, rather than selection on birth rates and survival probabilities (Sacher, 1978; Lindstedt and Calder, 1981; Western and Ssemakula, 1982). Indeed, these authors can be quite emphatic about the contrast between what they see as their point of view and that of someone like Williams, seeing them as "diametrically opposed hypotheses about the nature of the factors responsible for the aging process" (Sacher, 1978).

An unfair reading of the publications of these authors could lead a critic to suggest that they imagine that selection can proceed on some basis other than differences in net reproduction, and thus Darwinian fitness. For example, in an apparently critical vein, Western and Ssemakula (1982) write: "Under the aegis of the adaptationist paradigm it is acceptable to construct theories, of for instance, the evolution of birth rates, of death rates and of life span, without having to justify them as primary adaptive traits or epiphenomena." Instead, they suggest that "reproductive rates would be constrained within a narrow envelope of possibility by size selection." But how is such selection to proceed, unless via differences in net reproductive rates?

Sacher (1968, 1978) often asserted that there is no evidence for the kind of age-specific or pleiotropic effects assumed in the evolutionary theory and its population-genetic mechanisms. In a population-genetic sense, the alternative that he seemed to emphasize, in which "every successful species has an evolved degree of molecular and organizational stability sufficient to assure for it a survival characteristic that confers an adequate level of fitness in its ecological niche" (Sacher, 1978), seems to be that aging is unitary with fitness. The evidence discussed in Chapters 3 and 4 directly refutes this view. (See also Johnson, 1988a.)

The language of these authors is, however, rarely coherent in a population-genetics sense. Perhaps it is fairer to propose instead that some of these authors are simply offering the same views formulated in greater mechanistic detail, or perhaps from an "organismal," as opposed to "population," vantage point, and that they fail to understand the fit between their findings and the predictions of Williams (1957) and other traditional evolutionary biologists. At present, it is hard to say if this interpretation is correct.

## Conclusion

Ultimately, the comparative method can provide the broadest tests of the evolutionary theory of aging. At present, there are few taxonomic groups for which sufficient data have been assembled. A great deal more should be done, since it is unlikely that the intensive experiments on genetic variation in aging discussed in Chapters 3 and 4 will ever be performed on more than the handful of exceptionally convenient laboratory animals, such as *D. melanogaster* and *C. elegans,* or short-lived plant species, such as *Poa annua.*

A potentially falsifying corollary of the general evolutionary theory of aging is that aging should evolve if and only if there is evolutionary age structure. Evolutionary age structure arises when there is a separation between soma and germ line; it does not arise when reproduction is fissile. Taxonomic groups in which there is a consistent separation of the soma and germ line, such as vertebrates, insects, and rotifers, appear to lack species that do not senesce. Taxonomic groups in which all reproduction occurs by fission, such as bacteria, many protozoa, and a miscellany of coelenterates and other simple invertebrates, appear to lack aging. There are a number of groups that have more ambiguous methods of reproduction, such as ciliates, colonial coelenterates, and grasses. The evolutionary theory does not make clear predictions about these cases, and aging is indeed often difficult to sort out in these species. Nonetheless, it seems clear that the evolutionary theory's prediction concerning the presence or absence of aging has not been falsified. Thus the comparative evidence provides dramatic support for the validity of the evolutionary theory of aging.

To a limited extent, the evolutionary theory of aging can be used to make sense of some of the comparative patterns of aging. The theory predicts that aging should occur at slower rates in organisms that have lower mortality rates in the wild or higher fertility rates at later ages, all other things being equal. Certain broad taxonomic comparisons bear out this prediction. Birds and bats, which can fly away from terrestrial predators, generally exhibit lower rates of aging compared with other like-sized terrestrial vertebrates. Similarly, animals with thick shells, like turtles and bivalves, tend to live longer than animals without armor. It has also been predicted that higher early reproductive rates should be associated with faster aging, and this has been borne out particularly in comparative studies of mammals, in which the contrast between mouse and elephant appears to be generally valid: small, fecund, and short-lived versus large, less fecund, and long-lived. However, all these patterns have exceptions, and the comparative predictions of the theory concerning rates of aging do not provide material for critical tests. In a way, the evolutionary theory of aging chiefly provides an explanatory framework for comparative patterns of aging, rather than a predictive tool, leaving aside the presence or absence of aging.

# 6

# An Evolutionary Perspective on Organismal Theories of Aging

The physiological mechanisms of aging have been the primary focus of gerontological research. Up until the late 1970s, the study of these mechanisms usually proceeded as if knowledge of such mechanisms were all that was required to understand aging fully (vide Comfort, 1979). In this respect, gerontology was typical of much reductionist physiological research. But unlike other physiological research, the field of gerontology could not use the concept of "function," which provides the implicit underpinning of most physiological investigations. On the other hand, the concept of "pathology," which might at first seem an appropriate replacement for function, could hardly be stretched to cover the dramatic association between reproduction and aging in semelparous salmon and monocarpic plants, as indeed the discomfort of gerontologists with such cases illustrates (e.g., Kirkwood and Cremer, 1982). Thus gerontology lacked solid conceptual foundations to guide its research. This lack of basic conceptual foundations was paired with a proliferation of unsuccessful theories. The result was a diffuse field in which little sense was made of a large mass of well-established empirical findings.

It is the gravamen of this book that the fundamental explanatory theory for the existence and features of aging is that developed by evolutionary biologists. Given this perspective, it is appropriate to reconsider extant gerontological findings, with a view to incorporating them within an evolutionary biology of aging considered in its widest sense. This is the goal of Chapters 6–8. It should be emphasized that the present discussion is *not* intended to summarize this body of research on its own terms. Rather, this research will be presented, analyzed, and synthesized according to the degree to which it makes sense within the evolutionary biology of aging. There is a vast literature on aging, very little of which is interpretable in terms of evolutionary thinking. That literature is not reviewed here.

To begin this process of re-evaluation, one point is obvious at once. Since aging is a result of the declining force of natural selection in age-structured populations, according to the theory of Chapter 1, there is no purely physiological cause of aging. While the evolution of any set of characters involves physiological means, the search for an ultimate physiological cause of aging is no more cogent than a search for a physiological cause of evolutionary adaptation would be. (The latter is in fact a Lamarckian project.) This implies that one of the basic goals of gerontology, that of finding the physiological cause(s) of aging, is misconceived. On the other hand, it does *not* imply that the substantive findings of gerontology are worthless. Rather, it implies that these findings should be integrated within the framework provided by the evolutionary theory of aging.

The highest level of physiological integration is that of the whole organism, and aging is evidently manifest at this level. It is natural, therefore, that there should be physiological theories based on the idea that aging is a result of a failure of function at the organismal level. Such theories and the experiments that bear upon them are considered in this chapter. The physiological theories and experiments confined to cellular and molecular levels are the concern of the next chapter.

## Extrinsic Theories

The simplest way to explain aging as a strictly physiological process is to propose that it arises because of external "insult." One may broadly split such extrinsic mechanisms into two subsidiary categories: "wear and tear" and infectious disease.

### Wear and Tear

Cars get old, too. That is, they become progressively more subject to mechanical breakdown with "age" from the date of manufacture. This aging process is not due to some internal disorder, at least if you own a Toyota, still less infectious disease. The cause is the many physical and chemical factors that tend to move physical systems towards high values of entropy: oxidation, metal fatigue, cracks due to mechanical stress, accumulation of combustion byproducts, and so on. All of these processes are evoked by the phrase *wear and tear*.

Any organism that lacks complete self-renewal must be as subject to eventual disintegration as any car, all of which of course lack such self-renewal capacity. That many organisms lack some renewal capacities is obvious in the common absence of limb-regeneration capability. Many metazoan tissues consist of cells that undergo very little division, after the cessation of growth in the adult. Thus it is easy to proceed to the conclusion that aging is an inevitable consequence of the wear and tear undergone by living things, and so of little scientific interest.

Before proceeding any further with this discussion, it should be made clear just what sort of hypotheses are under consideration. The idea of wear and tear can be regarded as an all-inclusive category for a large number of molecular and cellular theories of aging. Such theories will be dealt with in Chapter 7. Here the concern is with much less sophisticated theories, those that involve the wearing out and breaking down of macroscopic body parts.

Two simple examples should indicate the type of theories under consideration. (1) After reproductive maturity, the teeth of many mammalian species are not replaced, and in many orders they also cease to grow. Mammalian teeth wear out, most obviously in herbivores, which process large quantities of plant matter and grit (Pearson, 1945; Perry, 1953). If the teeth wear out completely and are not replaced, such mammals may starve. As wear proceeds, the quality of nutrition may fall with age, resulting in a weakening of disease resistance, musculature, and so on. All these together could engender a general collapse in the herbivore's capacity to survive and reproduce, such that it dies.

(2) An analogous theory can be concocted about mechanical damage to insect wings. Any gerontologist who customarily allows large cohorts of flies to age in good culture conditions will have noticed the way their wings fray at the edges, sometimes large panels of the wing being lost (Rockstein, 1966). Entire wings are often broken off near their base. In effect, the power of flight is decreasing by stages, so that older laboratory flies rarely take flight, moving about instead on their legs, with only occasional wing-assisted "hops." In the wild, such mechanical damage would materially impede the fly's ability to get from one food source to another, to say nothing of avoiding predation. Such problems would have major deleterious effects on the fly's capacity to survive and reproduce, analogous to the effects of tooth wear for a herbivore. In both of these examples, the nature of the wear and tear is not elusive, nor are its consequences.

Such simple examples are readily generalized: wear of mouth parts, such as arthropod mandibles; wear of joints in animals with skeletons; tearing of connective tissues that contribute to limb movement, like tendons; wearing out of protective structures, such as spines, shells, etc.; and so on, indefinitely. Wear and tear must affect all machinery in a world subject to the Second Law of thermodynamics, and the machinery of living things cannot be an exception.

The major problem that besets any general wear-and-tear theory of aging is the capacity of some organisms to repair damage, and apparently to undergo thorough renewal. All cells alive today are descendants of an unbroken lineage of cells stretching back at least a billion years. Throughout that time, the ancestral cells must have been continually renewed and repaired, whether autonomously or through the action of associated cells in multicellular structures. Living things are not incapable of resisting the forces that act to destroy all inanimate machinery. Such resistance is evidently not confined to single cell lineages, as the apparent absence of aging in paratomically reproducing animals and some vegetative plants attests. (See Chapter 5.) So the question facing any general wear-and-tear theory of aging is: Why are some organisms apparently susceptible to it, while others are not?

This question is of course easily answered in terms of the evolutionary theory of aging. If the effects of a particular type of wear and tear are sufficiently delayed in age-structured populations, then natural selection will not favor the evolution of repair to counter the wear involved. This point has been understood by evolutionary biologists for some time (e.g., Maynard Smith, 1962) and has gained some currency within the gerontological community (Kirkwood, 1981). In keeping with the two possible population-genetic mechanisms of senescence, discussed in Chapter 4, there are two ways in which this failure of repair could evolve. The first is that such repair mechanisms are cost-free but do not evolve because of the strict indifference of natural selection. The second is that such repair mechanisms trade off against enhanced early reproduction, and thus fitness, and so their evolution is actively opposed by natural selection (Kirkwood, 1981). The first mechanism implies that the requirements of repair can be met out of organismal resources at later ages only, while the second implies that some advance investment must be made. Regenerating a lost limb or tail may not require any standing investment of "regrowth capacity," regeneration occurring simply by reactivation of dormant ontogenetic programs in stem cells required for ordinary tissue functioning. Other repair capacities may require specific cannibalization and reconstruction mechanisms that are costly to maintain. It does not seem reasonable to exclude either possibility *a priori*, as either is sufficient to explain the absence of any particular repair capacity in organisms from populations with age structure.

A theory that proposes that aging is only a result of wear and tear contradicts both the evolutionary theory of aging and the apparent absence of senescence in some organisms. On the other hand, any theory that completely dismisses wear and tear as a part of aging is also at variance with the wearing out of essential, unreplaced structures in a variety of organisms, from mammals to insects. And there must be still more instances that are not yet known. This is not to say that all aging organisms senesce in part because of wear and tear at the organismal level. Many organisms may never live long enough to undergo mechanical wear with significant consequences, even under the best possible laboratory conditions. They may die of other mechanisms of aging first. In general terms, though, wear and tear is a perfectly credible organismal mechanism of aging.

## Infectious Disease

Another plausible mechanism of aging is that it is a result of the chronic effects of persistent infectious disease. One of the seminal founders of gerontology in its modern form, Elie Metchnikoff (1904, 1908) proposed that aging in vertebrates was due in large part to intestinal bacteria that produce toxins that are absorbed by the body and chronically poison it. Such chronic disease was also supposed to stimulate phagocytotic cells to scavenge the body's own cells, causing diverse senescent pathologies. Accordingly, Metchnikoff (1908) proposed that differences between vertebrate longevities were to be explained in terms of the size and contents of the large intestine, as well as their frequency of evacuation. Thus the generally greater bird life span was explained in terms of the bird's smaller large intestine and its relative lack of bacterial and protozoan intestinal flora and fauna. Patterns of longevity in other species were similarly explained by Metchnikoff as resulting from patterns of chronic poisoning, from external or internal toxins. The evolution of such autotoxification was discussed by Metchnikoff partly in terms of group selection, although in such a confused way that there is little point going into it here. In addition to intestinal problems, Metchnikoff also discussed syphilis as an aging factor, establishing himself as the foremost proponent of infection as a mechanism of aging.

The suggestion that disease is a primary determinant of aging had some degree of plausibility in the aftermath of the general acceptance of the germ theory of contagious disease, in the late nineteenth century. Not enough work had yet been done with organisms reared in germ-free environments. Since then, experiments of this kind have been performed, most often on rodents and *Drosophila*. Summarizing the evidence, Strehler (1977, p. 299) and Lamb (1978, p. 22) find no indication that maximum life span is increased under such conditions, although mean life span may be.

On the other hand, in man the age dependence of death from *acute* infection, such as influenza and pneumonia, is strikingly like that of cancer or cardiovascular disease (Dublin, Lotka, and Spiegelman, 1949), rising dramatically with increasing adult age. This implicates disease in aging, although perhaps only as a final cause of death. Evidently, there must be a weakening in the capacity of the mammalian body to resist acute infection. To the extent that contagious diseases are eliminated by isolation and hygiene, medically or in the laboratory, this type of endogenous aging must be of less consequence for mortality patterns. But this is hardly a plausible extrinsic mechanism of senescence. Human chronic infectious disease, such as tuberculosis, displays a very different pattern of age dependence (Dublin, Lotka, and Spiegelman, 1949). The old show little increase in morbidity due to such diseases. Since these are the diseases most plausibly considered extrinsic forces establishing aging, the idea that infectious disease constitutes a strictly extrinsic mechanism underlying the physiology of aging is left rather tattered.

## Exhaustion Theories

Since Metchnikoff, few gerontologists have favored the idea that aging is a result of extrinsic factors. Instead, they have searched for some internal mechanism inevitably leading to death.

### Simple Depletion

The simplest idea of this kind is simply that there is some finite, indispensable, and incompletely replaced resource or substance that is depleted during adult life. Its eventual exhaustion must then lead to death. The most unequivocal instances of aging that can be attributed to such depletion of resources are those involving semelparous organisms. In particular, many adult insects lack mouthparts, especially among the Ephemeroptera and Lepidoptera, and have no other mechanism of obtaining nutrition. Adult lamprey do not feed either, to give a chordate example. The eventual cause of death and reproductive failure is not difficult to ascertain in such cases. Though it may seem trite to say so, natural selection has evidently failed to maintain the mouthparts of these insects, presumably because (1) there is only a slight chance of adults surviving to starve to death in the wild, so mouthparts evolutionarily atrophied by mutation accumulation, or (2) alleles were favored that diverted resources from the adult soma to immediate reproduction, a type of antagonistic pleiotropy. Whatever the population-genetic mechanism(s) in such cases, there can be little doubt that depletion of caloric reserves required for adult survival is one of the principal proximate mechanisms of aging in such organisms.

### Reproductive Exhaustion

Other semelparous organisms, such as Pacific salmon and monocarpic plants, do not senesce in a way so readily explained in terms of depletion. In these cases, structures like the digestive system in some semelparous fish and leaves in monocarpic plants are present, but they often appear to deteriorate in the course of, or immediately after, reproduction. Such cases can be characterized as "reproductive exhaustion." The validity of this characterization is borne out by the consequences of removing the gonads of mature Pacific salmon or the flowering structures of monocarpic plants. Captive salmon that are castrated live much longer than those that are not, as much as 18 years longer (Robertson, 1961). Similarly, cultivated soybean plants that have had all flowers and fruits systematically removed during the growing season thrive long after their reproducing controls have died (Leopold, 1961). At the other end of the scale, giving males more females to mate with each day shortens life in *Drosophila melanogaster* (Partridge and Farquhar, 1981; Partridge, 1986), just as virgin *Drosophila* females live longer than those that are mated (Maynard Smith, 1958; Partridge, 1986). Patently, increasing reproductive activity is associated with early death, while preventing reproductive activity is associated with prolonged life span.

This sort of antagonism between reproduction and survival has been interpreted in terms of a depletion of nutrients from somatic tissues due to their diversion to reproductive organs (e.g., Molisch, 1938). This mechanistic hypothesis has elicited a great deal of experimental investigation, particularly in plants (vide Noodén, 1980). In its barest form, it needs to be qualified. Some monocarpic plants increase their uptake of nutrients from the environment before reproduction, depleting the vegetative structures of their nutrients only when the nutrients available from the environment are not sufficient (Noodén, 1980). But others, such as soybeans, may deplete the vegetative structures even with experimental provision of supplements, and some, like oats, may do so especially under such circumstances (Noodén, 1980).

Experiments of this kind are in any case somewhat tricky to interpret, in that they are typically conducted under conditions of cultivation or laboratory rearing. Thus it is likely that they involve environmental nutrient levels in excess of those in the wild, suggesting that nutrient depletion is indeed the normal proximate cause of death, at least in monocarpic plants that survive to reproduce. On the other hand, aging is a phenomenon of fitness-component deterioration in the absence of deficiencies in the environment, making experiments with nutrient supplementation defensible. Furthermore, there are monocarpic plants in which nutrient depletion has not been detected, such as spinach and cocklebur (Noodén, 1980).

The failure to find simple depletion hypotheses sufficient to explain monocarpic plant aging has led to the development of hormone theories of plant aging (Noodén, 1980). Analogous "death hormone" theories have been proposed for mammalian aging (Denckla, 1975). There is evidence in favor of these theories in experiments that either directly manipulate hormone levels (Noodén, 1980) or involve removal of hormone-producing organs (Denckla, 1974). It has been suggested that group selection on species favors those that senesce early, fostering turnover of the individuals within a population and thereby reducing mean generation time (Denckla, 1975). But the evolutionary theory of aging renders such proposals supererogatory: Few organisms in nature are likely to senesce, and individual selection mechanisms like antagonistic pleiotropy actively foster aging with a selection intensity far greater than that likely from such group selection.

The simplest way to explain the material evidence for reproductive exhaustion and "aging hormones" is to invoke antagonistic pleiotropy. In terms of genetic mechanisms for their evolution, semelparous animals and monocarpic plants can be taken as the extreme on a continuum of evolutionary allocation between reproduction and adult survival. Mobilization of all organismal functions for a single burst of reproduction has the side effect of precluding adult survival after reproduction. Transfer of nutrients from vegetative to reproductive structures in monocarpic plants is only one of the most obvious forms that such an allocation can take. Other processes could involve cessation of maintenance of somatic structures so as to reduce their metabolic burden upon the organism. Each semelparous species would have a unique set of possibilities for evolutionary allocation. Furthermore, it should be noted that, in the later evolution of semelparity, once subsequent episodes of reproduction have been rendered extremely unlikely, selection acting on loci that possess alleles that exhibit antagonistic pleiotropy between initial reproduction and subsequent adult survival will favor alleles that foster semelparity still more. In effect, the adult life span collapses as the evolutionary balance between adult survival and early reproduction falls entirely on the side of early reproduction. If antagonistic pleiotropy is a prevalent mechanism in the evolution of aging, then it is inevitable that there should be some cases like Pacific salmon and soybean.

An unusual case of coexistence of semelparous and iteroparous forms in a colonial sea squirt, *Botryllus schlosseri,* illustrates this evolutionary scenario (Grosberg, 1988). In this species, semelparous colonies die immediately after reproduction. Relative to iteroparous colonies, the semelparous colonies have rapid growth, with an earlier age at first reproduction. The number of embryos produced per zooid per clutch is higher, indicating increased reproductive activity. This seems to be a clear case of alternative life-history "strategies," with life span and reproduction antagonistically covarying.

Hormones are obvious candidates for mediating controls of the allocation between reproduction and survival. One of their known functions is reproductive maturation itself, making variation in the intensity of their "mobilization signals" a plausible avenue for genetic variation in degree of reproductive exhaustion. Experimental manipulation of hormone levels in monocarpic plants (vide Noodén, 1980) could be analogous to the effects of allelic variants at hormone-related loci. With the present interpretation, however, such hormones are not "aging hormones" or "death hormones." Rather such hormones would be reproductive hormones, functioning to prepare the organism for reproduction in the fashion characteristic of the type of organism involved, with the side effect of greatly accelerated aging.

Few more dramatic instances of this exist than aging in the marsupial "mouse," *Antechinus stuartii.* In this organism, males engage in extraordinary levels of reproductive effort, fighting for access to females and copulating for protracted periods. This pattern is associated with a striking rise in plasma androgen concentration and progressive breakdown in disease resistance (Bradley, McDonald, and Lee, 1980). Shortly after the mating period, all males are dead, at about one year of age. Castration allows survival well into a second or third year. This is analogous to the pattern in Pacific salmon or soybean. In the case of marsupial mice, the connections between hormone levels, reproductive activity, and pathology clearly reveal the physiology of antagonistic pleiotropy.

Such phenomena in semelparous organisms may be of great relevance to iteroparous species as well (Finch, 1987). Iteroparous organisms of varying longevity, between or within species, could similarly be subject to survival-impairing effects of reproduction that vary according to the intensity of hormonal "signals." This variation in intensity of signal could in turn be a result of variations in hormone structure, the structure or number of cell-surface hormone receptors, and so on. If this is a valid suggestion, then the study of physiological mechanisms of aging in semelparous and other organisms could be fostered by concentrating on hormonal mechanisms that link reproductive with somatic functions.

## Rate-of-Living Theory

As discussed in Chapter 2, patterns of aging are subject to a variety of environmental influences. Many of these patterns of modulation of life span, fertility, and other life-history characters have long been taken to reflect some tradeoff between "speed" of life and its total duration: *In general, the duration of life varies inversely as the rate of energy expenditure during its continuance. In short, the length of life depends inversely on the rate of living"* (Pearl, 1928, pp. 150–51, emphasis in original). In Pearl's (1928) *The Rate of Living,* two aspects of "living" are confounded, growth and metabolic rate, rapidity of growth also being taken as an aspect of rapidity of "living." [See Sohal (1986) for a modern view.] There are many organismal theories of aging that involve growth pattern, and in any case confounding growth rate and metabolic rate hardly seems scientifically precise. Accordingly, this section treats modulation of senescence that does not involve variation in growth patterns. All such growth phenomena, and their associated theories, will be discussed in the next section.

### The Basic Observations

The best data relating life span to some aspect of the "rate of living," separate from rates of growth, come from studies of the dependence of insect longevity on ambient temperature in laboratory cultures. Some of the earliest results of this kind were obtained with *Drosophila* by Loeb and Northrop (1916, 1917), flies at lower temperatures living longer than flies at higher temperatures. Along with life-span pattern, at low temperatures the fruit flies appeared sluggish and inactive, while at high temperatures they appeared to be very active. Indeed, Loeb and Northrop proposed the existence of a coefficient relating life span duration to ambient temperature with a magnitude of 2–3, like that of chemical reactions. And indeed the simplest interpretation of these results is that they reflect a general modulation of the rate of chemical reactions in the fly body, and thus its metabolic rate, which in turn inevitably modulates the "wearing out" or "using up" of the whole organism.

   These basic results have been reproduced with *Drosophila* by a number of workers (e.g., Alpatov and Pearl, 1929; Strehler, 1961, 1962; Shaw and Bercaw, 1962). Characteristic results are shown in Figure 6.1. Whatever the interpretation to be placed upon the mechanistic basis of temperature's effects on insect life span, there can be little doubt of the existence of the phenomenon to be explained.

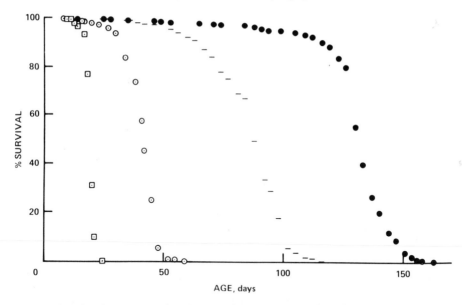

FIGURE 6.1. Survival curves of male *D. melanogaster* kept as adults at different ambient temperatures. The solid dots represent the 18 °C results. The dashes give the 21 °C results, circles the 27 °C results, and squares 30 °C. (From Miquel et al., 1976.)

and life span was provided by Trout and Kaplan (1970), using *shaker* mutants in *Drosophila melanogaster*. These mutants affect the neurological system, producing high levels of activity, such activity in turn being strongly correlated with oxygen consumption, and thus metabolic rate. Different *shaker* alleles have different degrees of increased activity, and thus metabolic rate. Figure 6.2 shows the relationship between metabolic rate and mean life span in *shaker* stocks. Evidently, this relationship conforms to the basic notion of an antagonistic relationship between rate of living and duration of life.

## Problems of Interpretation

A series of experiments by Maynard Smith and Clarke (Maynard Smith, 1958, 1963; Clarke and Maynard Smith, 1961a,b) cast a considerable shadow over the simple rate-of-living theory of Pearl. These experiments indicated that, once egg laying was controlled, flies kept first at a high temperature and then transferred to a lower temperature for the remainder of their lives had mean longevities that are the same as flies kept continuously at the lower temperature. This type of result is shown in Figure 6.3, where the expectations of the rate-of-living theory are clearly not met.

In order to explain these quite different results, Maynard Smith and Clarke (Clarke and Maynard Smith, 1961b; Maynard Smith, 1963) proposed a "threshold theory" for the dependence of longevity on temperature. Reverting to the type of graphical model discussed in Chapter 2 (Maynard Smith, 1966; Lamb, 1977, pp.

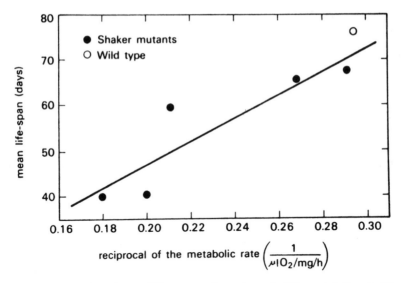

FIGURE 6.2. Regression of mean life span on the reciprocal of the metabolic rate ($O_2$ consumption) for wild type and *shaker* stocks of *D. melanogaster*. The graph indicates that higher metabolic rates are associated with depressed longevity. Reprinted with permission from *Experimental Gerontology* 5, Trout, W.E. and W.D. Kaplan. A relation between longevity, metabolic rate, and activity in Shaker mutants of *Drosophila melanogaster*. Copyright 1970, Pergamon Press plc.

73–75), Maynard Smith (1963) outlined two basic models for the dependence of longevity on ambient temperature, shown in Figure 6.4. Both models presume the existence of some lower "vitality" threshold, below which life is not sustained. Both models also assume that there is some strictly decreasing function relating vitality to adult age. The models differ with respect to the factor influenced by ambient temperature. In the rate-of-living model, the function relating vitality to age declines more rapidly at higher temperatures. In the threshold model, the pattern of vitality decline is not altered. Instead, the vitality threshold is raised by the higher temperatures, presumably because of metabolic disruptions. Either variant explains the reduction in mean life span with age. Only the threshold model explains the results of Figure 6.3.

Experiments on the annual fish *Cynolebias bellottii* by Liu and Walford (1975) also conformed to the threshold model. Fish kept continuously at 20 °C had life spans of 14.0 ± 3.9 (mean plus or minus the standard deviation) months, while fish kept continuously at 15 °C had life spans of 18.9 ± 5.5 months. Fish kept for 8 months at 15 °C and then switched to 20 °C until death had life spans of 15.2 ± 4.4 months, while fish kept for 8 months at 20 °C and then switched to 15 °C had life spans of 23.5 ± 9.1 months. These experiments also suggest that the ambient temperature during the later period of life seems to have greater influence than that during the earlier. This is in broad conformity with the threshold model. An interesting aspect of these experiments is that the fish grown at 15 °C were more active and

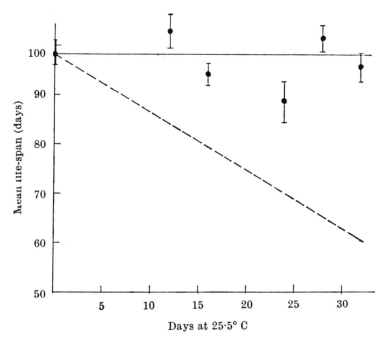

FIGURE 6.3. Results of an experiment in which *D. subobscura* were shifted from high temperature (25.5 °C) at early ages to low temperature (20 °C) at later ages. The number of days spent at the high temperature appears to have little effect on mean life span, contrary to the expectations of the rate-of-living theory, plotted as a dashed line. Reprinted by permission from *Nature*, Vol. 199, pp. 400–2. Copyright (C) 1963 Macmillan Magazines Ltd.

grew faster than those reared at 20 °C, so that the greater life span of the former does not really fit with the rate-of-living theory in any case.

However, it should not be concluded that the threshold model has vanquished the rate-of-living model. Hollingsworth (1966, 1968, 1969) and Lamb (1968) performed further experiments on the dependence of the *Drosophila* life span on temperature, obtaining results that often did not fit the threshold model . In some experiments, their results fit the rate-of-living model quite well. In other experiments, neither model seemed to fit. The biology of life-span modulation is evidently more complex than had been supposed up until the late 1960s. Neither simple rate-of-living nor threshold theories can be regarded as tenable (Sohal, 1986).

## Evolutionary Biology of Life-Span Modulation

There are two obvious problems with the rate-of-living experiments discussed so far. First, they neglect to assay the vitality levels and aging rates that are presumed to underlie the life-span patterns. The organism's life history is being treated as a black box with only one meaningful output: the age at death. Under such circum-

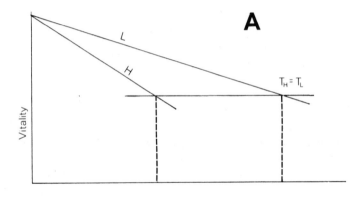

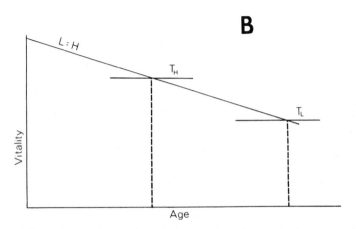

FIGURE 6.4. Diagrammatic representation of the contrast between the rate-of-living and "threshold" theories for loss of vitality under different temperature regimes. (A) In the rate-of-living theory, the loss of vitality is more rapid at higher temperatures, but the threshold for death is unchanged. (B) In the threshold theory, the loss of vitality is the same at the two temperatures, but the threshold for death is elevated at higher temperatures. L and H indicate the features of the process of senescence at low and high temperatures, respectively. Reprinted by permission from *Nature*, Vol. 199, pp. 400–2. Copyright (C) 1963 Macmillan Magazines Ltd.

stances, it is not surprising that experimental investigation should finally become stymied.

Second, the simple experimental results relate temperature to life span after the fashion of the dependence of chemical reactions on reaction kinetics. This rests on an intellectual sleight-of-hand: At more extreme temperatures, such relationships must break down, because of the organism's limits for thermal tolerance. There are thus at least two different types of temperature dependence where longevity is concerned, that of the "normal" or "physiological" temperature range, and that of pathological extremes. But a problem arises from the fact that not all life-span variation that seems normal at the level of the timing of death need be normal physiologically. There could be pathological changes in the organism at less extreme temperatures that are not expressed at the level of life span. So long as life history is studied as a black box producing the single result of an age at death, the biological interpretation of that age at death must be hazardous.

Miquel et al. (1976) have gone a considerable distance towards clarifying the ambiguities of *Drosophila* research on the dependence of life span on temperature. Their experiments had many good design features: (1) They used a range of four temperatures: 18, 21, 27, and 30 °C; (2) they measured oxygen consumption in order to estimate metabolic rate; (3) they determined age-specific "vitality" levels, using (a) negative geotaxis and (b) mating behavior as indices; (4) flies were switched from one temperature to another, from lower to higher temperatures *and* from higher to lower temperatures, symmetrically; (5) they studied the histology of flies kept at different temperatures. With this intensive and extensive regime of data collection, it was inevitable that Miquel et al. (1976) would collect some of the best data yet obtained concerning the relationship of life span to metabolic rate.

Their results are significant in several respects. First, they showed that the timing with which flies are exposed to relatively higher temperatures had little effect on their mean life span, although there was some tendency for flies exposed to higher temperatures at later ages to have lower mean longevities, as shown in Figure 6.5 and 6.6. The fit of their data to a rate-of-living equation that does not take into account threshold variation is excellent, as shown in Figure 6.7.

Second, Miquel et al. (1976) showed that there is a straightforward tradeoff between metabolic rate and mean longevity, such that the total adult consumption of oxygen is roughly constant. These results are shown in Figure 6.8. This is a concrete demonstration of Pearl's (1928) thesis that the total amount of "living" should be roughly constant.

Third, Miquel et al. (1976) showed that some life-span effects appear to be compensatory, with losses at some times being made up at other times, while other effects, at more extreme temperatures, are strictly pathological. The age-specific vitality measures provide some of this evidence. As shown in Figure 6.9, there is an interesting contrast between age-specific negative geotaxis patterns at 18 and 21 °C. At 21 °C, there is a relatively higher level of performance in the first part of the life history, but later the 18 °C flies perform better. At 27 °C, the vitality level is always lower than that at 21 or 18 °C, having collapsed entirely by 40 days of age, up to 10 days before death at 27 °C. Essentially the same pattern occurs in male mating behavior, as shown in Figure 6.10. In addition, it should be noted that total oxygen consumption appears to be lower at 27 °C, as shown in Figure 6.8. Thus, while the life-span differences between 18 and 21 °C appear to involve shifts in temporal allocation of a roughly constant total performance capacity, 27 °C life spans seem to be partly a result of extreme stress, with an overall loss in performance. This arises *in spite* of the apparent conformity of life-span modulation between 18 and 27 °C to the rate-of-living theory. Patterns of mean life span alone do not reveal whether or not the assumptions of the rate-of-living theory are met.

What, then, is to be made of the other published research on the rate-of-living

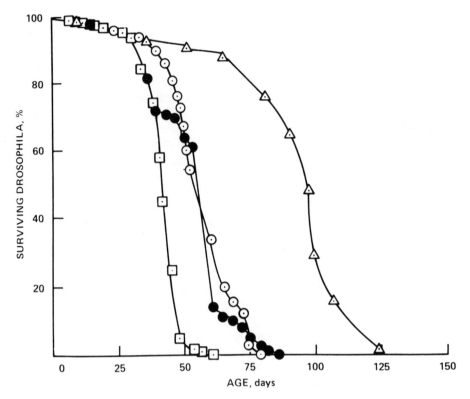

FIGURE 6.5. Survival curves for male *D. melanogaster* exposed to different temperature regimes during adult life. The triangles plot survival data for flies kept at 21 °C, while the squares represent flies kept at 27 °C. The circles represent flies kept at 21 °C until the thirty-fifth day of adult life, whereupon they were transferred to 27 °C for the rest of their lives. The solid dots represent flies kept at 27 °C until the thirty-fifth day of adult life, whereupon they were transferred to 21 °C for the rest of their lives. (From Miquel et al., 1976.)

theory, including that which apparently fits the threshold model? It seems reasonable to suggest that the rate-of-living theory has some validity in the immediate neighborhood of a population's normal temperature range. [The fruit flies studied in the experiments of Miquel et al.'s (1976) had been maintained at 21 °C for some generations.] If a simple rate-of-chemical-reactions theory is not viable because of the breakdown of the rate-of-living pattern at more extreme temperatures, then how is this to be explained?

Perhaps an evolutionary viewpoint can provide a way of creating some sense of the seeming disorder. Poikilotherms must be routinely subject to varying body temperatures, particularly small poikilotherms like insects. Natural selection accordingly will favor the capacity to respond to such temperatures so as both to minimize pathological disruption and to maximize the potential for net reproduction

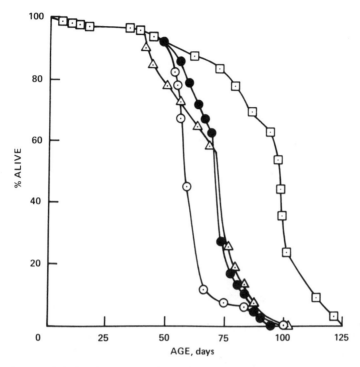

FIGURE 6.6. Survival curves for male *D. melanogaster* exposed to different temperature regimes during adult life. The squares plot survival data for flies kept at 21 °C throughout adult life. The other three curves are for flies kept at 27 °C for 20 days at varying periods of adult life: solid dots, from the third to the twenty-fourth day; triangles, from the twenty-fifth to the forty-fifth day; and circles, from the forty-sixth to the sixty-sixth day. It is notable that exposure to higher temperatures later in life results in a sharp drop in survivorship, in keeping with some aspects of the threshold theory. (From Miquel et al., 1976.)

at such temperatures. The latter will be discussed first. At slightly elevated temperatures, it may be possible for the poikilotherm to accumulate and convert calories for reproduction more rapidly, giving rise to a sharper initial peak in "performance" characters, such as female fecundity, male mating success, or negative geotaxis. The same physiological antagonisms that underlie antagonistic pleiotropy may then engender reductions in later performance, as well as longevity. This type of pattern is exhibited in the contrast between negative geotaxis and longevity in the 18 and 21 °C data of Miquel et al. (1976). Such antagonism between early performance and later survival may be at the center of rate-of-living ideas. However, it can be seen as an ontogenetic variant of the hypothesis of physiological tradeoffs that underlies the antagonistic pleiotropy mechanism for the evolution of aging.

Natural selection will also foster the capacity to resist thermal injury due to temperature extremes, all other things being equal. But natural selection is neither all-powerful nor free of constraints. If an organism is rarely exposed to particular

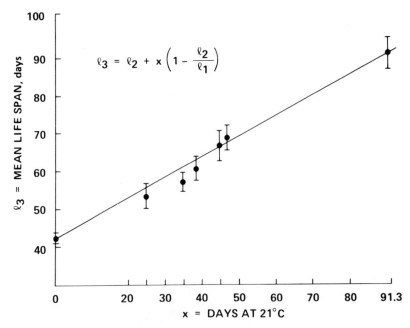

FIGURE 6.7. Fit of life-span patterns for male *D. melanogaster* under temperature variation to the expectations of the rate-of-living theory. The data are shown as means with error bars. The solid line shows the theoretical expectation, as a function of the number of days spent at 21 °C when the temperature regime involves a mixture of days at 21 and 27 °C. The fit appears to be quite good, in spite of some anomalous results shown in Figure 6.6. (From Miquel et al., 1976.)

temperature extremes, or improved performance at such temperatures would require reduced performance in its normal temperature range, selection will not adapt the organism to such temperatures. Then exposure to such temperature extremes will result in thermal injury, which will lower early performance and life span, without any associated benefit. So long as rate-of-living experiments do not incorporate age-specific performance measures, then they will not be able to distinguish ontogenetic physiological antagonisms during adult life from the effects of thermal injury. As the results of the study of Miquel et al. (1976) show, either may fit rate-of-living expectations. The cases for which the threshold model seems to fit the data best (e.g., Maynard Smith, 1963) could be those in which thermal injury is the cause of death. Resistance to such thermal injury may have little to do with performance levels early in life, instead depending on other physiological mechanisms that senesce without shifts in temporal allocation at different temperatures. Such allocative shifts will usually be specific to some of an organism's functions. They are not universal accelerations or decelerations in a general rate of living. Therefore, there is no reason to expect all poikilothermic organisms to conform to rate-of-living theories under all temperature regimes.

As a general theory of aging, Pearl's (1928) rate-of-living theory is untenable. It does nonetheless point out the potential for physiological antagonisms in interac-

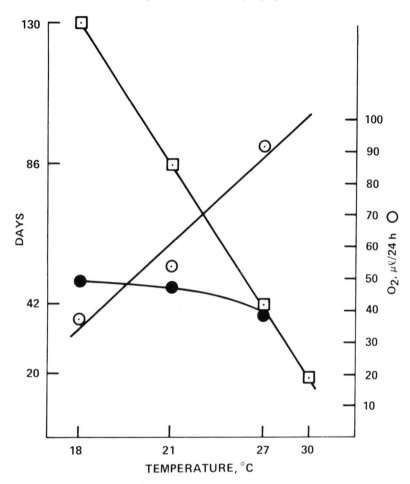

FIGURE 6.8. The relationship between life span and metabolic rate for male *D. melanogaster* kept at different ambient temperatures. Mean longevity is plotted as squares, metabolic rates as circles, and total $O_2$ consumption as solid dots. The roughly uniform total $O_2$ consumption is in accord with the rate-of-living theory. (From Miquel et al., 1976.)

tions between early performance and later survival in organisms with appropriate allocative flexibility. Such allocative antagonism has undoubtedly been important in the evolution of aging in many organisms.

## Growth and Nutrition Theories

In the early years of the century, the notion that growth and development were critical determinants of aging was widespread. These theories still survive in diverse guises within the cellular and molecular subdisciplines of gerontology, as will be

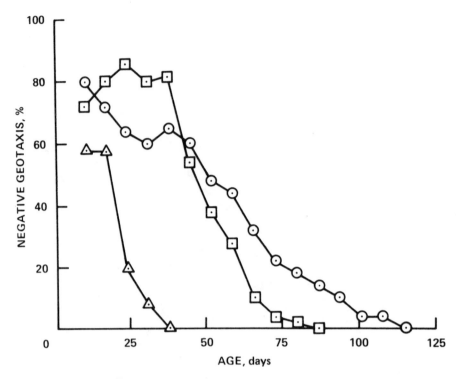

FIGURE 6.9. Age-specific patterns of negative geotaxis in male *D. melanogaster* kept at various ambient temperatures. The circles represent the data for males kept at 18 °C, while the squares are for 21 °C and the triangles are for 27 °C. The pattern at 27 °C can be fairly described as an early breakdown of vitality. (From Miquel et al., 1976.)

discussed in Chapter 7. Here the focus will be on the simpler issue of the relationship between whole organism growth and aging.

## Aging as a Result of Growth Cessation

One of the most straightforward theories of aging was that put forward by Bidder (1932), whose incontestable starting point was selection for determinate body size in birds and mammals, selection that, he proposed, centered on efficiency of locomotion. He then argued as follows:

> Adequate efficiency could only be obtained by the evolution of some mechanism to stop natural growth so soon as specific size is reached. This mechanism may be called the regulator . . . senescence is the result of the continued action of the regulator after the growth is stopped. (Bidder, 1932)

This argument rests on a number of empirical postulates of some plausibility. One is the idea that nonsenescent protozoa, sea anemones, sponges, etc. are free from aging because of their unceasing growth. In a sense, this is valid, because the

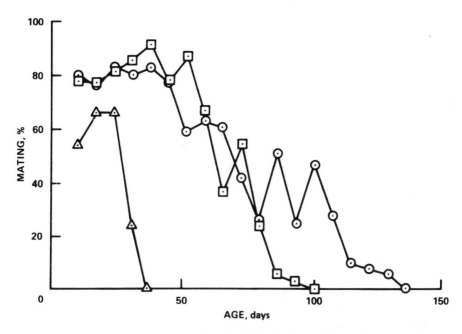

FIGURE 6.10. Age-specific patterns of mating initiation in male *D. melanogaster* kept at various ambient temperatures. The circles represent the data for males kept at 18 °C, while the squares are for 21 °C and the triangles are for 27 °C. The pattern at 27 °C can be fairly described as an early breakdown of vitality. (From Miquel et al., 1976.)

absence of defined germ-cell lineages allows the possibility of unlimited replication of all cells within the "body." Another plausible postulate is that multicellular organisms with indefinite growth, like giant trees and some fish, many of which have never been directly observed to age, do not do so for the same reason. Unfortunately for this postulate, there is evidence that growing fish do in fact age, and many trees do so as well (Chapter 5). While some plant species may not age, these are again cases in which the germ- and somatic-cell lineages are not fully distinct.

Bidder's (1932) theory is one of those unfortunate victims of the empirical method: a neat and fairly logical theory that initially appears to fit the observed patterns well, yet is demonstrably wrong in a few concrete instances. Perhaps the only thing that can be salvaged from it lies in the relationship between growth and fecundity, and thus the dependence of the force of natural selection on age. Growth that continues after the onset of reproduction is normally associated with increasing fecundity, sometimes markedly increasing fecundity. As discussed in Chapter 5, this will result in a slower rate of decline in the force of selection acting on age-specific fecundity, higher values of later fecundity then increasing the force of selection acting on age-specific survival probability, assuming no physiological effect on the survivorship curve arising from such increasing fecundity. Indeed, for some organisms, such as trees and marine fish, it is reasonable to suppose that increasing size in and of itself enhances age-specific survival rates, thus augmenting the potential association between continued growth and low rates of aging. If rates of aging in a species are sufficiently slow, and no laboratory rearing studies of sufficient length have been conducted, then aging will often go undetected. This may account for Bidder's (1925, 1932) unfounded conclusion that no fish senesce, and thus his argument that selection for efficient terrestrial locomotion led to the evolution of aging. In any case, Bidder's ideas are now only of historical interest.

## Prolongation of Life Span by Nutritional Restriction

Life span responds to varying nutritional levels in at least as many species as it does to varying temperature (Lamb, 1977; Comfort, 1979). In particular, if the supply of food during laboratory rearing is restricted, then life span is prolonged in a wide range of invertebrates, and even in some mammalian species. However, some cases of life-span prolongation do not result from prolonged adult life; instead, prolongation of juvenile development may be involved. Cases of life-span prolongation due to prolongation of aging must be distinguished from those due to postponed maturation.

Among the invertebrates in which the existence of aging is well established, the best data concerning the relationship between nutrition and longevity come from the arthropods. Ingle et al. (1937) varied duration of nutritional restriction in *Daphnia longispina,* all starvation treatments commencing at birth and ceasing at different instars. The total duration of life, as measured in instars, did not vary over treatments, but the temporal duration of life increased as the rate of growth from molt to molt slowed. The greatest increases in life span were achieved when nutritional restriction ceased in the later instars. Most of the insect results are surprisingly ambiguous. Loeb and Northrop (1917) and Northrop (1917) prolonged the larval period, and thus total life span, by underfeeding, but did not detect any increase in imaginal life span. Surveying disparate studies, Comfort (1979, p. 182) offers the general conclusion that life-span prolongation by nutritional restriction of growth in holometabolous insects involves prolongation of larval phases, with adult life span prolonged by enhanced nutrition during the adult phase. However, it is remarkable how little systematic research there has been on this problem with *D. melanogaster* or other well-known insect species.

One growth restriction effect that is known to prolong adult life span substantially is larval crowding in *Drosophila.* It is a commonplace of *Drosophila* laboratory culture that crowding of larvae results in smaller adults with reduced early fecundity and greatly increased adult longevity (e.g., Lints and Lints, 1969). The problem, however, is that this effect could be partly due to pheromonal or other interactions between larvae that result in a developmental shift, rather than a simple nutritional effect. Overall, it is possible that nutritional and growth patterns do not have the relatively simple sort of effect on *adult* arthropod life span that temperature has.

Historically, the great excitement in studies of the relationship between nutritional deprivation, growth restriction, and longevity came from work on rodents. It is the only body of experimental work on mammals in which life span has been substantially prolonged. The classic experiments were performed by McCay and his colleagues (McCay and Crowell, 1934; McCay, Crowell, and Maynard, 1935; McCay et al., 1939; McCay, Sperling, and Barnes, 1943) using rats. The experimental treatment involved rearing rats from the time of weaning on diets restricted in calories, such that growth to adult size and reproductive maturity was prevented. This treatment is generally referred to as "retardation" in the literature. Retardation was eventually terminated, and the rats were given enough calories to grow to adulthood. As already shown in Figure 2.10, one of the most frequently reprinted figures in gerontology, this treatment resulted in a great increase in *total* life span. These results are readily reproducible and are not generally due to peculiar dietary constituents or experimental stocks.

Experiments with adult dietary restriction appear to give increased longevity by means other than obesity prevention or prolonged development (Weindruch and Walford, 1982, 1988; Masoro, 1988; Yu, Masoro, and McMahan, 1985). A healthy feature of research on dietary restriction in rodents is that a great deal of physiological information about the "restricted" rodent has accumulated (Barrows and Kokkonen, 1978; Bertrand, 1983; Yu, 1985; Masoro, 1988; Weindruch and Walford, 1988). The restricted rodent is in no sense a "sick" animal. With respect to many physiological performance measures, it is equal or superior to the ad libitum fed animal. Food restriction has been associated with reduced or delayed incidence of tumors as well as reduced levels of atherosclerotic and autoimmune lesions. Significantly, the metabolic rate per unit mass of restricted rodents does not appear to be reduced, contrary to the rate-of-living theory. An interesting mechanistic feature of the physiology of the restricted rodent is that it appears to retard age-related declines in protein synthesis (Birchenall-Sparks et al., 1985; Richardson et al., 1987). Recently, a flood of papers on the physiology of dietary restriction has appeared, papers that continue to indicate the physiological robustness of the restricted rodent (Duffy et al., 1989; Lipman, Turturro, and Hart, 1989; Leakey et al., 1989a,b; Pegram, Allaben, and Chou, 1989; Feuers et al., 1989; Kolta et al., 1989; Nakamura et al., 1989; Laganiere and Yu, 1989a,b).

The commonly whispered criticism of all this research is that the ad libitum feeding of laboratory mammals is pathological, as discussed by Masoro (1988). Such individuals are said to die sooner of an excess of calories, much as Western man is thought to. The restricted feeding regime then is offered as the "natural" feeding pattern, to which the organism is adapted. This is proposed to be the cause of its increased life span.

The problem with this criticism is that it is very difficult to answer experimentally. How could laboratory workers that employ mostly inbred or hybrid mammals ascertain what the "natural" feeding pattern for their organism would be? Unfortunately, it is very difficult to make any kind of assertion about "normal" conditions for an inbred stock or hybrid derivatives of it. Such organisms could not have maintained all their adaptations to life in the wild, nor can they be fully adapted to laboratory conditions. (See Chapters 3 and 4 for more on this problem.) For the time being, the demonstrably predictable phenomenon of life-span extension by food restriction will be taken as genuine. The problem then becomes how to explain it.

## Evolution of Nutritional Effects on Life Span

All organisms are exposed to variation in the environment that affects their capacity to develop towards reproductive maturity. Most organisms have therefore evolved ontogenetic mechanisms that foster eventual reproductive success in spite of temporary deprivations or that exploit temporary abundance so as to increase early reproductive output when possible. Many invertebrates exhibit facultative diapause contingent upon environmental extremes. A similar phenomenon is the capacity of arthropod ectoparasites, such as ticks, to wait for periods of up to a year or more between hosts. It is self-evident that natural selection should often favor an ontogenetic "stretching" capacity that lengthens the prereproductive period under nutritional conditions in which reproductive maturity cannot be achieved, or would entail an overwhelming reduction in reproductive success. This type of "stretching" in fact occurs with juvenile dietary restriction in rodents (Asdell and Crowell, 1935). All such adaptations reflect the accomplishments of natural selection when it is at its full force, and while they may affect the total duration of life, from start to end, they have no direct relevance to aging. The primary interest of studies involving juvenile dietary restriction is their significance for studies of mammalian development, not mammalian aging.

A different question is the extent to which natural selection has favored life-span "stretching" after the onset of reproduction, the phenomenon observed by Weindruch and Walford (1982) and Yu, Masoro, and McMahan (1985). In the case of temperature effects on longevity and vitality in *Drosophila*, near optimal temperatures for laboratory cultures, it seems as if there is relative life-span stretching at lower temperatures, as discussed in the preceding section. In rodents, dietary restriction is known to result in collapse of early reproduction (Visscher, King, and Lee, 1952; Holehan and Merry, 1985), but it should be borne in mind that the evolutionary context is different for adults, in that there is the evolutionary option of a "suicidal" episode of reproduction in cases where continued survival is unlikely. Thus it might be predicted that life-span stretching under conditions of nutritional deprivation should be more common among the prereproductive age classes than among adults.

The idea of life-span stretching evolving to overcome a period of nutritional deprivation in which reproduction is unlikely has surfaced in the gerontological literature (Harrison and Archer, 1988; Holliday, 1989). Harrison and Archer (1988) propose that it enables females in nature to live long enough to reproduce when severe environmental conditions are encountered. Holliday's (1989) idea is similar. He also points out that the restricted animals do not have higher Darwinian fitness relative to the ad libitum animals, because the latter are far more fertile. Thus Holliday is explicit on the point that the restricted mammals are probably "making the best of a bad lot." Holliday also points out the relevance of this type of nongenetic allocative response to theories that invoke an evolutionary tradeoff between early reproduction and later survival.

These ideas have been criticized on the grounds that later reproduction is unlikely to be selected for in nature (Phelan and Austad, 1989). It is argued instead that dietary restriction in mammals increases life span by direct physiological enhancement of survival because of reduced reproductive effort. This hypothesis seems tenable, also. However, it should be noted that this line of reasoning likewise requires an evolutionary antagonism between survival and reproduction. Thus these different lines of explanation really have a great deal in common, in terms of their underlying assumptions.

## Integrated Organismal Aging Theories

There is no simple physiological mechanism that is known to be responsible for all aspects of aging in all vertebrates, to say nothing of all other metazoa. Indeed, a great diversity of deteriorating processes appear to comprise aging. Nonetheless, many of these processes seem to deteriorate in parallel, as if coordinated in some fashion. This is of course readily explicable in the evolutionary theory of aging, in which the mechanism of coordination is the declining force of selection affecting all particular contributors to survival or reproduction. (This will be discussed further in Chapter 8.)

Within gerontology, however, two alternative types of theory have been proposed that attempt to account for such "unity in diversity" in terms of immanent physiological mechanisms. (1) Aging is the result of a single fundamental cellular or molecular process of deterioration with consequences that are expressed in diverse ways in the wide array of tissues and structures making up complex metazoa like vertebrates and insects or metaphyta like angiosperms and gymnosperms. This type of theory will be discussed in Chapter 7. (2) Alternatively, aging is the result of mechanisms acting at the highest levels of organismal integration, with consequences affecting a wide range of lower-level physiological processes. Theories of this type are discussed in this section.

### *Global Feedforward Failure*

A popular type of theory of aging is that it arises from a failure of organismal integration. Rosen (1978) has provided a rather abstract type of "integrated organismal aging" theory. He transforms the organism into a multidimensional system with a mapping that represents the physiological dynamics occurring from time $t$ to a future time $t + h$. The particular focus of Rosen's (1978) study is that "it is possible for a complex system to exhibit global modes of failure which are not associated with local subsystem failures." This idea leads Rosen to "a comprehensive theory of aging, resting on global and universal principles," without the slightest element of biological detail, as he notes in his concluding paragraph, which relates his model to the work of Spengler and Toynbee on the decline of civilizations. The central line of argument in Rosen's analysis is as follows. (1) Organisms depend on "feedforward" processes that ensure that the later steps of multistep biochemical processes, such as biosynthetic pathways, are primed to function by activators from earlier steps in the process. Presumably such multistep processes could involve sequences such as hunting–feeding–digestion, growth–differentiation–sexual maturation, and so on. (2) Rosen then mentions that it can be shown that "*any* predictive model tends to become increasingly erroneous with time," giving rise to progressive breakdown of feedforward control of organismal physiology, since the feedforward control systems built into the organism implicitly presume a predictive model of some kind. (3) Rosen emphasizes that the loss of feedforward control is *not* a result of a complete failure to function. Rather, it is a result of the necessary imperfections of any feedforward control system for real systems that have too many degrees of freedom.

An empirically testable assumption of Rosen's analysis is the hypothesis that organisms do in fact have important feedforward control systems. If they do not, then there is no reason to accept Rosen's analysis. The other empirical problem with Rosen's theory is that it leaves the continuation of life itself somewhat anomalous. All cells alive today are descendants of cells alive at least one billion years ago. If the relevant feedforward processes are at the cellular level, then it is difficult to see how these cell lineages have been preserved. Rosen allows that feedforward loops can be "recalibrated," and considers the possibility that mitosis may play such a role of recalibration. But if mitosis can recalibrate feedforward, why can not other processes at the supracellular level do so in metazoa, preserving life indefinitely? If they can not, how can some sea anemones perpetuate themselves without aging? If they can, then Rosen needs a theory explaining why some metazoa reset feedforward loops, while others do not. Rosen's theory does not account for the comparative biology of aging, nor does it seem to have any obvious points of connection with other empirical approaches to aging.

## Hormonal Theories of Aging

The fact that hormones control diverse aspects of whole organism functioning, as well as regulating sexual maturation and behavior, naturally led to an early espousal of the theory that hormones were the key to aging (e.g., Brown-Sequard, 1889). This theory has continued up to the present day, with active vertebrate experimental research pursued by Korenchevsky, Finch, and many others (vide Comfort, 1979, pp. 221–37; Finch, 1987). While it has proved difficult to increase life span materially by means of hormone treatments, there is considerable evidence that the effects of food restriction on life span are at least partly mediated by endocrine mechanisms (Masoro, 1988). Evidently, a major problem with endocrinological research in gerontology is the sensitivity of the endocrine system to environmental factors, such as nutrition. Since aging itself is also sensitive to some of these factors, this problem must be regarded as a technical one, rather than evidence against the involvement of hormones in controlling aging.

There are two actuarial components of senescence, declining survival probabilities and declining fertility, and while there are hormonal aspects to both of these, the involvement of hormones in fertility is obvious. Unfortunately, simple administration of gonadal hormones cannot be used to restore vertebrate fertility directly (Wise, 1983), no doubt reflecting exhaustion of the oocytes.

Work on the effect of hormones on survival seems to be more promising. There are claims of more successful intervention in the hormonal regulation of vertebrate somatic function in rodent experiments involving removal of the pituitary, leading to the hypothesized elimination of a hormone that directly determines the timing of death (Denckla, 1974, 1975), dubbed by some journalists an "aging hormone" or "death hormone." Work on the rat has also implicated hyperadrenocorticism and a breakdown in the feedback control of plasma glucocorticoid concentrations in aging and death (Sapolsky et al., 1986a,b). It is not clear how well this work will generalize to other mammals, to say nothing of other animal phyla.

Three general points should be borne in mind when considering endocrine theories of aging. First, hormones do not act in isolation, or even in tandem. Rather, they form parts of elaborate feedback networks that, in vertebrates for example, extend from the hypothalamus to the gonads. Their experimental study calls for considerable sophistication and reluctance to generalize, particularly when working with mammals. Endocrine mechanisms of aging are certainly among the most difficult of all organismal mechanisms of aging to approach experimentally.

Second, the theory that there are death hormones that neatly and efficiently kill off organisms, once it is their "time to die" for the sake of species survival (Denckla, 1975), cannot be taken seriously. If such death takes place when we find aging normally occurring in the laboratory, then these organisms would have been long dead in the wild, so that there is no target for group selection (Williams, 1957). Predators, disease, etc. normally kill off organisms long before endogenous aging has much effect. The great exception to this is semelparous organisms, from Pacific salmon to univoltine moths to soybean. [Of course, the rodents that provide the empirical foundation for this theory (vide Denckla, 1974, 1975) are not semelparous in the same sense as Pacific salmon or marsupial mice.] But aging in such organisms is readily explicable in terms of antagonistic pleiotropy, a demonstrably important factor in the evolution of aging (Chapter 4). The hypothesis of group selection for death hormones is neither cogent nor necessary.

Third, hormones are likely components of physiological mechanisms that give rise to antagonistic pleiotropy between survival and reproduction. Hormones control the onset and intensity of reproductive functioning, and thereby no doubt also have major secondary effects on mortality levels through the direct physiological costs of reproduction, the shunting of resources from somatic maintenance to reproduction, or both. Genetic loci affecting hormone production or function would be obvious loci to examine for alleles exhibiting antagonistic pleiotropy. This suggests, in turn, that rather than examining solely the effects of reproductive hormones on reproductive aging, the impact of reproductive hormones on survival should also be studied. Similar studies should be done on other hormones. However, there is no reason to expect this line of research to be any easier than present gerontological work on hormones; so this suggestion is hardly an answer to the material problems of sorting out the endocrinology of aging.

## A Hierarchy of Clocks

Neither general systems theories nor endocrinological theories have yet solved the problem of the apparent temporal synchronization of the diverse, seemingly independent, phenomena of aging. The most powerful attack on this problem from the physiological standpoint is that mounted by Comfort (1979, pp. 200–203) in his "Concept of Hierarchy of Clocks." Rather than propose that there is a single all-important subsystem responsible for aging, or a master regulator that tightly controls all subsidiary processes of aging, Comfort allows three elements in his hierarchy: (1) a master clock, (2) regulated peripheral clocks, and (3) unregulated peripheral clocks. All clocks can function as fuses, capable of setting a "charge" that is actually responsible for eventual physiological breakdown and death. What is of greatest interest here is his view of the coordination of the multiple processes of aging.

Some of these are autonomous, like the accumulation of mutational events. Others, such as clonal and immunological senescence, are probably subject to timing by an overall life-span-determining clock. In turn, this clock itself directly detonates the charge, and also activates dependent clocks with varying time intervals; we witness the activation of these clocks in the process of ageing, and they contribute to its features, but the terminal event is probably initiated by the master clock. Or possibly the master clock, rather than itself detonating the charge, arms the detonating circuit, but the charge is not exploded until one or more of the dependent clocks runs out its time interval and is also armed. The apparently "gradual" appearance of senile dyshomeostasis, expressed in the notion that "ageing begins at birth," may well be an illusion generated by the successive activation of these dependent processes, while actual deterioration and death are relatively late processes, reflecting the arming of a neuroendocrine destruct mechanism, which is the most likely candidate for the life-span-setting master. Reprinted by permission of the publisher from *The Biology of Senescence*, A. Comfort, p. 201. Copyright 1979 by Elsevier Science Publishing Co., Inc.

The most direct empirical consequence of this model is that, while it allows the possibility of substantial prolongation of life by means of a slowing of the master clock, "rather as a conventional clock can be regulated fast or slow" (p. 202), one of the unregulated clocks would then establish a new leading process of aging that would "detonate the charge." This model runs counter to "the predictions, based on unitary models of ageing, that once the nature of 'the' ageing process is identified, and that process modified, vast life spans can be predicated on the mortality rates existing at the time of life when mortality is lowest" (p. 202). This makes Comfort's model quite distinct from the classic gerontological fantasy of virtual immortality, and its modern recastings.

On the other hand, Comfort's model is largely, albeit not wholly, devoid of empirical content. All it requires is (1) a major mechanism of aging that plays a leading role in determining age at death, and (2) multiple mechanisms of aging independent of this major one that prevent the achievement of potential immortality upon control of any other mechanism of aging. Requirement (2) would be conceded by almost all gerontologists. Requirement (1) is somewhat ambiguous, in that it is not clear how a "master clock" is to be distinguished from any mechanism of aging that happens to act somewhat before others in most organisms of a species. Since, as Comfort (1979, p. 201) admits, "various alterations of this model can accommodate most credible hypotheses of ageing," the model primarily seems to be a post hoc restatement of gerontological knowledge in the face of the failure of unitary physiological theories of senescence.

## Conclusion

An important point to make about organismal theories of aging is that in some cases they provide the apparent mechanistic basis for the evolution of aging. Lepidopterans lacking adult mouth parts eventually die because they cannot feed. Semelparous *Antechinus* males die because of hormonally triggered efforts to mate.

Some organismal theories, therefore, are patently valid, as well as being compatible with evolutionary theories of aging.

Other organismal theories of aging may have some validity, after considerable redefinition. The rate-of-living theory can be seen as analogous to antagonistic pleiotropy. Within the context of the latter type of theory, it retains some intuitive value. Similarly, nutritional theories concerning caloric allocation between present and future reproduction, and thus survival, are evidently natural mechanistic complements to antagonistic pleiotropy, once the evolutionary context is taken into account.

Then there are those theories that account for little or are logically incompatible with the evolutionary theory of aging. "Death-hormone" theories and global feed-forward theories are disposable parts of the corpus of gerontological theories.

Overall, a remarkable amount of progress has been made in gerontological research on organismal hypotheses for the physiology of senescence. Much of this research, however, seems to have been given little attention in the biomedical research community. Perhaps a major reason for this neglect is that this type of research does not fit in as well with the prevailing cellular and molecular fashions of biomedical research. By contrast, organismal research in gerontology is readily assimilable within the evolutionary biology of aging. Indeed, it provides a great deal of useful physiological detail with which to illuminate somewhat dry hypotheses like antagonistic pleiotropy.

# 7

# An Evolutionary Perspective on Cellular and Molecular Theories of Aging

In this chapter cellular and molecular theories of aging will be evaluated in terms of evolutionary research on aging. Again, this will not constitute a review of such theories simply on their own merits, as their proponents would have them judged. Rather, the intent is to evaluate theoretical proposals and salient experimental results within the framework developed in Chapters 1–5. Most important, this framework is incompatible with the idea that there can be any such thing as an absolute physiological cause of aging.

An additional point that should be made is that a huge amount of empirical material in cellular and molecular gerontology has little theoretical significance, at least at present. Many results that describe some biochemical difference between tissues from old and young organisms, or longstanding and initial cell cultures, have little apparent value for testing alternative theories. They may some day, when that particular observation bears upon an important corollary of a theory, but often that day seems far away. The present review of this field, then, concentrates entirely on findings that seem to have some immediate bearing on a mechanistic theory of aging. Furthermore, because of the vastness of this part of biological gerontology, much will necessarily be omitted or only alluded to in passing. This may give rise to ill-advised omissions, but the purpose of this book is to erect a framework for research, so these omissions should be remediable later.

Since 1960, gerontology has largely become reductionist in the sense of studying cells and molecules, rather than whole organisms or populations of organisms. Several factors may have been responsible for this. Biology as a whole has become more reductionist, with molecular biology and biochemistry emerging as preeminent disciplines. Experiments in which cohorts of organisms are kept for sufficient time to allow the observation and/or manipulation of aging are inherently time consuming, relative to experiments on almost any other feature of life. Thus there has always been practical pressure to avoid organismal research on aging. Finally, the early 1960s saw publication of evidence that aging might be a process affecting autonomous cells, with organismal aging a secondary byproduct of cellular aging, at least in vertebrates. Today, a large part of gerontological research involves in vitro cell cultures: the limits to their proliferation and survival, their metabolic changes during proliferation, and their molecular biology. In addition, biochemical assays of in vivo cell constituents are common, along with some trail-blazing work on the molecular genetics of aging. This spectrum of work would not have developed without the proposal of an interesting collection of theories of aging that are rooted in cell biology and biochemistry. But these theories in turn would not have been proposed without the acceptance of evidence that cells senesce autonomously of organismal aging. So this is where the chapter will begin.

## The Hayflick Limit

### *Carrel's Myth*

Before 1960 it was generally thought that aging was a property of whole organisms which could only be explained in terms of organismal physiology. The reason for this was the claim by Alexis Carrel that chick cell cultures had been kept alive for many years (Witkowski, 1985). Pearl's (1922) contemporaneous discussion of this claim should indicate its impact:

> By the method of transfer to fresh nutrient media, Carrel has been able to keep cultures of tissue from the heart of the chick embryo alive for a long period of years. . . . It should be understood that this long continued culture has gone on at body temperature in an incubator, and not by keeping the culture at a low temperature and merely slowing down the vital processes. This is indeed a remarkable result. It completes the demonstration of the potential immortality of somatic cells, when removed from the body to conditions which permit of their continued existence. Somatic cells have lived and are living outside the body for a far longer time than the normal duration of life of the species from which they came. (Pearl, 1922, pp. 62–63)

Carrel's results were not unique: Other cell lines had been kept growing indefinitely, those that appeared to have undergone transformation to a tumorous condition (Hayflick, 1977). This work dated back to the turn of the century, when tumor cell lines were kept alive by repeated transplantation (Pearl, 1922, pp. 64–67). The cytological abnormality of such transformed cells was not of particular concern to biologists then. Instead, it was supposed that cultures of transformed cells had simply escaped organismal controls. Pearl (1922, p. 67) concluded "that all the essential tissues of the metazoan body are immortal. . . . It is the differentiation and specialization of function of the mutually dependent aggregate of cells and tissues which constitute the metazoan body which brings about death; and not any inherent or inevitable mortal process in the individual cells themselves."

Since these early decades of the century, many cancerous or "transformed" in vitro cell lines have been kept replicating indefinitely, particularly mouse cell lines (Hayflick, 1977). But no one has succeeded in keeping mammalian or avian cultures of normal diploid cells growing indefinitely since Carrel (Phillips and Cristofalo,

1983). Thus Hayflick (e.g., 1977) has proposed that Carrel's cultures were not what Carrel claimed they were:

> An alternative explanation is that the method of preparation of chick embryo extract, used as a source of nutrients for his cultures and prepared daily under conditions easily permitting cell survival, contributed new, viable embryonic cells to the chicken heart strain at each feeding. Although it cannot be proven, we believe that the low-speed centrifugation used in Carrel's laboratory allowed for the presence of viable chick cells in the supernatant fluid of the chick embryo extract used to feed his alleged "immortal" chick heart cells.

In any case, Carrel's myth is dead, and organismal theories of aging have not been fashionable since the early 1960s.

## Hayflick's Limit

The man most responsible for the demolition of Carrel's myth, and thus the development of "cytogerontology" (Kirkwood and Cremer, 1982), is Leonard Hayflick.

To explain Hayflick's findings properly, some background information about in vitro, vertebrate, cell culture must be given. [This description is drawn from Hayflick and Moorhead (1961) and Hayflick (1965, 1977).] Once cells have been extracted from their original tissue matrix, they are normally placed in glass or plastic culture vessels containing a nutritive medium, usually cell-free plasma, and incubated at 37 °C. The cells attach to the vessel surface and soon begin to divide. After a matter of days, the cells will have completely covered the vessel surface, at which point the rate of cell division falls, a situation referred to as "confluency." This initial culturing period is called *Phase I* by Hayflick. The practice at this point has been to discard half the cultured cells and transfer the remainder to a new culture vessel. These cells are then again allowed to divide until confluency is reached once more. This process of 1:2 subcultivation gives rise to regular cell number doubling, each doubling called a *passage,* with the total number of doublings a culture has undergone since in vitro cultivation called the *passage number.* So long as doubling times are short, Hayflick calls the culture a *Phase II* culture. (In this terminology, Carrel claimed to have maintained cultures in Phase II indefinitely.) Such Phase II cultures are evidently healthy, in view of their proliferative capacity.

Hayflick's discovery was that, with in vitro human diploid cell strains, Phase II is succeeded by a *Phase III* in which cell division first slows and finally ceases (Hayflick and Moorhead, 1961; Hayflick, 1965). This is shown in Figure 7.1. In normal human cell cultures, the transition to Phase III beings at 50 ± 10 passages. Other terrestrial vertebrate species have since been cultured to check for the occurrence of Phase III in normal cell strains, and all have been found to undergo it, each with characteristic passage numbers at which the transition occurs. Some of these transition values are given in Table 7.1.

The obvious question is whether or not there was some nutrient deficiency in the cell culture media Hayflick used. In a sense, this is not a question that can be firmly answered in the negative, only the positive. For the time being, no laboratory has

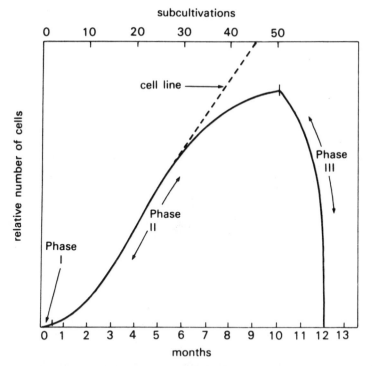

FIGURE 7.1. Schematic representation of the three phases of vertebrate cell culture. The vertical axis represents relative number of cells under repeated halving, so that it amounts to a measure of replicative potential. In Phase I, the culture is just establishing itself. In Phase II, the culture is growing vigorously. The dashed line indicates the replicative trajectory of a transformed cell line. In Phase III, the culture ceases to grow, although its cells need not immediately die. (After Hayflick, 1966, via Lamb, 1977, p. 128.) © 1966 John Wiley & Sons, Inc.

discovered a medium for in vitro cell culture that allows indefinite proliferation of diploid cells having normal histological features (Phillips and Cristofalo, 1983, 1987). Hayflick's limit stands as one of the very few important findings of gerontology that have no exceptions. (However, the interpretation and explanation of the

TABLE 7.1. Correspondence between species maximal life span and the passage number until Phase III of in vitro cell cultures, starting from normal embryonic fibroblasts

| *Species* | *Passage number* | *Maximal life span (yrs)* |
|---|---|---|
| Galapagos tortoise | 90–125 | 175+ |
| Man | 40–60 | 110 |
| Mink | 30–34 | 10 |
| Chicken | 15–35 | 30 |
| Mouse | 14–28 | 3.5 |

From Hayflick (1977), which in turn compiles from other sources.

Hayflick limit have not been straightforward, as will be discussed in the next section.)

## Factors Affecting the Hayflick Limit

It has long been known that cell transformation enables cell cultures to proliferate indefinitely (e.g., Pearl, 1922). (Transformed cell lines are defined by histological aberrations, particularly heteroploidy, but the criteria are somewhat elastic.) However, not all transformed cell lines are abnormal on first inspection, resulting in claims of immortal "normal" cell cultures that prove to be abnormal on closer examination (Hayflick, 1977). Infection of normal cell cultures with the oncogenic SV40 virus readily establishes transformed cell lines (Phillips and Cristofalo, 1983), and such cell lines are of obvious interest in oncology. An interesting line of in vitro cell research is that using cell lines created by fusion of normal cells with transformed cells. It was originally thought that indefinite proliferation was dominant over finite replicative capacity, but more recent work suggests that finite replication is dominant (Stanulis-Praeger, 1987). Evidently this research is related to the recent efflorescence of research on oncogenes (which will be discussed later in this chapter) in that some of the oncogenes, at least when mutated, can play a considerable role in controlling cell proliferation. In any case, transformation leading to indefinite cell proliferation is hardly a recipe for overcoming aging. Rather, transformation constitutes an alternative, pathological, developmental pathway.

There are also human pathological conditions that give rise to reductions in the capacity for cell proliferation. For example, cells from individuals suffering from Werner's syndrome exhibit much less proliferative capacity upon in vitro cell culture (Salk, 1982). These results are of particular interest, because Werner's syndrome is progeroid, with sufferers having the appearance of premature aging. (See Chapter 2 for a discussion of progeria.) On the other hand, not all progeroid syndromes result in diminished proliferative capacity (Wertz et al., 1981).

Even more significant is the relationship between donor age and culture proliferation. Hayflick (1965) found 14–29 passages before culture failure when fibroblast cells were sampled from adult human lung, as opposed to the 35–63 passages obtainable from fetal human lung fibroblasts. Martin, Sprague, and Epstein (1970) made an extensive study of the replicative potential of human skin fibroblast cultures taken from donors of various ages. As shown in Figure 7.2, the relationship is well defined: Culture proliferative capacity is a monotonically decreasing function of donor age. Thus in vivo cellular life "uses up" in vitro cellular life, suggesting some correspondence between in vivo and in vitro processes of cellular development.

Many methods of culturing cells in vitro have been tried, but only two substances have been found to prolong in vitro fibroblast replication significantly: hydrocortisone and dexamethasone, a synthetic glucocorticoid (Phillips and Cristofalo, 1983). The basic process of in vitro proliferative failure remains; the period of proliferation is only extended. An interesting side issue is the nature of standard culture media. If bovine serum is not used, the basal medium requires supplementation with a range of hormonal factors, such as epidermal growth factor (EGF) and

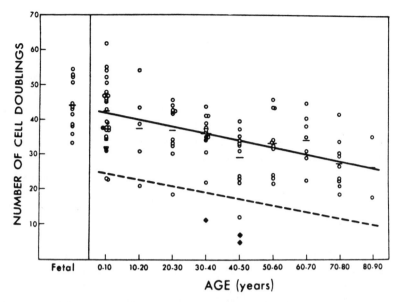

FIGURE 7.2. Number of in vitro cell culture doublings before Phase III for human skin fibroblasts from donors of various ages. The circles give the mean for culture samples from each age class, while the line gives a linear regression through the data. Reprinted with permission from G.M. Martin, C.A. Sprague, and C.J. Epstein. Replication lifespan of cultivated human cells: Effect of donor's age, tissue, and genotype. *Laboratory Investigation* 23: 86–92, 1970. © by the United States and Canadian Academy of Pathology.

insulin (Phillips and Cristofalo, 1983), with EGF in particular prolonging cell proliferation considerably in some in vitro systems (Stanulis-Praeger, 1987). In vitro cell cultures do not appear to be true "cells in isolation." Their proliferation is dependent upon hormones or hormone analogs in a way that suggests the importance of organismal physiology for in vivo proliferation.

## Theories of Cell Proliferation

Few now doubt the empirical validity of the Hayflick limit, at least among home-othermic vertebrates. The problem is that the biological significance of this limit is open to alternative interpretations. These alternative views of the Hayflick limit may be sorted into three main groups: (1) artifact, (2) spurious differentiation, and (3) genuine aging. Each of these alternatives will be considered in turn.

### Cell Culture Artifact

The most straightforward theory is that the Hayflick limit is simply an artifact of in vitro culture, with no relevance to in vivo cell physiology, in general, and of no value in the study of aging, in particular. The simplest version of this theory is that there is no proliferative failure among in vivo cells, and such failure in vitro is a result of deficient culture conditions. The most convincing way to buttress this theory would be to discover culture methods that enable indefinite in vitro cell proliferation without cancerous transformation. There is the possibility of an as yet unknown "cell immortality" hormone, which prevents in vivo cessation of proliferation. The problem with this notion is that in vitro cell proliferative capacities seem so great that it is doubtful that there would ever be a shortage in vivo of necessary stem-cell lineages, if in vitro proliferative limits indeed apply in vivo. Therefore, there would be no natural selection on the whole organism for such "cell immortality" hormones in somatic cell tissue. In any case, as already discussed in the previous section, no one has found a plausible in vitro culture deficiency to remedy, and thereby exceed Hayflick's limit, excepting cell transformation.

Switching to the other side of the argument, Hayflick (e.g., 1965, 1977) has argued that transplantation experiments suggest that in vitro proliferative cessation corresponds to in vivo proliferative dynamics. It has long been known that tumors are capable of indefinite survival if transplanted from host to host. Similarly, in vitro cultures of tumorous cells are apparently capable of indefinite proliferation. The critical question is whether or not repeated transplantation of normal diploid tissues can keep them alive indefinitely. Three lines of evidence suggest that normal cells cannot be so maintained. First, it has turned out that no such repeated transplantation experiments have kept normal tissues alive indefinitely; all have ultimately died (e.g., Krohn, 1962; vide Hayflick, 1977). [Such results by themselves are open to the objection that the stresses of surgery in repeated transplantation are responsible for the eventual loss of the transplanted tissue (Lamb, 1977, pp. 106–110).] Second, the physiology of the transplanted tissue appears to reflect the "age" of the tissue rather than that of the host (Krohn, 1962, 1966), suggesting an autonomous aging process. Third, there is some evidence that suggests the existence of a decline in the proliferative capacity of serially transplanted tissue, analogous to the in vitro decline (Daniel, 1977). In total, these findings suggest that serial transplantation runs into proliferative cell limits.

Perhaps the best single piece of evidence for a correspondence between in vitro and in vivo cell proliferation is the relationship between donor age and in vitro proliferative capacity. As already shown in Figure 7.2, from Martin, Sprague, and Epstein (1970), cells aged in vivo resemble in vitro cells that have undergone more passages. [This result has been extensively replicated, in terms of numbers of cell cultures, types of tissue, and species sampled (Stanulis-Praeger, 1987).] The simplest explanation for this finding is that the in vivo cells have undergone rounds of cell division just like the in vitro cells, with parallel diminution of proliferative capacity.

Any scientific result is open to doubt, and interpretations of those results are still more justifiably subject to dissent. But there is no critical evidence against the biological importance of the Hayflick limit, even though a number of potentially "fatal" experiments have been performed. Whatever its significance, it seems doubtful that it is a mere artifact of in vitro cultivation. Therefore it seems appropriate to turn to hypotheses that attempt to place limited cell proliferation within the context of in vivo physiology.

## *Spurious Differentiation*

A biologist can accept the importance of the Hayflick limit for cell biology in vivo, and yet deny that it has any significance for aging. The alternative is that cessation of cell proliferation in vitro is a result of the eventual spurious differentiation of cells that had been functioning as the in vitro analog of in vivo stem cells. After all, a great number of the cells in the vertebrate body are largely postmitotic, neurons being the typically cited instance, so that maintenance of proliferative capacity is hardly an unfailing guide to maintenance of cell function. Most importantly, loss of cell mitotic capacity in vivo is specifically associated with long-term maturational processes, and therefore it is these processes that could be spuriously, and perhaps somewhat chaotically, echoed by in vitro cell cultures.

The original Hayflick and Moorhead (1961) study contained results bearing on this point. They obtained explants from fetal tissue of different organ types, and the cultures from different organs gave rise to in vitro cell cultures having different replicative capacities, from 5–26 passages in the case of heart tissue to 35–55 passages in the case of lung tissue. Along with this range of replicative capacities, Hayflick and Moorhead (1961) also found a great deal of variation in the ease of initiating in vitro cultures from fetal organs of different types. While all these cell cultures apparently contained fibroblastlike cells, many other cell types have since been cultured in vitro (Stanulis-Praeger, 1987). These have a number of differences from fibroblast cultures, including different proliferative capacities, although none of these cells, when normal, transgresses the Hayflick limit. Again, this conforms to the expectations of a proponent of the view that proliferative limits reflect some type of spurious differentiation.

There are a great many studies of the metabolic changes undergone by cells kept in vitro, as reviewed by Stanulis-Praeger (1987) and Phillips and Cristofalo (1987). Measures of overall metabolic rate do not appear to decrease during Phase II, although there is evidence of a greater degree of variability in Phase III cultures. On the other hand, there is evidence of a decrease in responsiveness of later Phase II cells to hormones and hormonelike factors. The content of several classes of molecules increases in later Phase II cells: glycogen, lipid, total protein, and RNA. On the other hand, DNA content and DNA synthesis decrease. Other cell components that decrease include mucopolysaccharides, collagen, and ribosomal RNA. Quite unlike whole organism physiology, pervasive deterioration is not apparent in these cell physiology changes.

Studies of cell morphology have also failed to yield obvious aging patterns (Martin et al., 1974; Bell et al., 1978; Phillips and Cristofalo, 1983). Cell size increases and becomes more variable. Cells become less regular in shape. There are a number of changes in organelle structure that are difficult to interpret: Like the cell itself, the nuclei become less regular in shape; more mitochondria lack transverse cristae; the endoplasmic reticulum has fewer ribosomes associated with it; lysosomes increase in number; and the Golgi apparatus becomes more prominent.

One of the most penetrating studies of cell morphology in proliferating cultures is that of Mets and Verdank (1981a,b) using stromal cells from human bone marrow. In vitro cultures of these cells appear to be composed of two distinguishable morphological types, which are proliferating and nonproliferating. With increasing passage level, the proportion of nonproliferating cells increased. As one would expect, nonproliferating cells appear to be derived from proliferating cells. The number of proliferating cells in explants decreases with donor age, and some electron-microscopic studies of bone marrow indicate the presence of both proliferating and nonproliferating cells in vivo, suggesting that the in vitro dynamics correspond to those of in vivo cells. The morphological specificity of the derivation of nonproliferating from proliferating cells conforms well to the hypothesis that cessation of in vitro cell proliferation corresponds to differentiation of mitotic cell types to postmitotic cell types. The lack of such apparent specificity in fibroblast in vitro cultures could, on such a view, be due to some lack of determined ontogenetic trajectory in cells of that type. If true, this theory requires that stem cells that are more differentiated than fibroblasts should exhibit a relatively specific set of postmitotic descendant cells.

A final point that has been made in favor of the differentiation theory of in vitro proliferative termination is that Phase III cells do not appear to be as frankly moribund as Hayflick has described (Bell et al., 1978). Such cells can be kept alive for more than a year in vitro after complete cessation of cell division, and, as already mentioned, many of their biochemical features are indistinguishable from those of Phase II cells. Martin et al. (1974) and Bell et al. (1978) proposed that the differences between cells from these two phases may reflect differentiation, rather than deterioration.

## Autonomous Cellular Aging

The simplest way to relate the Hayflick limit to aging is to suppose that in vivo cells proliferate during Phase II, the body remaining healthy, and then upon achieving Phase III the cells cease division, resulting in the diverse organismal malfunctions that comprise senescence. There are three material problems with this hypothesis. First, most in vitro cell cultures have the capacity to produce vast numbers of cells, far more than any vertebrate body could need, even if it had a rate of cell loss as great as any now known. Second, cells from old human donors (80–90 years of age) still have about 20 Phase II passages of proliferative capacity, yet the donors themselves are obviously senescent (Martin et al., 1970). Third, transplanted vertebrate tissues can be kept alive much longer than their hosts (Krohn, 1962), again suggesting that Phase III is not normally achieved in vivo. Therefore, the idea of explaining aging as a result of a failure of cell proliferation is given little credence (e.g., Kirkwood and Cremer, 1982).

Hayflick's (e.g., 1974) own view is that "functional losses that occur in cells prior to their loss of division capacity produce age changes in animals much before their normal cells have reached their maximum division limit." Thus Hayflick is proposing the existence of an autonomous cellular process of aging that has two independent consequences, organismal aging and an in vitro proliferative limit, consequences that are not causally related to each other. A major problem for this view is the difficulty of characterizing the changes exhibited by Phase II cultures as deterioration. After all, Bell et al. (1978) could plausibly argue that Phase III cells were not moribund, so how could Phase II cells be pathological in their physiology? There is in any case no direct evidence for the existence of Hayflick's hypothesized cellular aging process.

On the other hand, there is indirect evidence bearing on Hayflick's thesis coming from genetic diseases and interspecific comparisons. Some human genetic diseases that have been characterized as exhibiting "accelerated aging," such as Werner's syndrome (Martin, 1978), exhibit reduced proliferative capacity in vitro (Phillips and Cristofalo, 1983), as has been mentioned already. This suggests that some unknown metabolic process is responsible for both the accelerated organismal aging and the reduced proliferative capacity in vitro. There are two empirical anomalies in this evidence, however, that call into question its value as support for Hayflick's theory. First, not all "progeroid" syndromes exhibit reduced proliferative capacity in vitro, myotonic dystrophy being an example (Wertz et al., 1981). Second, diabetes is associated with reduced proliferative potential (Goldstein, 1978), yet it is a specific pathology that hardly seems to be a disease affecting a "master control" of aging. Many deleterious mutant alleles could severely disrupt cell function and thereby *both* restrict in vitro proliferation *and* hasten death or sterility, as Werner's syndrome apparently does. The existence of alleles with pleiotropic deleterious effects upon both organismal function and in vitro cell proliferation is not very substantial support for Hayflick's theory. It would be surprising if such genetic syndromes did not exist.

By far the best available evidence in favor of Hayflick's theory is the positive correlation between in vitro cell proliferation limits and maximum species life span. Hayflick (e.g., 1977) has presented the data of Table 7.1 as evidence of this correlation. Stanley, Pye, and MacGregor (1975) claimed to find cell culture results substantially at variance with this pattern, but their work had methodological deficiencies, and they obtained some in vitro results out of keeping with those from other laboratories, making their study suspect (Röhme, 1981). The best study of the comparative correlation between in vitro proliferation and organismal life span is that of Röhme (1981). As shown in Figure 7.3, he obtained an excellent correlation between species maximum life span and fibroblast proliferation limits, with a correlation coefficient of 0.95. These results suggest that the evolution of longevity in vertebrates is bound up with the evolution of cell proliferation capacity, presumably because of processes that affect both in a similar manner. While this does not preclude the involvement of differentiation processes in the Hayflick limit, it does suggest that any such processes may also be physiologically entangled with organismal aging. It seems ironic that the best evidence available for the importance of research on in vitro cell proliferation in gerontology comes from comparative research. This situation accords with the view argued here that evolutionary analysis provides the only secure theoretical foundation for gerontological research.

## Nonproliferative Theories of Cell Aging

Many organisms have few actively dividing cells as adults, insects, nematodes, and rotifers being well-known examples. Among mammals, muscle cells and neurons

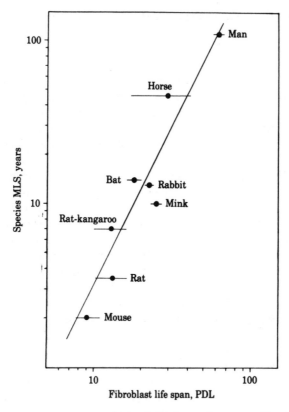

FIGURE 7.3. Correlation between maximum species life span (MLS) and in vitro cell population doubling limits (PDL). The correlation coefficient is 0.95. (From Röhme, 1981.)

do not normally divide. Many other metazoan cell types do not divide to such an extent that proliferative limits are likely to play much role in the aging of their function(s). Therefore, it is appropriate to consider possible mechanisms of cell aging that do not involve proliferation.

When cells do not normally proliferate, they can be viewed as fixed "building blocks" of tissues and organs. Broadly speaking, one may divide postmitotic cell functions into two broad categories: metabolism and differentiation. Metabolism primarily involves the efficient functioning of cytoplasmic components, such as organelles, ribosomes, and so on. Differentiation, on the other hand, is thought to involve controls on gene expression, particularly transcription, possibly reflecting modifications of chromosomal DNA. Thus to some extent there is a simple material division in the cell components involved in the two cellular roles.

## Pathologies of Metabolism

### MITOCHONDRIAL FUNCTION

Mitochondria are obviously organelles that could plausibly play a fundamental and widespread role in aging, because they are the catabolic engines of eukaryotic cells.

Strehler (1977, pp. 243–47) and Miquel et al. (1980) have reviewed the available evidence for and against the importance of mitochondria in aging. Interestingly, mitochondria from proliferating cells in vivo show no reproducible sign of deterioration. In insects, mitochondria from the postmitotic cells of older adults show structural abnormalities, as well as a decrease in their total number. This is associated with a decrease in respiratory activity, which in turn seems to give rise to a decline in flight ability and negative geotaxis. In mammals, the evidence has not been as clear, possibly because of technical problems in mitochondrial isolation. However, some studies suggest that tissues like cardiac muscle exhibit a pattern like that of insect postmitotic cells, with age-associated declines in mitochondrial quality and quantity. Much research on mitochondrial aging has dealt with the biochemistry of their deterioration, which will be discussed later in the chapter. At this point, it is enough to note that strictly postmitotic cells exhibit declining mitochondrial, and thus respiratory, function with age.

## LIPOFUSCIN

One of the most widely observed features of aging in postmitotic cells is the accumulation of debris referred to as "lipofuscin" (Brandes, 1966; Lippman, 1983). In fact, this term is probably misleading, in that the substance is quite heterogeneous in molecular content. This accumulation of lipofuscin granules has been found in nematodes, molluscs, insects, and vertebrates (Lippman, 1983). Apparently, lipofuscin accumulation is a function of total metabolic activity, rather than chronological age alone (Lippman, 1983). Figure 7.4 shows the age dependence of lipofuscin content in human myocardium. Strehler (1977, pp. 252–264) and Lippman (1983) provide critical reviews of the distribution and importance of lipofuscin in postmitotic metazoan cells. Among the rather slight lines of evidence for the importance of lipofuscin in aging is a human hereditary disease, Batten's syndrome, which entails a rapid accumulation of lipofuscin in the central nervous system, followed by blindness and mental deterioration. But even if normal levels of lipofuscin accumulation with age have no deleterious effects, radically higher levels could still be pathological. It is generally reasonable to suppose that the accumulation of ostensibly inert debris in cells should impair their function, but direct physiological evidence for this has been difficult to obtain. Comparison of rodent, canine, and human lipofuscin accumulation patterns indicates an inverse relationship between rate of accumulation and species longevity. This is the best evidence implicating the involvement of some factor relating to lipofuscin accumulation in organismal aging.

## SELF-DIGESTION BY LYSOSOMES

The third aspect of cellular metabolism that has often been discussed in the context of aging is self-digestion. Evidently, if postmitotic cells digest their constituents more rapidly than they are replaced, eventual breakdown would be unavoidable. The critical organelles in proteolysis and most intracellular digestion are the lysosomes. [In fact, it is generally thought that lysosomes give rise to fuscin as a waste breakdown byproduct (Brandes, 1966; Lippman, 1983).] Lysosomes certainly have enzymes that could digest most cell components, and secretory cells that self-destruct in order to release their secretions do so by releasing the contents of

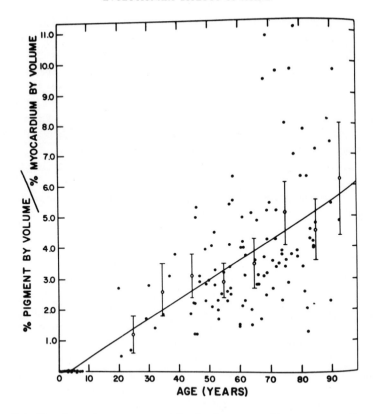

FIGURE 7.4. Correlation between age and lipofuscin content of human myocardium. (From Strehler, 1962, p. 186.)

lysosomes into the cytoplasm (Brandes, 1966). The tempting hypothesis is that cells may age because of a slow degradation brought on by a protracted, presumably accidental, analog of this process. Other than lipofuscin accumulation, there is no material evidence relating cell aging to normal lysosome function. A further problem is that the indefinite survival of germ-cell lineages becomes problematic on this hypothesis, unless it can be shown that germ cells lack lysosomes, or have vastly fewer of them.

## Differentiation and Loss of Maintenance Capacity

One of the most obvious physiological hypotheses that could explain aging is that it is an inevitable consequence of cellular differentiation in metazoa, particularly since almost all metazoa senesce, while almost all unicellular microorganisms do not. (See Chapter 5.) As Comfort (1979, pp. 7–16) has discussed, few ideas have been accepted less critically than the proposal that "aging is the price paid for differentiation." However, while early discussion of this idea was uncritical and somewhat vacuous, more recent treatments have not been as lacking in cogency or empirical foundation.

Bernard Strehler (e.g., Strehler, 1962; Strehler et al., 1971; Strehler, 1977) has been responsible for the most intensive exploration of the relationship between cell differentiation and cellular aging. [This may reflect his conviction that the Hayflick limit in vitro is of little or no importance for senescence (vide Strehler, 1977, pp. 42–55).] Strehler (1977, pp. 295–307) has contributed a thoughtful discussion of the range of possibilities for an association between cell differentiation and aging, a treatment that will be outlined briefly here. Strehler begins with an incontrovertible starting point, that differentiated cells must differ in their synthetic activities, broadly conceived. In particular, differentiated cells must impose restrictions on their synthetic activities. Any theory of aging starting from cell differentiation must presume that such restrictions on synthesis impede the cell's maintenance of itself. The problem then centers on alternative theories of postmitotic cell maintenance and the way(s) in which it fails.

Strehler distinguishes between four such theories. (1) Cell maintenance may involve "a continual monitoring process in which the chemical constitution of a cell is compared with a certain fraction of the genome or of some alternative molecular representation of the genome." In effect, in this theory maintenance involves feedback monitoring of correspondence to an encoded goal, presumably that which corresponds to sustaining the differentiated cell's function(s). Aging could then occur as a result of molecular damage to the coded form of the cell's goal, resulting in mistaken redirection of the cell towards loss of function. (2) Differentiated cells could be subject to general negative feedback mechanisms that function to return disrupted cells to their state before disruption. The necessary imperfection of such self-correction without an encoded goal could result in "slow drift" away from the optimum cell state (cf. Rosen, 1978). (3) It is implausible to assume that every constituent of a differentiated cell has its own repair system. In particular, stable structures that can endure for some time on their own might not be replenished after their initial synthesis during cellular differentiation. Aging of differentiated cells could then be a result of the autonomous deterioration of the macromolecules making up such structures, a possibility discussed later in this chapter. (4) By a similar argument to that of (3), cells may not dispose of deleterious molecules that accumulate sufficiently slowly. Lipofuscin is the example of choice for such mechanisms, and it has already been discussed.

These four hypotheses fall into two groups of two. The latter pair are simple "molecular" hypotheses that are amenable to some degree of empirical investigation, at least from the standpoint of whether or not the hypothesized form of deterioration occurs or not. The former pair of hypotheses involves breakdown in cellular organization at the "control system" level and as such are extremely difficult to probe empirically. Evidently, they turn on the nature of the control systems of differentiated multicellular eukaryotes, a problem of enormous scientific difficulty.

Strehler (Strehler et al., 1971; Strehler, 1977) has also proposed a specific model of cellular differentiation that, if correct, would provide a concrete framework for discussion of the relationship between cellular differentiation and aging. The model presumes that "*different cell types possess restricted codon-decoding properties* and that these capacities are precisely those required to translate a restricted group of messages—namely, those 'needed' by a cell at a particular time in its ontogeny" (Strehler, 1977, p. 309, emphasis in the original). Strehler (1977, pp. 307–324) discusses a variety of lines of evidence that conform to the postulates of his theory, as well as a few that do not. Such theories of differentiation are beyond the scope of the present volume, because they are not primarily theories of cell senescence.

## Somatic Mutation Theories

Clearly articulated somatic mutation theories of aging surfaced in the literature at the end of the 1950s (Szilard, 1959; Failla, 1960). They soon attracted a great deal of attention, ingenious experiments were performed, and many aspects of aging were interpreted in terms of somatic mutation (e.g., Curtis, 1966). These early theories were generalized: Senescence was explained as a result of multifold cellular incapacitation due to the loss of functional genetic information of all kinds. One source of the attractiveness of such a theory in the 1960s was that it had become apparent to all gerontologists that aging involved diverse pathologies, within and between species. Only mechanisms that could disrupt almost any organismal function were plausible sole, or primary, causes of aging. In addition, such nonspecific theories of aging have the disciplinary advantage of being difficult to refute directly.

The critical problem for the evaluation of the somatic mutation theory is the lack of good estimates of the rate of physiologically important damage to the DNA of somatic cells (Fulder, 1975; Hirsch, 1978). It should be borne in mind that this damage need not result in altered proteins. Some of it could affect transcriptionally important DNA so as to prevent transcription or greatly reduce transcription rates. Still less directly, DNA lesions could disrupt DNA between sequences involved in transcription in such a way as to cause structural problems for the chromosome that would then secondarily disrupt gene expression. Since little of the DNA of some multicellular organisms has any apparent function (Doolittle and Sapienza, 1980; Orgel and Crick, 1980), this may be the most important type of DNA damage affecting somatic cells, depending on the importance of such nonfunctional DNA lesions for chromosomal function.

Though they may often reflect only a small portion of all DNA changes in vivo, the rate of change in translated protein products in somatic cells provides some evidence as to somatic mutation rates with possible effects on cell function. One of the best tests of such mutations was performed using human hemoglobin. Since isoleucine is not incorporated in normal human hemoglobin, measurement of isoleucine levels in hemoglobin provides a joint estimate of somatic mutation as well as errors of transcription and translation. As shown in Figure 7.5, no increase in isoleucine levels was statistically detectable (Popp et al., 1976), suggesting a low rate of increase in somatic mutation. Other, less direct, evidence that may reflect changes in amino acid coding by DNA sequences is reviewed by Hirsch (1978). Much of it suggests little important somatic mutation, although there are cases in which inactive enzymes increase in frequency (e.g., Gershon and Gershon, 1970). Such cases could of course reflect transcriptional aberrations, translation errors, or post-translational modification. (See the next two sections.)

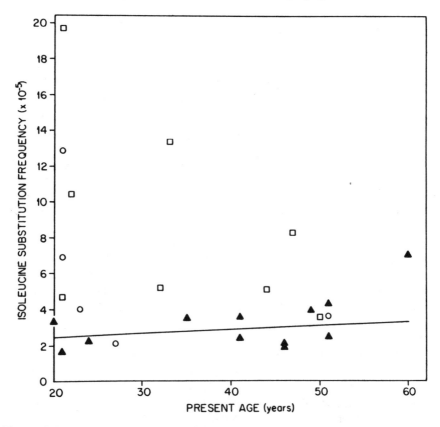

FIGURE 7.5. Isoleucine levels in hemoglobin from inhabitants of the Marshall Islands as a function of age. The isoleucine level is generally low and does not rise much with age. Individuals represented by hollow symbols were exposed to radiation. Individuals represented by solid triangles were not. (From Popp et al., 1976.)

In vitro cell cultures are another source of somatic mutation rate estimates. Albertini and DeMars (1973) estimated in vitro human fibroblast mutation rates using an enzyme inactivation assay, with a result of about $10^{-7}$ mutations per cell per hour. The comparable human germ-line mutation rate is about $10^{-11}$ (Stern, 1973). But in vitro estimates of mutation rates vary widely (Fulder, 1975), for reasons that may in part be technical. On the other hand, it should be mentioned that, from what is now known of the importance of transposable elements in mutagenesis as well as the variation in transposable element distribution between individuals within species (Shapiro, 1983), there is every reason to expect cell strain mutation rates to vary, both in vitro and in vivo. It is clear that in vitro mutation rates are generally higher than those in germ-line cells. Two explanations for this disparity come to mind. One is that, since in vitro culture forces cell division to high rates, it may also give rise to elevated mutation rates because of more frequent DNA replication. The other is that organisms are stringently selected for germ-line DNA replication fidelity, while somatic cells can undergo more frequent DNA replication failures without much impact on organismal fitness. These explanations are not incompatible with each other, but the first at least calls into question the relevance of in vitro somatic mutation rate estimates.

Perhaps the best data bearing on the frequency of somatic cell DNA damage come from studies of cytogenetic aberrations in vivo. A number of independent studies have found increased chromosomal abnormalities with age in mammals (Hirsch, 1978). Chromosomes appear to be lost with age but do not appear to exhibit increasing levels of hyperdiploidy with age. Not only do liver chromosome aberrations appear to increase in frequency with age, they do so more rapidly in strains with shorter life span (Crowley and Curtis, 1963). Similar results have been obtained for kidney tissue (Martin et al., 1985), but not for some other tissue types, such as bone marrow and lymphocytes, which raises doubts about the relevance of particular tissues as indicators of a general process of somatic mutation (Tice, 1978).

A particularly damning finding for somatic mutation theories of aging is that xeroderma pigmentosum, a human DNA repair-deficient disorder, is not associated with a decreased maximum life span, in vivo or in vitro (Hanawalt and Sarasin, 1986). Similarly, DNA repair-deficient mutants in *C. elegans* do not have shorter life spans relative to normal organisms (Johnson and Hartman, 1988). These results indicate that susceptibility to somatic mutation, under normal physiological conditions, plays little role in determining longevity.

Thus the direct evidence bearing on the incidence of somatic mutation, and its potential importance for organismal aging, hardly makes an impressive case for somatic mutation as the primary cause of aging (pace Curtis, 1966). But there are other, less direct, lines of evidence and more subtle somatic mutation theories of aging, all of which merit some consideration here.

## Radiation, Accelerated Aging, and Somatic Mutation

Much of the original inspiration for the somatic mutation theory was the ostensible similarity between the chronic effects of radiation exposure and normal aging. These similarities are twofold. The first is at the level of mortality curves. As shown in Figure 7.6, the mortality pattern of irradiated animals sometimes resembles accelerated aging. Unlike many types of stress, radiation does not simply impose a short-term rise in mortality with little later effect. Rather, the typical mortality curve is shifted to the left, so that the irradiated survivorship pattern is a "pre-echo" of the control survivorship pattern. The second similarity between the effects of radiation and normal aging is at the level of pathology. Generally speaking, it is accepted that the causes of death in irradiated mice resemble those in mice dying "normal senescent" deaths (Lindop and Rotblat, 1961; Lamb, 1977, p. 86; Comfort, 1979, p. 245). Superficially, the effect of low-level radiation seems to be simply accelerated aging.

This interpretation of the effects of irradiation is a critical argument in favor of somatic mutation theories, since irradiation is well known to be mutagenic. For example, Curtis (1963) was able to show that x rays increase the frequency of those liver chromosome aberrations that he found to increase with age in the liver cells of

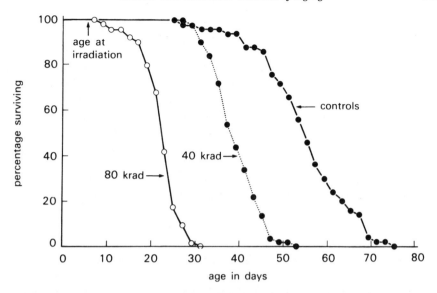

FIGURE 7.6. Survival patterns for irradiated male *D. melanogaster*. The solid dots plotted with solid lines indicate the control pattern. The dotted lines plot the data when there was a 40 krad exposure. The circles with the solid lines give the results when there was an 80 krad exposure. The survival curves with irradiation qualitatively resemble those associated with normal senescence. (From Lamb, M.J. 1977, *Biology of Aging*, Blackie, Glasgow and London, p. 85.)

mice that have *not* been irradiated. Thus, proponents of somatic mutation theories can argue, there are two independent types of parallelism between the premature deaths due to irradiation, demographic and pathological, while x rays have been shown to increase the level of somatic mutation. This evidence, together with the evidence for normal somatic mutation, was perhaps the best case ever built in support of a strictly physiological theory that endeavored to explain aging as a result of a single primary cause (vide Curtis, 1966).

It was not long before these arguments were to be unravelled. The most obvious anomaly was that some populations exhibited *increased* longevity as a result of irradiation (Strehler, 1977, pp. 276–77). At least some of this longevity enhancement appears to be associated with sterilization, since no increase in longevity with irradiation is found in genetically sterile *Drosophila* females, such as those lacking ovaries (Lamb, 1964). Although this problem is easily controlled for by the use of genetically sterile females, it is obvious that somatic mutation cannot in any case be the sole factor controlling life span, since the indubitably deleterious mutagenic effects of irradiation on somatic cells can be overcome by the reduction in the physiological burdens of reproduction resulting from sterilization.

Another damning line of evidence is the lack of increased sensitivity with respect to aging shown by irradiated *C. elegans rad* mutants (Johnson and Hartman, 1988). These mutants were selected on the basis of increased immediate lethality levels under irradiation and had normal aging patterns when unirradiated. This indicates that sensitivity to irradiation is not a simple function of one variable, somatic mutation.

Whether it is supposed that somatic mutations are dominant or recessive in effects, an organism's chromosomal ploidy must have a considerable effect on the accumulation of deleterious effects on cell function (cf. Szilard, 1959; Failla, 1960; Maynard Smith, 1966). *Habrobracon* is a parasitic wasp genus with both diploid and haploid males. While haploid males show much greater sensitivity to irradiation than diploid, there is little difference between unirradiated haploid and diploid male longevities (Clark and Rubin, 1961). This too is dramatic evidence against somatic mutation theories of aging.

At the level of pathology, the assertion that there is a strict parallelism between normal aging and the pathologies of irradiation has also come under attack (Maynard Smith, 1966). However, what differences there are could be confined to aging processes with no impact on *aging*, meaning declining age-specific survival or fertility rates, as such.

Even the relationship between artificial mutagenesis and accelerated aging is subject to experimental problems. The most straightforward of these problems is that some powerful mutagens, such as ethyl methane sulfonate (EMS) and mustard gas, do not produce any detectable life-shortening effect (Maynard Smith, 1966; Lamb, 1977, p. 87). Another difficulty is that of the dose–response relationship between irradiation and chromosome abnormality versus that between irradiation and life-span reduction (Curtis, 1966; Strehler, 1977, pp. 280–82): Levels of irradiation sufficient to produce chromosomal aberrations equal in frequency to those in very old mice do *not* appreciably shorten life span. Finally, as shown in Table 7.2, there is no correlation between maximum species life span and the sensitivity of the species to irradiation.

The interpretation of the effects of irradiation on survival as a *simple* reflection of accelerated somatic mutation giving rise to accelerated aging (e.g., Curtis, 1966) is no longer tenable. This does not preclude the development of more elaborate theories, especially if different combinations of dominant and recessive mutations are allowed, if effects on dividing cells are separated from those on nondividing cells, and if different organs are thought to be subject to different degrees of

TABLE 7.2.    $LD_{50}$ values for different organisms
when subjected to ionizing radiation

| Species | 50% lethal dose (rads) |
|---|---|
| Man | 450 |
| Mouse | 550 |
| Rat | 750 |
| Goldfish | 2,300 |
| *Drosophila* (adult) | 64,000 |
| *Paramecium* | 300,000 |

Note that, while maximal life span tends to decrease from the top of the table to the bottom, the $LD_{50}$ follows the reverse pattern.

From Sinex (1974).

functional disruption (Maynard Smith, 1966). But this involves a substantial departure from the appealing elegance and generality of the original somatic mutation theory. Generalized somatic mutation is no longer given much attention as *the* cause of aging (vide Rothstein, 1983). Instead, those who still regard somatic mutation as an important factor in aging (e.g., Burnet, 1974) have turned to less general hypotheses that relate somatic mutation to specific functional aberrations that are thought to afflict senescent vertebrates. The hope that somatic mutation might directly explain aging in all organisms has been essentially abandoned.

## Autoimmune Malfunction

The immune system of vertebrates undergoes a process of somatic mutation as an integral part of the production of antibodies (Baltimore, 1981; Hood, Weissman, and Wood, 1982; Tonegawa, 1983). Intrachromosomal recombination is used to splice together exons in heterogeneous ways, so as to produce antibody protein of widely varying antigenic specificity. Differential replication of lymphocytes that have produced appropriate antibody then results in the development of an immune response specific to particular types of antigen.

Walford (e.g., 1962, 1966, 1969) has related the process of somatic mutation to the immune system by pointing out that an organism's own cells must not be subject to antibody attack by its own immune system, which in turn requires (1) maintenance of host cells within a range of permitted genotypes and (2) inhibition of autoantibody production. Both of these requirements may be violated as a result of somatic mutation, either inside or outside the immune system.

There is a respectable range of evidence that conforms to the expectations of the autoimmune theory (Walford, 1969; Burnet, 1974; Lamb, 1977, pp. 116–18). The level of autoantibody does tend to increase with age in man. The immune system's lymphocytes are found to accumulate in the tissues of older individuals. Conversely, when acute autoimmune disease is deliberately engendered by transfer of foreign lymphocytes to a new host, there is a "graft-versus-host" interaction that resembles aging in the deterioration of skin and hair, weight loss, renal malfunction, and so on. A further point in favor of the autoimmune theory is that nutritional restriction is known to delay the deterioration of the immune system, and such restriction is the only generally effective way of prolonging mammalian life span (Weindruch and Walford, 1988, pp. 179–97). Finally, strains of mice, such as NZB, which exhibit high levels of autoantibody, also have relatively short life spans in conjunction with pathological symptoms ostensibly of accelerated aging (Walford et al., 1978).

The main problem for the autoimmune theory is that increasing levels of autoantibodies among individuals within populations are not associated with an increase in clinical autoimmune disease (Nagel, 1983). If autoimmune malfunction were the primary cause of aging in vertebrates, one would expect some clear etiological connection between autoantibodies and aging in organisms as extensively studied as man and mouse. The lack of such findings in spite of a search for them suggests that autoimmune pathology cannot be considered the primary cause of normal vertebrate aging. This in no way precludes some contributory role for autoimmune pathology in aging.

## Vertebrate Oncogenes

A characteristic problem of basic physiological theories of aging is that, while the proposed process of deterioration may be shown to occur, it is often not clear whether it plays any major part in the reduction of age-specific survival probabilities and fertilities, which is the crux of aging. Any process that plays a critical role in the development of cancer in vertebrates is not subject to this problem. Cancer evidently militates against continued survival and reproduction in those organisms that have it.

Two lines of research suggest that somatic mutation is the critical factor in the genesis of cancer. The first is that showing the virtual identity of the set of mutagenic chemicals with the set of carcinogenic chemicals (Ames et al., 1973). This, of course, is only circumstantial evidence. The second line of research is that involving oncogenes. These are genes incorporated in retroviruses that are unrelated to the virion genes essential for viral replication and that cause tumorous transformation of somatic cells in vivo and in vitro (Duesberg, 1983). In the early 1980s, it was found that these *onc* genes have closely related "proto-oncogenes" in normal vertebrate genomes (Land, Parada, and Weinberg, 1983a,b), leading to the conclusion that tumors that do not involve retroviruses arise by somatic mutation of these proto-oncogenes. This conclusion has been disputed (Duesberg, 1983, 1985) and cannot be regarded as established with certainty. These findings nonetheless bear careful consideration as evidence in favor of the hypothesis that cancer is usually a result of somatic mutation.

The experiments bearing on this hypothesis primarily involve either (1) transfection of oncogenes, altered proto-oncogenes, or the protein products of such genes into somatic cells in vitro, or (2) molecular analysis of proto-oncogene changes in tumor cells cultured in vitro. Type (1) experiments show that, if somatic mutations are responsible for cancer, then at least two distinct proto-oncogenes must undergo appropriate mutations (Land, Parada, and Weinberg, 1983a,b; Newbold and Overell, 1983; Ruley, 1983). A diversity of proto-oncogenes are available for such cooperative tumorigenesis, allowing multiple pathways for the process. The empirical ambiguities have been made much of by critics of this research (e.g., Duesberg, 1985). Furthermore, oncogenes may be derived from proto-oncogenes in any one of three basic ways: (a) change of amino acid sequence, (b) regulatory mutation resulting in increased transcription rate, and (c) increased proto-oncogene copy number (Land, Parada, and Weinberg, 1983b). The *ras* oncogene, for example, can arise by either of two amino acid substitutions (Yuasa et al., 1983), resulting in a functionally modified protein (Feramisco et al., 1984; McGrath et al., 1984), although it may also be subject to regulatory mutation and amplification of gene copy number (Schwab et al., 1983). Type (2) experiments suggest that *myc* oncogenes, on the other hand, arise from mutations causing quantitatively increased levels of gene transcript, without amino acid substitutions (Hayday et al., 1984; Stewart, Kattengale, and Leder, 1984; Taub et al., 1984). This complexity is not particularly surprising for oncologists, who have long been of the opinion that cancer cannot normally have a single or simple cause.

One of the better lines of evidence in support of the somatic mutation hypothesis of oncogenesis is that pointing to a regulatory role of proto-oncogenes in mitogenesis (Heldim and Westermark, 1984). If proto-oncogenes normally control cell division, then it is reasonable to suppose that they could undergo mutations that lead to unrestricted cell proliferation, and thus cancer.

## Comparative Evidence

Particularly in light of oncogene research, the apparent association between frequency of in vitro transformation and species life span (e.g., Sacher and Hart, 1978) suggests that longer-lived species have lower rates of somatic mutation, assuming that in vitro transformation is analogous to oncogenesis. Human somatic cell cultures, in particular, show great stability of karyotype and proliferative limitation, quite unlike rodent cells (Hayflick, 1977).

The first molecular biological data collected bearing on this point were obtained by Hart and Setlow (1974). They examined the capacity of in vitro fibroblasts to repair uv-damaged DNA, where these fibroblasts were obtained from dermal explants of young individuals of different mammalian species. The extent of DNA repair was closely correlated with maximum species life span. On the other hand, Woodhead, Setlow, and Grist, (1980) and Kato et al. (1980) failed to reproduce these findings using other vertebrate species. But Francis, Lee, and Regan, (1981) did corroborate the findings of Hart and Setlow (1974) over a wide range of mammals. Hall et al. (1984) found that uv-induced DNA repair in primate lymphocytes positively correlates with maximum species life span. Maslansky and Williams (1985) found positive correlations between unscheduled DNA repair and species longevity at low but not high doses of uv radiation. The reasons for this heterogeneity of findings are elusive. In any case, the relevance of unscheduled DNA repair to normal DNA repair in mammals has been questioned (Hanawalt, 1987). At present, it would seem that the comparative data bearing on DNA repair do not point one way or the other.

## Translation Error Catastrophe Theory

Most types of macromolecules in living cells are degraded and replaced, unlike DNA, which seemingly precludes their playing much role in the aging of the cells making up multicellular organisms. RNA molecules, in particular, are almost entirely produced in order to generate protein molecules according to the instructions of the genetic information encoded by the cell's DNA. As such, they would seem poor candidates for key roles in a molecular mechanism of aging. This line of thought, however, implicitly assumes that molecular aging must depend upon *structural* deterioration of inert molecules. This is not the only path available to molecular aging *a priori*, as will now be illustrated.

## Error Catastrophe: Positive Feedback of Translation Errors

In 1963, L.E. Orgel proposed that errors of translation could be subject to positive feedback, leading to an exponential increase in error levels, an "error catastrophe," and resultant cell aging. Orgel argued as follows:

. . . the ability of a cell to produce its complement of functional proteins depends
not only on the correct specification of the various polypeptide sequences, but also
on the competence of the protein-synthetic apparatus. A cell inherits, in addition to
its genetic DNA, the enzymes necessary for the transcription of that material into
polypeptide sequences; the inheritance of inadequate protein-synthesizing enzymes
can be as disastrous as the inheritance of a mutated gene. Similarly, a cell may
deteriorate through a progressive decrease in the adequacy of its transcription
mechanism. (Orgel, 1963)

From this perspective, Orgel turns to the consequences of errors in the synthesis
of components of the transcription/translation apparatus: "errors which lead to a
reduced specificity of an information-handling enzyme lead to an increasing error
frequency." This process "must lead ultimately to an error catastrophe; that is, the
error frequency must reach a value at which one of the processes necessary for the
existence of [a] viable cell becomes critically inefficient."

This conclusion of Orgel's (1963) hinged on a mathematical model that he later
realized was deficient (Orgel, 1970). Orgel (1970) then proposed a simple mathematical model that has since provided a starting point for further mathematical
analysis. It is assumed that the dynamics of the translation apparatus can be represented in terms of a sequence of discrete "cell generations," where these generations are not clearly defined. Let $p_n$ be defined as the error frequency of generation
$n$. Let $E$ be the "residual" or inherent error frequency. Let $k$ give the extent to which
errors in one cell generation contribute to the error frequency of the next generation.
Then Orgel's (1970) model can be given as

$$p_{n+1} = E + kp_n. \tag{7.1}$$

If $k$ is greater than or equal to one, $p_n$ increases without bound as $n$ goes to infinity.
If $k < 1$, then $p_n$ approaches a steady-state value, such that an error catastrophe does
*not* occur. Thus, as Orgel (1970) conceded, a translation error catastrophe is not a
necessary result of errors in the synthesis of components of the translation machinery. Even in the very simple model of Eq. (7.1). the occurrence of an error catastrophe hinges on the value of an unspecified parameter $k$. Thus Orgel himself realized
that there was no inevitability of error catastrophe, contrary to his initial sup-
position.

The model defined by Eq. (7.1) lacks sufficient detail to allow interpretation in
terms of basic features of translation mechanics. Others have since provided models
of greater complexity (Hoffman, 1974; Kirkwood and Holliday, 1975; Goel and
Islam, 1977; Kirkwood, 1980). All models currently available make unrealistic
simplifying assumptions, so that none is truly "correct"; this is only a typical
situation in scientific theory, of course. All these models share with Orgel's (1970)
the feature that error catastrophes occur only under specific parametric regimes. For
example, two parameters in the model of Kirkwood and Holliday (1975) are $R$,
defined as the activity of an erroneous and error-prone translation-apparatus molecule relative to the activity of an error-free molecule, and $S$, a parameter that reflects
the accuracy of specification of translation-apparatus components by the translation

apparatus. Error catastrophe occurs when $R$ is large and $S$ is small, which is not too surprising in the case of $S$. The $R$ parameter's effect may be a bit more obscure. One way to understand it is to realize that if $R$ is zero, then erroneous molecules are completely inactive, so that errors cannot feed back on themselves. If $R$ is large, then erroneous molecules are able to do their mischief by fathering still more erroneous molecules. In any case, the basic pattern of parametric dependence is rather like that of Orgel's (1970) model, error catastrophe requiring structural investment in translation fidelity that is sufficiently low.

So why should the translation apparatus of multicellular organisms ever evolve values of fidelity parameters that allow error catastrophe? This question has been explicitly addressed as part of the "disposable soma" theory (Kirkwood, 1977, 1981; Kirkwood and Holliday, 1979). This theory ingeniously invokes an argument exactly parallel to that of Williams (1957): Low values of $R$ and/or high values of $S$ require the diversion of substantial biological resources in order to ensure somatic immortality, while natural selection favors diversion of those resources to reproduction. The soma is in fact "disposable": Its physiological collapse as a result of eventual error catastrophe is of no importance to natural selection and will be actively fostered if net fitness is thereby increased through greater reproductive rates. It has been supposed that this type of argument provides support specifically for the error catastrophe mechanism of aging (Kirkwood, 1977), but not the many alternative physiological mechanisms that could exhibit antagonistic pleiotropy. This is obviously erroneous, but it does at least suggest a good reason for supposing that the somatic cells of multicellular organisms are subject to aging as a result of error catastrophe. In no way does this argument preclude the action of other physiological mechanisms of aging.

## Experimental Tests of Error Catastrophe Theory

Orgel's (1970) reformulation of his earlier model (Orgel, 1963) was indeed appropriate, since the earlier version implied the inevitability of error catastrophe for all cell lineages. This corollary, of course, is empirically refuted by the many strictly asexual unicellular organisms that have maintained themselves indefinitely. Nor can this be a result of selection among cells (cf. Orgel, 1963), since fissile metazoa, such as some sea anemones, also do not senesce (Chapter 5). Thus, in terms of Orgel's (1970) model, such lineages must have $k < 1$, with analogous parametric characteristics if the other error catastrophe models are invoked. Whatever the mathematical form, any formal version of the error catastrophe theory must allow parameter combinations in which aging does not occur, such as higher translation fidelity, in order to account for immortal lineages of somatic cells. Thus organisms like fissile annelids, which can lack aging (Bell, 1984c), must have considerably increased translation fidelity compared with closely related organisms that do exhibit aging. As yet, this has not been ascertained.

Aside from the death of the cell, error catastrophe should be associated with two major changes in the molecular properties of the cell: (1) increasing levels of abnormal protein, especially protein lacking functional activity; and (2) decreased fidelity of translation. A major empirical problem in the evaluation of error catastrophe theory is that post-translational modification of proteins could produce the first of these two effects in the absence of an error catastrophe. On the other hand, absence of this effect would constitute evidence against the error catastrophe theory. If the second effect is measured simply as production of proteins with incorrect amino acid sequences, then it could be due to somatic mutation as well as an error catastrophe (Hirsch, 1978).

The dynamics of error catastrophe are handily illustrated by a *Neurospora* mutant, *leu*-5. This mutant produces a defective leucyl-t-RNA synthetase protein that allows incorporation of amino acids other than leucine when leucine is specified by the mRNA codon. At 37 °C, *leu*-5 cultures cease growing after a few days. During this period, the cells produce proportionately less and less active protein (Lewis and Holliday, 1970). In this case, an error catastrophe has been deliberately contrived. These results do not show that error catastrophes play any role in the deterioration of somatic cells with chronological age, in vivo or in vitro. What they reveal is the kind of dramatic breakdown in production of functional protein that is to be expected when error catastrophes disrupt the functioning of cells.

The question outstanding is, then, to what extent do the somatic cells of metazoa exhibit a progressive failure to produce functional protein? On the whole, the evidence suggests that there is no overwhelming collapse of enzyme activity in senescent cells (Samis, 1978). However, particular instances of enzymes with decreasing activity (e.g., isocitrate lysase, in *Turbatrix aceti,* Gershon and Gershon, 1970), increasing heat lability (e.g., G-6-PD in human fibroblast, Holliday and Tarrant, 1972), or reduced functional accuracy (e.g., DNA polymerase-$\alpha$, in human fibroblast, Linn, Kairis, and Holliday, 1976) have been found. Several criticisms have been made of this work (e.g., Samis, 1978; Rothstein, 1983). One such criticism is that proteins from older cells may be subject to partial degradation during isolation, because older cells may have more lysosomes. Furthermore, there may be more dead or dying cells in older tissues, or old in vitro cultures, with the proteins from such cells being damaged by extensive proteolysis. Methods of protein isolation that employ cell fractionation exacerbate these problems. A different line of criticism is that, if protein turnover is slower in older cells, then there may be more time for accidental post-translational modification of proteins, perhaps by free radicals. (See the next section for discussion of free radicals.)

In any event, there are many instances in which particular proteins do *not* appear to be altered with age. Several enzymes have been found to exhibit increasing activity with in vitro age of human fibroblast culture (Fulder and Tarrant, 1975). DNA polymerase-$\beta$ from the liver tissue of two species of mice showed no dependence of either activity or accuracy on tissue age or species longevity (Fry, Loeb, and Martin, 1981). Many other examples of unaltered enzymes are given in Rothstein (1983). In summary, it appears that: (1) some proteins do undergo some loss of function with age, but this loss is rarely severe; (2) other proteins show no loss of function with age; (3) in those cases in which the cause of functional deterioration can be ascertained, it seems to be consistently due to postsynthetic modification (Rothstein, 1983).

More direct tests of the error catastrophe theory focus upon the accuracy of translation, as measured by changes in protein products that cannot be due to post-translational modification. One of the earliest such tests assayed the extent to which human fibroblast cells from old in vitro cultures could support viral replication (Holland, Kohne, and Doyle, 1973). Viruses grown in old cells were indistinguishable from those grown in young cells in every character measured: thermal stability, mutation rate, and subsequent infective potency. Since isoleucine is not normally coded for in human hemoglobin exons, its incorporation in hemoglobin is a sensitive measure of translation fidelity, as well as somatic mutation. As was shown in Figure 7.5, there is no statistically significant increase in isoleucine levels with age (Popp et al., 1976). This combined measure of somatic mutation and translation error indicates no trend to decreased fidelity of protein synthesis with age. "Stuttering" occurs in two-dimensional protein gels when there is incorrect amino acid incorporation during protein synthesis. It too is thus a sensitive measure of translation fidelity. Two-dimensional gels of somatic tissue from young and old *D. melanogaster* reveal little stuttering at either age (Parker et al., 1981; Fleming et al., 1986). There does not appear to be any stuttering in gels from old *C. elegans* either (Johnson and McCaffrey, 1985). Other studies have also failed to find evidence for decreases in translation fidelity with age (Richardson and Birchenall-Sparks, 1983; Richardson, Birchenall-Sparks, and Staecker, 1983; Richardson and Semsei, 1987).

Finally, there are experiments that directly test error feedback itself. Translation fidelity and error feedback have been directly measured in *Escherichia coli* (Edelman and Gallant, 1977; Gallant and Palmer, 1979; Gallant and Prothero, 1980). While *E. coli* cells are not somatic cells, and thus are not "disposable" (cf. Kirkwood, 1977), they nonetheless can be used to unravel some of the basic features of error propagation in living cells more directly than is possible with eukaryotic cells. This work has supported Orgel's original ideas to the extent that it has shown that error feedback does occur. Interestingly, the observed, normal, error frequencies are so low in magnitude that all extant error catastrophe models essentially reduce to that given by Orgel (1970), Eq. (7.1) (Gallant and Prothero, 1980). In terms of this model, the critical error feedback parameter, $k$ in Eq. (7.1), appears to be substantially lower than its critical threshold value of one, at least in *E. coli*. Indeed, deliberate attempts to push these cells into an error catastrophe failed (Gallant and Palmer, 1979), suggesting that prokaryotic cells may not be near the region of error catastrophe instability.

The closest comparable experiments in eukaryotes are those using amino acid analogs to induce high levels of translation error in order to induce error catastrophes. The first experiment of this kind fed amino acid analogs to late-instar larvae of *D. melanogaster* and then compared the resulting survivorship pattern with controls (Harrison and Holliday, 1967). The result was a substantial decrease in longevity, as would be expected from error catastrophe theory. A problem with these experiments, however, is that 80 percent of the protein in the adult somatic tissues of insects, other than the fat body, does not turn over (Bozcuk, 1972). Thus the life-shortening effect observed by Harrison and Holliday (1967) could have been due to physiological deficiencies resulting from incorrectly specified protein incorporated in the adult body during the later larval and pupal stages. The life-shortening effects of amino acid analogs fed to young *Drosophila* adults have been tested in other studies (Dingley and Maynard Smith, 1969; Bozcuk, 1976). There was no life-shortening effect, once flies immediately dying from the experimental treatment were removed. Thus the ostensible corroboration of the error catastrophe theory provided by Harrison and Holliday (1967) is in fact of doubtful relevance to the theory. Those experiments with amino acid analog feeding in *Drosophila* that are correctly designed suggest insufficient error feedback to generate error catastrophes, even when errors are forced, in conformity with the results from *E. coli*.

The evidence bearing on the error catastrophe theory is negative overall, particularly in view of the fact that corroborative results can be readily explained in terms of other known mechanisms, such as post-translational modification of proteins (Gallant, 1981; Rothstein, 1987). This suggests that the arguments of Orgel and his colleagues have critical deficiencies. Perhaps one oversight is that all cells that synthesize proteins are selected to minimize error feedback, so as to foster accuracy when young, in the face of transient perturbations that may be imposed by ingestion of naturally occurring toxins or solar radiation. This may have given rise to translation machinery that has error feedback levels that never allow error catastrophe before the cell has died of other causes. Another possibility is that metazoa may simply destroy cells producing a broad spectrum of aberrant protein, as a result of an error catastrophe, the vertebrate immune system providing an example of such a recognition/destruction device. In any case, the translation error catastrophe theory is one of the most thoroughly refuted of modern physiological theories of aging. This is not to say that error catastrophes never occur, only that they appear to be of little importance in the aging of those organisms studied sufficiently carefully so far.


## Postsynthetic Deterioration Theories

Up to this point, it is clear that the evidence for autonomous molecular mechanisms of aging is slim at best. The mechanism that seems most plausible at present is somatic mutation of multiple proto-oncogenes, giving rise to cancer in vertebrates. Even in vertebrates, however, cancer is only one type of life-threatening pathology, evidently distinct from cardiovascular disease, declining pathogen resistance, and so on. In other organisms, cancer is of even less apparent significance. If there are autonomous molecular–cellular mechanisms that give rise to the pervasive pathologies of aging, then they must involve deterioration of the constituents of the cell after synthesis.

In considering this possibility, the immediate question must concern rates of turnover. Molecules that are rapidly degraded and then synthesized again are not going to be sources of aging due to postsynthetic deterioration, because rapidly degraded molecules are not retained for sufficient time. At the other extreme, some extracellular proteins in vertebrates, such as collagen, appear to be virtually permanent; once synthesized in adults, they are not normally replaced. In insects, a large fraction of total adult protein does not appear to turn over (Maynard Smith, Bozcuk, and Tebbutt, 1970). In addition, the evidence that total protein synthesis declines with age in a wide variety of organisms is extensive (Richardson and Birchenall-Sparks, 1983). Therefore, the absence of a similar decline in the protein content of the tissues of most organisms implies that protein turnover must also fall in the great majority of senescing organisms. The ineluctable conclusion must be that aging adults have macromolecules that are not being replaced as rapidly and so are potentially subject to postsynthetic deterioration over the life of the adult.

## Agents of Damage

While there are evidently macromolecules that are not regularly replaced in adult cells, their deterioration requires active agents of damage. It cannot be simply assumed that that which does not turn over must somehow deteriorate within the lifetime of the organism. Indeed, the required agents of damage are well known.

### THERMAL DENATURATION AND HYDROLYSIS

Two minor damage agents that should be mentioned are thermal denaturation and hydrolysis. The first depends on the loss of secondary or tertiary structure due to conformational changes requiring high activation energy levels, such that, once such changes have taken place, the molecule is unlikely to resume its original form readily. Patterns of aging among survivors of heat shock treatment in poikilotherm species provide one means of assessing the importance of this mechanism of aging. Strehler (1962) performed this experiment in *Drosophila melanogaster,* subjecting the experimental flies to 38.5 °C for a short period. There was no apparent acceleration of aging. This does not preclude some role for thermal denaturation in aging, but it does suggest that it is either not universal or not large.

Strehler (1977, pp. 270–74) has also argued for the importance of simple hydrolysis in aging, because the process of anabolism after all normally proceeds by synthetic processes in which water molecules are produced as byproducts. (The most typical reaction is the replacement of an –OH terminus and an –H terminus by a covalent bond, freeing an $H_2O$ molecule.) Yet, as Strehler points out, the thermodynamic coefficients of these reactions generally favor hydrolysis. Furthermore, cellular metabolism evidently proceeds in an environment in which water molecules are in high concentration. Nucleotide bonds are readily broken by hydrolysis, but it is unlikely that conventional DNA repair mechanisms would have much difficulty restoring them. On the other hand, proteins, lipids, and carbohydrate polymers that do not turn over have no such repair systems, so that all may be subject to a progressive "loosening" of the bonds that make them functional macromolecules, giving rise to a pervasive deterioration of the cellular machinery.

### FREE RADICALS

Free radicals are the agents of damage that have received the most attention, some authors having argued quite strongly for their primacy as a mechanism of aging (e.g., Harman, 1956; Gordon, 1974). Free radicals arise when reactions produce molecular species with unpaired electrons, such as superoxide,

$$O_2 + e^- = O\cdot_2$$

or the hydroxy radical ·OH. An interesting aspect of free-radical chemistry is that free radicals are produced by both normal enzymic reactions and such environmental perturbations as x rays and toxic chemicals. Thus they could be used to explain both normal aging and the accelerated aging sometimes exhibited under irradiation (Harman, 1956).

Among the many types of molecular damage that free radicals can cause, lipid peroxidation is perhaps the best characterized (Lippman, 1983). Lipid peroxidation involves free-radical reaction with double bonds in unsaturated lipids, a process that can proceed as a chain reaction and result in the formation of toxic products such as ethane, pentane, and malondialdehyde, a known mutagen. Though the chemistry involved is incompletely characterized, lipid peroxidation also gives rise to many of the components of lipofuscin, the mysterious intracellular detritus discussed previously. The list of the different types of damage to which lipid peroxides may give rise is quite long and suggests the potential for diverse pathologies (Lippman, 1983).

Cells contain many protective mechanisms that eliminate free radicals. For example, the class of enzymes known as superoxide dismutase specifically eliminates superoxide radicals. Vitamin E is thought to be an antioxidant that protects polyunsaturated fatty acids against peroxidation, and vitamin E deficiency has been associated with increased levels of lipofuscin accumulation in a variety of vertebrates. Moreover, vitamin E provision has been associated with reduced levels of lipid peroxidation (Lippman, 1983). Since vitamin E is readily ingested, as are other such simple antioxidants, the possibility of prolonging life span by enhancing organismal defense against free radicals is clear.

Comfort (1979, pp. 267–76) has reviewed such antioxidant experiments with a somewhat jaundiced eye. In many of these experiments, mean life span is prolonged compared to that of controls, but the maximum life span often is not. In many cases, it is not clear that the diet of the control animals is really adequate. Comfort, Youhotsky-Gore, and Pathmanathan (1971) performed one of the few antioxidant experiments which one can be sure was not performed deliberately to confirm the free-radical hypothesis of aging. As shown in Figure 7.7, the group given the antioxidant ethoxyquin had significantly increased mean and maximum longevities. However, there is good reason to doubt that the effect of this drug was confined to free-radical chemistry, because the mice treated with ethoxyquin became significantly lighter than the controls as shown in Table 7.3. The manifest possibility, then, is that these mice underwent some type of nutritional restriction, perhaps due to suppression of appetite or reduced digestive efficiency.

The argument that reduced free-radical damage could explain the increased longevity of food-restricted rodents in terms of a reduced metabolic rate has been refuted by the lack of a long-term reduction in metabolic rate among restricted rodents (Masoro, 1988). One piece of evidence for the free-radical theory was the prolongation of in vitro human cell cultures obtained with provision of vitamin E (Packer and Smith, 1974). This finding has since proved irreproducible (Balin et al., 1977). Another problematic experiment for free-radical theories of aging comes from work on *C. elegans* (Harrington and Harley, 1988). Vitamin E does extend life span in *C. elegans,* but at the same time it decreases total fecundity and postpones peak fecundity. Thus the life-span increase could have been due to diminished reproductive effort via the type of pathway that produces the diminished reproduc-

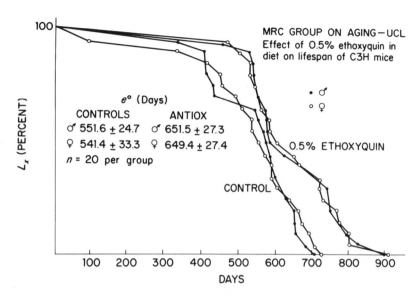

FIGURE 7.7. Life-span effects of the antioxidant ethoxyquin on $C_3H$ mice. The antioxidant appears to lengthen life, but see the text. (From Comfort, 1979, p. 267.)

tion and extended life span of the *age*-1 mutant in *C. elegans* (Friedman and Johnson, 1988; also Chapter 4).

Therefore, at present there is no clear evidence that antioxidants can be used to prolong life span by means of free-radical inhibition specifically. Alternative dietary restriction and reproductive inhibition hypotheses seem to fit the experimental results better. However, this in no way precludes the possibility that free radicals give rise to forms of molecular senescence that experimentally administered antioxidants cannot retard (Sohal, 1987).

A further elaboration of the free-radical theory that takes into account many of the failures of its original version has been offered (Pryor, 1987). This theory focuses on the chronic diseases of mammals, particularly man. This "positioning" ensures that it will not be possible to subject this theory to tests using in vitro cell culture or organisms like *D. melanogaster* and *C. elegans*, because experiments

TABLE 7.3. Average weights of $C_3H$ mice fed normal diets (control) or diets containing the antioxidant ethoxyquin (treated). Weights are in grams and age is in days.

| | *Age (d)* | | | |
|---|---|---|---|---|
| | *97* | *197* | *310* | *533* |
| Male control (g) | 25.4 | 31.9 | 30.5 | 29.2 |
| Male treated (g) | 26.0 | 28.9 | 25.2 | 26.0 |
| Female control (g) | 20.2 | 26.8 | 27.3 | 25.9 |
| Female treated (g) | 20.9 | 24.4 | 20.6 | 20.3 |

Data from Comfort, Youhotsky-Gore, and Paramanathan (1971).

with mammals necessarily take longer and are smaller in scale. In this respect, the original theory was certainly preferable.

## GLYCATION

Even the seemingly innocuous glucose molecule has been proposed as an agent of molecular damage giving rise to aging among cell constituents and extracellular proteins (Cerami, 1985). Specifically, it appears that glucose molecules can cross-link proteins, when the glucose molecules have undergone what is called an Amadori rearrangement and attach themselves to amino acids, in the absence of any catalyst. Such glycated proteins are thought to be more resistant to proteolysis, and there is some experimental evidence that they resist degradation. Glycated proteins are also thought to be toxic to some degree. The degree to which diabetics are progeroid is also thought to support the involvement of glycation in aging, since diabetics have much higher levels of serum glucose.

Corroborative evidence for this hypothesis comes from food-restricted rodents. Masoro, Katz, and McMahan (1989) have shown that food-restricted rats have plasma glucose concentrations and hemoglobin glycosylation percentages significantly lower than those of ad libitum fed rats. This is in keeping with Cerami's (1985) hypothesis. However, an alternative analysis would be that the ad libitum rats are like diabetics due to pathological overeating. The restricted rodent is then the normal rodent that does not suffer from diverse pathologies associated with overfeeding, including glycation.

## Collagen Cross-Linkage

If cellular DNA is efficiently repaired and most important cellular components undergo synthesis and turnover at rates sufficient to preserve cellular function, then extracellular molecules are the most plausible foci for molecular mechanisms of aging. In vertebrates, the most durable, common, extracellular molecule is the primary protein component of rigid extracellular tissue: collagen. While collagen does undergo some degree of turnover under exceptional conditions, such as pregnancy and the growth of scar tissue upon wounding, it is still a remarkably inert molecule (Kohn, 1971). Indeed, in vertebrates, collagen has six key properties that could be required of any molecular candidate for primacy in the process of aging. (1) As stated, it has a low rate of turnover. (2) It is present in large quantities in many body structures. (3) It undergoes aging; that is, it changes measurably in biologically important properties during adult life. (4) An autonomous molecular mechanism of change has been identified, and there is no reason to suppose that changes in other organismal functions are responsible for the molecule's aging. (5) The aging of the molecule can be related to pervasive functional deficiencies, at least in principle. (6) Some life-prolongation treatments also slow the aging of the molecule. Having already discussed the first point in this list, the remaining five will be discussed in turn.

Kohn (1971, p. 20) has estimated that about 23 percent of the mammalian body consists of extracellular connective tissue. That part of the connective tissue that is rigid contains a high proportion of collagen. Of the total protein in the body, collagen is thought to comprise 25–30 percent (Kohn, 1971, p. 23).

There are a number of studies that have dealt with aging changes in collagen. Three types of change will be mentioned here. One attribute that has been repeatedly studied is the resistance of collagen to thermal contraction, in effect a measure of the rigidity of collagen fibers. This rigidity increases throughout life (Verzar and Thoenen, 1960). A problem with this finding is that the rate of increase in rigidity is faster before the onset of reproduction, suggesting that such "aging" is more developmental than senescent. Another attribute that increases with age in collagen is its resistance to degradation in corrosive solution (Hamlin and Kohn, 1972), as shown in Figure 7.8. Finally, collagen is progressively more resistant with age to osmotic swelling (Kohn and Rollerson, 1958). To some extent, both these measures reflect increasing chemical obduracy; even if there were much evidence for turnover of collagen in normal connective tissue, and there is not, the collagen of older individuals would be substantially more resistant to proteolysis. In a sense, collagen seems to age in such a way as to become metabolically inert.

Cross-linkage has long been a favored biochemical mechanism of molecular aging (e.g., Bjorksten, 1974, and references therein). Collagen is one of the few biological molecules for which the evidence of cumulative cross-linkage is good, in that the type of aging changes just described can be readily explained in terms of cross-linkage (vide Kohn, 1971, pp. 33–39).

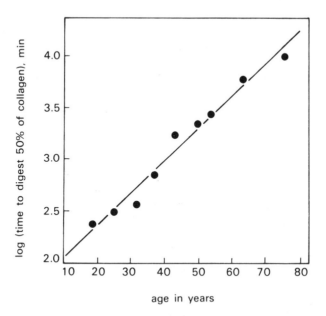

FIGURE 7.8. Effect of age on the time to digest collagen from human diaphragm tendons. Reprinted with permission from *Experimental Gerontology* 7, Hamlin, C.R. and R.R. Kohn. Determination of human chronological age by study of a collagen sample. Copyright 1972, Pergamon Press plc.

It is easy to develop speculative connections between collagen cross-linkage and declining organismal functions. Kohn (1971, pp. 153–56) has done a thorough job of this, suggesting the following consequences of collagen aging. (1) Connective tissue may generally become rocklike, immobile. (2) Cardiac muscle may lose contractile efficiency because of stiffening induced by collagen; and indeed it is known that heart muscle becomes more rigid with age. (3) Arterial linings could lose their ability to transmit contractile force, reducing efficiency of blood circulation. (4) Cross-linked collagen may function as a barrier to perfusion of nutrients from blood to tissue and of metabolic waste products from tissue to blood. These four types of deterioration are then linked by Kohn to arteriosclerosis, hypertension, carcinogenesis, and kidney malfunction, all diseases that increase in frequency with age. Finally, it is now well established that collagen becomes more "youthful" in nutritionally restricted, and longer-lived, rodents (Bertrand, 1983).

In general, collagen cross-linkage meets more criteria for molecular aging than any other process. Its only rival is free-radical peroxidation of lipids leading to lipofuscin accumulation. But like lipofuscin accumulation (vide Davies and Fotheringham, 1981), the question remains whether or not collagen cross-linkage constitutes aging. Strehler (1977, p. 208) has suggested that "It may well be the case that the changes in quantity and properties of collagen mentioned are reflections of an adaptively useful continuation of a developmental process." As we have seen throughout this chapter, this is a generic problem for putative suborganismal mechanisms of aging. It is a problem that will be considered further in Chapter 8.

## Conclusion

A possibly mortal problem for any simple cellular or molecular theory of aging is that it is difficult to argue that cells, as such, undergo aging, as discussed at length at the start of the chapter. There certainly is good evidence that in vitro proliferative limits are evolutionarily, and thus genetically, related to the processes that limit life span among species. However, since patterns of pleiotropy can be remarkably subtle, this does *not* constitute evidence that in vitro proliferation reflects organismal aging mechanisms. Theories of cell aging that revolve around differentiation suffer from the problem that there is no powerful, general, well-attested theory of cellular differentiation available for application to the problem of aging. Thus a great deal of research on cells has to be regarded as ambiguous with respect to the mechanistic particulars of the dependence of organismal aging on cell biology.

Indeed, the general situation with respect to cellular and molecular theories of aging is that it is hard to find a theory with much generality that has fared well under testing. The somatic mutation theory has clearly received some devastating experimental hits, obliterating old claims that it was the fundamental cause of aging (e.g., Curtis, 1966). Still, it is likely that somatic mutation plays some role in the development of cancer, clearly a component of the mammalian aging syndrome. The translation error catastrophe theory has to be about as dead as any major, modern, scientific theory can be (vide Rothstein, 1987). While agents of damage like free radicals would seem to be unavoidable hazards of life, the amount of direct evidence for their action in determining rates of aging is quite limited. Cross-linkage of collagen has been demonstrated, and conceivably it could have diverse pathological effects (vide Kohn, 1971). But others are inclined to the view that collagen undergoes development, not deteriorative aging (Strehler, 1977, p. 208). Overall, the molecular theories of aging do not stand out as particularly successful, even when compared with organismal theories of aging.

# 8

# The Future of Gerontology

One hundred years without Darwinism are enough.
H. J. MULLER, 1959

Although this book is intended to be all of a piece, nonetheless the majority of the book has been concerned with theories of aging of quite heterogeneous kinds, from antagonistic pleiotropy to lipofuscin accumulation. The connections between these theories have only been alluded to in passing. In this final chapter the focus will be on the causal connections between physiology and evolution, and the implications of these connections for the study of the physiology of senescence, gerontology, with respect to both theory and experiment. In sum, this is the conclusion to what has been, in part, a long argument for the importance of the evolutionary theory of aging for all research in gerontology.

Here a program is presented for the organization of gerontological research along evolutionary lines. The first part of this program is a new theoretical foundation for the field. One of the most important starting points for such a foundation must be the admission of physiological diversity in mechanisms of aging, between and within species. The "unity in diversity" of aging, such as the synchronization of sources of mortality in some species, arises from evolutionary factors, not a common underlying molecular mechanism of aging. These will be the starting points for the reworking of theoretical gerontology.

The second front for the reform of gerontology is experimentation. One of the less constructive features of empirical research on aging has been its treatment of cases of shortened life span. The avoidance of artifacts with such experimental approaches is extremely difficult. Postponing aging, it will be argued, is the far more useful form of intervention. The comparative method can also be valuable, but it has its share of problems of interpretation, particularly confounding variables like body size and a lack of evolutionary independence between species.

One of the most important issues for experiments on aging is that of the choice of experimental system. Small, short-lived, invertebrate metazoa, especially *Drosophila* and *Caenorhabditis,* should have primacy in tests of fundamental theories, evolutionary or physiological. On the other hand, the problem of phylogenetic heterogeneity in mechanisms of aging must incline even the staunchest advocate of invertebrate research to the conclusion that rodent research is imperative. In the end, there will be no other way to attain the biomedical research goal of ameliorating

160

human aging. It is concluded that this goal is scientifically feasible, although practically demanding, thanks to the power that the evolutionary theory of aging affords for unraveling the causal mechanisms controlling the process.

## Theoretical Issues

Given the case made for the evolutionary theory of aging in Chapters 1–5, it is only natural to attempt to sort out the theoretical issues of gerontology using that theory. However, it should be borne in mind that the discussion to be presented is one in which present-day gerontological issues are digested from an evolutionary standpoint. What is offered here is an evolutionary paradigm for gerontology (vide Kuhn, 1970).

### The Causes of Aging

Nothing in biology has only one cause, in an absolute sense. In a more limited sense, the cause of aging is the falling intensity of natural selection with respect to age after the onset of reproduction, as discussed in Chapter 1. But the efficacy of this cause in the evolution of aging requires alleles with some degree of age specificity in their effects on adult survival and/or reproduction. To some extent, Chapter 6 includes considerable circumstantial evidence for the existence of such allelic effects. In this wider sense, the physiology of aging also plays a causal role in aging. However, Chapter 3 presents the critical evidence bearing on this hypothesis, evidence that concerns patterns of allelic pleiotropy.

A HIERARCHY OF CAUSES

The simplest schema for understanding the view of aging propounded here is given in Figure 8.1. Again, the ultimate cause of aging is seen as the attenuation of the force of natural selection with respect to the age of gene effects. Given this attenuation, alleles with deleterious effects at later ages may increase in frequency because of either of two alternative population-genetic mechanisms. The first is mutation accumulation, in which an allele with later deleterious effects has no, or very little, effect at ages when natural selection is sufficiently powerful to overcome mutation pressure. The second mechanism is antagonistic pleiotropy, in which alleles with beneficial effects at early ages have deleterious effects at later ages, the greater intensity of selection at earlier ages giving a selective advantage to such alleles. Mutation accumulation may give rise to senescence because of types of physiological deterioration with no significant effects, positive or negative, at early ages. Antagonistic pleiotropy gives rise to physiological features that are beneficial early but deleterious later, and thus it tends to leave aging bound up with adaptation. Some physiological mechanisms of aging may arise entirely because of one of these two population-genetic mechanisms, but others may involve both mechanisms. These points will be treated as matters of fact below, even though they evidently constitute scientific theory and as such must be considered susceptible to empirical refutation.

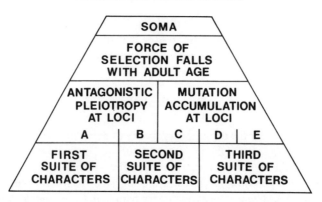

FIGURE 8.1. Hierarchy of causation of aging. At the top of the pyramid is the ultimate determinant of whether or not an organism senesces: the possession of a soma distinct from its germ line. This gives rise to a fall in the force of selection with adult age, in all cases where survivorship is concerned and in most cases where fecundity is concerned. There are then two subsidiary population-genetic mechanisms for the evolution of aging: antagonistic pleiotropy and mutation accumulation. Specific suites of characters may be subject to either or both of these mechanisms. In any case, multiple suites of interconnected physiological mechanisms are expected to determine the pattern of aging in any one species, with even greater diversity among species.

## ADAPTATION AND AGING

As discussed in Chapter 4, the evidence for the importance of the antagonistic pleiotropy mechanism in the evolution of aging is significant and growing. While antagonistic pleiotropy is not universal, this finding shows that aging is partly a result of adaptation. Therefore, later loss of physiological functions can have roots in earlier, beneficial, physiological functions. Thus the physiology of senescence is not a problem that can be cleanly divorced from the physiology of adaptation. The problem with this situation is that it leaves aging bound up with the nature and mechanisms of "peak performance" in the young organism. Such performance attributes cannot be taken as a mere reference point against which to gauge subsequent deterioration. The benefit is that, to some extent, clues to later mechanisms of aging may be provided by examination of physiological "design features" that give enhanced early performance at the expense of durability, much as one might compare the engineering of a racing car with that of a domestic sedan. It is not simply that the racing car is "better." Its design may also necessitate a shorter "lifetime" on the road. Thus there are both pitfalls and opportunities for the scientist in the mingling of the physiology of adaptation with the physiology of senescence. But if the possibility is simply discounted, then fundamental blunders may be made.

## AGING FROM ORGANISM TO MOLECULE

Something of the range of modern gerontological hypotheses was reviewed in Chapters 6 and 7. One conclusion that seems fair to offer is that the revolution in cellular and molecular biology that has been ongoing for the past three decades or so has not yielded the benefits for gerontology that it has in many other biological disciplines. Indeed, straightforward organismal theories of aging often seem the most tenable (vide Chapter 6). For example, the atrophied mouth parts in many adult insects are an example of a properly organismal feature that fosters death and the termination of reproduction. Reproductive exhaustion as a mechanism fostering death is abundantly demonstrated in organisms as distantly related as salmon and soybean (Chapter 6). By contrast, cellular and molecular theories of aging are only indirectly supported by the available evidence and are in fact often plainly refuted (Chapter 7). Cellular proliferation seems to be related in some way to species potential longevity (Röhme, 1981), but no one is claiming that organisms senesce because they exhaust their proliferative capacity (Hayflick, 1977; Phillips and Cristofalo, 1983). Lipofuscin accumulation and collagen cross-linkage are prominent age-correlated processes in adult vertebrates, but it is not yet clear that they are mechanisms of aging. Thus, as one proceeds from organismal to molecular levels in the analysis of the physiology of aging, things become more obscure, not less so.

It cannot be rationally maintained that organismal aging is preeminent, and there is no interesting molecular biology to be studied. All respectable biologists are reductionists of some stripe. Though organisms are of course *organized,* rather than structureless heaps of DNA, RNA, protein, and carbohydrate, that very organization must depend on the way specific molecules interact. Reproductive exhaustion in salmon and marsupial mice depends on hormones that channel resources into reproductive tissues and activities at the expense of those tissues and activities that would otherwise keep the animal alive (Chapter 6).

For some reason, it has proved difficult to find the crucial molecular foundations of aging. Perhaps the problem is that, with lack of knowledge of the organismal mechanisms, the *contexts* in which cellular or molecular mechanisms of aging might operate are usually not clear. This may not be too surprising, since there is little in the reductionist canon to suggest that the biologist can proceed directly to molecules isolated on a gel to solve all problems of interest.

Perhaps an example from population genetics will make this point more explicitly. The application of the techniques of electrophoresis to the problem of the nature of standing genetic variation was at first seen as a slice through a Gordian knot, but the lack of any context in which to interpret this variation led to an intensification, rather than a diminution, of controversy (cf. Lewontin, 1974; Kimura, 1983). When particular electrophoretic polymorphisms are subject to penetrating experimental analysis, the results often indicate a selective context of some complexity (e.g., Koehn, Zera, and Hall, 1983). The major desire of many population geneticists was to avoid such "slogging in the trenches," at least in the period from 1966 to 1975. But it is now seen that little is to be gained from scatter-shot studies of a wide range of molecular polymorphisms. Instead, selection acting at specific loci is being investigated (Powers, 1987; Koehn, 1987). Information about the specific physiological mechanisms of selection must be sought. Likewise, it may be the case that investigating changes in the lability of a large miscellany of enzymes with respect to adult age will not reveal the causal molecular mechanisms of aging, unless more is discovered of the organismal physiology of aging in the organism concerned.

An additional point that might be made in support of research on organismal mechanisms of aging is that such research may reveal whether these mechanisms arise from mutation accumulation, antagonistic pleiotropy, or both. For example, experiments involving castration, destruction of germ line cells in embryos, and the like can be used to some extent to ascertain whether or not antagonistic pleiotropy is critical to the aging of any particular component of an organism's physiology. Such experiments unavoidably require the use of whole organisms, although cellular or molecular samples could of course be taken, perhaps for transplantation.

## Multiplicity of Physiological Causes

The question of whether aging has one cause or many has been asked since Aristotle, if not earlier. Most writers from Aristotle's time until this century seemed to find the idea that aging has only one cause most congenial. Since 1970, if not earlier, few gerontologists have held this view.

In a sense, the present volume argues that aging has a single cause, the fading out of natural selection with the age of the soma. But this is probably not the sort of cause that most gerontologists have been thinking about. Of more interest to them is rather how many autonomous physiological mechanisms of aging exist. This is not a question that can be answered directly by reasoning from any particular evolutionary hypothesis. However, it seems worthwhile to discuss the question in terms of both evolutionary and physiological research on aging.

### MULTIPLICITY OF MECHANISMS WITHIN SPECIES

At present, there is no generally accepted theory that successfully explains all aspects of aging in terms of a single physiological mechanism. The slightest opportunity of uncovering such a mechanism has been assiduously explored since the turn of the century, without success. The straightforward explanation of this state of affairs is that aging involves a number of distinct physiological mechanisms, rather than one only.

What does the evolutionary theory suggest, where multiplicity of physiological mechanisms is concerned? Any locus at which alleles may have deleterious effects at later ages without deleterious effect at early ages will be subject to the spread of alleles that will foster aging. Thus the question becomes, how many such loci are there likely to be in any particular species? It would be simply astonishing if there were only one such locus. It would also be astonishing if every functional locus had such alleles. The correct answer must lie between $10^0$ and $10^5$, but this does not tell us much. One might want to know if the number is on the order of 10, 100, or $10^3$.

Some sort of minimum value can be obtained by selecting for increased life span and then estimating the number of loci involved in the response to selection, a research strategy now being actively pursued in both *Drosophila* and *Caenorhabditis elegans* laboratories (e.g., Luckinbill et al., 1987, 1988b, 1989; Johnson, 1987; Hutchinson and Rose, 1990). However, such estimates yield information only about loci that are polymorphic in the base population(s) used to initiate selection lines.

In any case, the evolutionary theory is quite compatible with the existence of more than enough loci to explain any degree of physiological diversity in aging. A large number of effective loci creates problems only for the unitary physiological theories prevalent before 1970.

## MULTIPLICITY OF MECHANISMS BETWEEN SPECIES

The implications of the evolutionary theory of aging for the question of the multiplicity of physiological mechanisms involved in aging are greatest where the diversity of species is concerned. So long as the evolutionary theory of aging is not adopted, then the most attractive way of explaining the universality of aging among groups such as arthropods or vertebrates is to suppose that there is some deep-seated physiological mechanism that gives rise to aging in all "higher" metazoa. Such a view is not as inherently unreasonable as it might at first seem. Eukaryotes have a large number of proteins in common, to say nothing of their similarities in ribosomal structure, transcriptional processing, chromosome packaging, catabolic pathways, and so on. There is no need for special evolutionary hypotheses to account for such homogeneities. Simple homology will do. Thus the initial temptation, at least before 1960 or 1970, was to suppose that one of these conserved physiological features would be found to be the cause of aging. As discussed, all such hopes have proved sterile. That leaves only the special evolutionary mechanism that molds aging in every species with an adult soma, as presented in Chapter 1.

There are many different ways of understanding this. One is that any "grand physiological theory of aging" is much like Lamarckism. It presumes some type of internal cause for the shaping of patterns of survival and reproduction when there is in fact a cause that is external, relative to the physiology of the organism: selection. In this sense, grand physiological theories of aging have the same status as grand physiological theories of flight or vision. All three of these processes arise because of evolutionary forces, but take on diverse physiological and anatomical forms. Moreover, the causal evolutionary forces need not always exist, and there are organisms that do not fly, see, or, indeed, senesce. The ultimate cause of aging is evolutionary, not physiological, and any theory that attempts to explain aging in terms of some fundamental feature of physiology by itself is therefore to be considered spurious.

This does not mean that the physiology of aging cannot display some degree of unity over species. All vertebrates share a common ancestral species, and all probably senesce (see Chapter 5); so the loci involved in the evolution of aging may be homologous over all or most vertebrates. Thus, in turn, the physiology of aging may be somewhat consistent among the vertebrates. Parallel arguments can be given for the insects, the mollusks, and so on, each in their turn.

However, the converse side of the point must be kept in mind. Similarity due to homology is the mirror image of diversity due to phylogenetic independence and consequent divergence. Physiological analyses of aging must show the same modesty as physiological analyses of adaptation. What is true of one taxon may not be true of another. The physiology of senescence in insects may be quite different from that of mammals, and indeed it is possible that the physiology of aging in rodents may be quite different from that of primates. These are questions that require empirical investigation using both experimental and comparative methods, as will be discussed in the following.

There is perhaps one factor that may mitigate the possibility of a virtually endless array of disparate physiological mechanisms of aging. Physiological mechanisms of aging all arise from the same two population-genetic mechanisms: mutation accumulation and antagonistic pleiotropy. There may be no limit to the diversity of mediating physiological mechanisms that can be subject to mutation accumulation. But there may be good reason to suppose that there are some possibilities for widespread homology where antagonistic pleiotropy is involved. The reason is that a primary source of loci that might exhibit antagonistic pleiotropy are those that control the mobilization of organismal resources for reproduction. These would include loci involved in the production of hormones, their secretion, and the reception of their signals at cell surfaces and the like. Such loci may be strongly conserved because they sit at the controls of the organism's most important act. While the features of reproduction vary radically among metazoa, the loci that control its timing and intensity behind this facade of diversity could be nearly universal. On the other hand, they may not be. This is a question that requires empirical investigation.

## Synchronization of Physiological Causes

Perhaps the most important fact motivating the pursuit of the idea that there is a single fundamental physiological cause of aging is the high degree of synchronization in the time course of deterioration with age in diverse physiological characters in many species. This synchrony can be readily explained in terms of the evolutionary theory of aging.

### TWO EVOLUTIONARY MECHANISMS

There are two distinct ways in which evolution may act to synchronize diverse mechanisms of aging, depending on the normal cause of death among adults. The first mechanism applies particularly to semelparous organisms, like Pacific salmon and soybean plants. Maynard Smith (1966) gives the clearest explanation of this mechanism, although Williams (1957) also discusses it:

> . . . natural selection will tend to synchronize different aging processes, even if these are physiologically independent. Suppose that in a particular natural population, one particular aging process—for example, atherosclerosis—proceeded much more rapidly than any other, so that any increase in the force of mortality occurred from this cause. Then any genetic change tending to delay the onset of atherosclerosis would be favored by selection, whereas genetic changes tending to cause an earlier onset of other aging changes would not be selected against. The result of such selection would be the synchrony of physiologically independent aging changes. (Maynard Smith, 1966) © 1966 John Wiley & Sons, Inc.

This mechanism will tend to give rise to simultaneous deterioration in a variety of functions having no simply physiological connection with each other. However, it is doubtful that this mechanism is of much importance in the evolution of aging in most iteroparous species, since such species usually die from external causes, rather than acute physiological malfunction. Man is perhaps the leading instance of an iteroparous species that could be subject to this evolutionary mechanism making for synchronization of autonomous physiological aging mechanisms. This is plausible because human populations have numerous deaths that are apparently due to aging. Thus deaths due to aging play some role in human mortality statistics and thus partly determine the intensity of selection with respect to age. This may also be true of some other large mammals (Nesse, 1988).

The majority of organisms that die from aging when carefully husbanded rarely do so in their normal habitat, dying instead from predation, disease, or accident. In such cases, the evolution of aging will still be subject to some degree of synchronization because the intensity of natural selection acting on characters contributing to either age-specific survival probabilities or age-specific fecundity will decline according to the same curves, since such curves depend on the fecundity and survival characters of the population (Chapter 1).

Three things should be noted about these patterns of decline. First, the evolution of reproductive aging is in principle independent of the evolution of aging in characters fostering survival. (Thus the early cessation of reproduction in female mammals, long before the physiological basis of survival collapses, is not an anomaly for the evolutionary theory of aging.) Second, the intensity of selection on a particular physiological attribute will be weighted according to its effect on age-specific survival or fecundity, not according to any features intrinsic to it, leaving pleiotropy aside. Thus, in the absence of pleiotropy, the rate of decline in a physiological character with age is to some degree an inverse measure of its importance in determining fitness components, with the further proviso of little heterogeneity in mutation rates. Third, all these arguments neglect pleiotropy, which ties together physiological mechanisms.

Some types of pleiotropy will positively link physiological mechanisms of aging, so that they foster one another, accelerating aging of the whole organism by means of positive feedback. Other types of pleiotropy will be antagonistic, so that one mechanism of physiological deterioration may mitigate others. For example, reproduction may impose major physiological burdens on the somatic tissues, but as reproductive aging proceeds, the organism's rate of deterioration in age-specific survival probabilities due to the physiological costs of reproduction may decelerate. Or the accumulation of substances such as lipofuscin could slow cellular metabolism and thereby secondarily decelerate the production of other deleterious by-products of cellular metabolism. All told, it is clearly difficult to say much about patterns of synchronization of the physiological mechanisms of aging characteristic of a species without unraveling its patterns of pleiotropy.

ARE THERE LEADING MECHANISMS OF AGING?

It has been common for evolutionary discussions of aging to preach pessimism where the prolongation of life is concerned (Williams, 1957; Maynard Smith, 1966; cf. Sacher, 1978). This view is based on the conclusion that aging is probably the result of many autonomous physiological mechanisms synchronized to such an extent that amelioration of the deterioration caused by one would only lead to death due to other mechanisms shortly thereafter. The implicit presupposition that underlies this argument is that there are no patterns of pleiotropy that could disrupt the fine synchronization of autonomous physiological mechanisms, as just discussed.

There are three lines of evidence against the pessimistic evolutionary view. First, as Comfort (e.g., 1979, pp. 325–29) discusses, even on the assumption of autonomous physiological aging mechanisms, one can still argue that elimination of only a few senescent pathologies could result in a significant increase in mean life span. For example, Rosenberg et al. (1973) calculate that eliminating heart disease would increase median human male life span by almost 9 years, which is plausible in view of the early incidence of heart disease in the men of some, but not all, countries. Eliminating cancer and vascular lesions as well, they calculate, would increase median life span by 27 years. [See Manton, Woodbury, and Stallard (1989) for other estimates along these lines.] The calculations need not be taken completely at face value, but they make the point that generalized collapse usually occurs in the 80s or 90s in human populations. Before that age, death normally has a well-defined etiology. Thus, in the context of diagnosed pathology, human aging does not appear to be particularly well synchronized. This suggests that, for some reason, some human physiological mechanisms of aging, such as those that give rise to cardiovascular disease in males, lead others in timing. Since little is known of mortality sources in senescing organisms of other species, it is not possible to say how unusual this pattern is.

Second, somewhat more directly, the experiments discussed in Chapter 4 indicate that pleiotropy is important in the evolution of aging. Therefore, the sort of ceteris paribus assumption that underlies the arguments of Maynard Smith (1966) and others is not generally valid. It is not always correct to assume that alleles having effects at later ages are indistinguishable at early ages. This does not by itself indicate the existence of leading physiological causes of aging, since patterns of pleiotropy could cancel each other out in such a way as to allow consistent synchronization of physiological mechanisms. But it does mitigate the apodictic quality of the argument against the existence of leading physiological mechanisms of aging.

Third, castration of some semelparous organisms can substantially prolong their life span. Salmon that have undergone castration can live up to 18 years longer than their normal time of spawning, and thus death (Robertson, 1961). Removal of reproductive structures from soybean plants substantially prolongs their lives as well (Leopold, 1961). Somewhat similarly, Maynard Smith (1958) himself has shown that prevention of egg laying in *Drosophila subobscura* can substantially prolong life span. All these results suggest that the deleterious effects of reproduction in these species precede, to some extent, aging due to other mechanisms, such that, once antagonistic pleiotropy is mitigated, there is an appreciable delay before the other mechanisms bring on death.

In conclusion, it can be said with confidence that there is no necessary association between the evolutionary theory of aging and the hypothesis that there are a large number of closely synchronized physiological mechanisms of aging, and thus little prospect of postponing aging (pace Sacher, 1978). Indeed, the available evidence suggests that there may well be leading physiological mechanisms of aging whose amelioration could effectively postpone aging.

## Evolutionary Issues in Theoretical Gerontology

This book offers a new framework for gerontological research of all kinds. However, gerontologists have for some years been developing their own, rather different, theoretical perspectives. Some gerontological theories have been concerned with more than particular mechanisms for the physiology of aging. They have also had "metatheoretical" content, especially where the evolution of aging is concerned. While these extant theoretical frameworks for gerontology are implicitly criticized throughout this book, a few aspects of the literature deserve special consideration within an evolutionary framework.

### EVOLUTIONARY MISCONCEPTIONS

More than almost any other field in the natural sciences, evolutionary biology is subject to depredations and misinterpretations by people with no professional background in the area. To some extent this is healthy. Many evolutionary biologists have become well trained in disposing of the intellectual errors of creationists, mystics, and assorted crackpots. But discussion of issues requiring detailed and abstract reasoning can be derailed by the interventions of the uninformed.

This has certainly occurred frequently where the evolution of aging is concerned. There are so many instances of it that any survey here would be exhausting. Rather than provide such a review, a single prominent example will be discussed as an illustration of the generic problem. This example is George Sacher's (1982) "Evolutionary Theory in Gerontology," a paper that effectively embodies much that is wrong in past evolutionary discussions of gerontology.

The first problem with this article is that it displays no real understanding of the literature on the evolution of aging that comes from population genetics. The critical work of Hamilton (1966) and Charlesworth (e.g., 1980) is not cited at all. The discussion of Medawar (1952) and Williams (1957) is radically misconceived. Some instances of this follow. (1) On p. 342, Sacher describes a "rejection by Medawar and Williams of an adaptive advantage for senescence." In fact, both authors supposed that antagonistic pleiotropy could lead to selection for increased rates of aging in association with enhanced fitness. (2) On p. 343, Sacher supposes that Medawar and Williams assume that "the lifespan can be partitioned into an initial phase of reproductive competence and a final, postreproductive phase, during which somatic senescence occurs." This is a misreading of their invocation of a declining force of natural selection, a force that both supposed to decline beginning around the onset of reproduction. (3) This leads Sacher (p. 343) to contrast the arguments of Medawar and Williams with "the better-supported hypothesis that whatever the factors that cause senescence, they are active throughout most of the lifespan." In fact, Williams (1957) in particular would agree with this hypothesis. If other gerontologists have taken the writings of Sacher and his like as their guide to the evolution of aging, then it is not surprising that little contribution was made by evolutionary theory to gerontology before 1980.

The second problem with this article is that, having disposed of population-genetics theory for the evolution of aging, it sets about constructing an alternative evolutionary theory of little cogency. This theory is based on the notion that immortality is not possible; limited life spans are simply the best that natural selection has achieved. This ignores the immortality of prokaryotes, fissile metazoa, and germ lines. Sacher invokes popular "longevity-assurance" ideas, especially longevity-assurance genes, which he contrasts with the "senescence genes" of population genetics. This comes out as "the antithetical hypothesis that length of life . . . is under positive genetic control" (p. 435). And so on. In fact, this theory is in no way antithetical to population genetics, in so far as it concerns genes that foster survival. It runs into trouble only when it comes to accounting for extant variation in life span, between and within species.

The third problem with this article is that it disparages the empirical salience of population genetics for aging research: "the senescence gene theory offers no assured path to fundamental discoveries" (p. 350). The experiments of Chapters 3 and 4 stand as adequate refutation of this assertion. Unfortunately, the views of Sacher had more currency within the gerontological literature than the population-genetic research on aging that he supposedly was qualified to address. Recently, evolutionary biologists have begun to publish in gerontological journals (e.g., Rose and Graves, 1989), so the present discussion may be mostly of historical value.

## GOMPERTZ FUNCTIONS AND MORTALITY PATTERNS

One of the fixations of gerontology concerns the shape of the curve relating the number of survivors of a cohort to their chronological age. As discussed in Chapter 2, some presume to measure the aging of individuals from such actuarial properties of cohorts. More generally, gerontologists have shared the conviction that such curves reveal fundamental features of the process of aging. Human mortality data in modern Western nations have tended to exhibit exponential increases in instantaneous mortality rates, a pattern noted by Benjamin Gompertz in the nineteenth century, and formalized as follows:

$$R_m = (-1/n)dn/dt = R_o e^{ct},$$

where $R_m$ gives the instantaneous mortality rate, $n$ is the size of the cohort at any moment, $R_o$ is the initial mortality rate at age zero, $c$ is a fitted constant, and $t$ is the chronological age of the cohort. A number of ingenious theories of mortality have been put forward to relate the Gompertz function to physiological deterioration with age, some of which are reviewed by Mildvan and Strehler (1960). Some gerontologists regard the conformity of mortality data to Gompertz functions as a test of the degree to which the cohort under study dies off because of aging.

The typical form of survival data from iteroparous species dying of aging is that of a plateau followed by a drop toward zero, shown in many of the figures throughout this book. It should be noted that this is necessarily the form of the curves generated by Eq. (1.6) for iteroparous species. Before the start of reproduction, the force of selection is high, and does not change with age. This should produce a plateau of high survival probability when young organisms are observed under good laboratory conditions. During the period of reproduction, the force of selection acting on survival steadily falls. This should give rise to declining survival probabilities and thus a declining survivorship curve. Finally, all organisms should be dead not too far into the postreproductive period, when the force of selection acting on survival probability is zero. Thus the "Gompertz" form of mortality iteroparous species may be due to a broad conformity of mortality to the intensity of natural selection acting on age-specific mortality rates. However, any direct relationship will be greatly clouded by patterns of pleiotropy, some of which may extend the plateau, while others may cause survivor numbers to drop off more rapidly.

## "PROGRAMMED" VERSUS "STOCHASTIC" AGING

At present, one of the most prevalent dichotomies according to which theories of aging are organized is that of programmed versus stochastic (or unprogrammed) theories (e.g., Davies, 1983, Chapter 4). The definition of this distinction is often both confused and confusing (Hayflick, 1987).

The category of programmed aging sometimes depends upon a conflation of evolutionary and physiological mechanisms. For example, we have the following:

> . . . to speak of programming is to postulate a definite set or sequence of events which have been built into the organism through selection pressures. In other words, it is to postulate that there are direct or indirect selective advantages to limiting life span through aging. (Wilson, 1974)

Wilson goes on to write as if any theory of aging that allows for evolution of interspecific heterogeneity of life span is a "programmed aging" theory. Yet Kirkwood's (1977) expansion of error catastrophe theory explicitly takes evolution into account while nonetheless relying on an apparently "stochastic" mechanism (Chapter 7). Indeed, Wilson (1974) points out the confusion himself:

> It is probably possible to subsume almost any of the "*how*" theories of aging under the programmed theory, as there are many mechanisms whereby aging could be built into an organism. Even the mutation theory, with the stipulation that some DNA repair mechanism be shut-off to trigger aging, *could* be incorporated as the aging mechanism programmed into an organism.

At other times, the term *programmed aging* seems to involve a conflation of genetic and developmental determination (e.g., Russell, 1987). Sometimes, programmed aging is regarded as aging that is determined in as precise a manner as normal developmental processes, a pattern that is characteristic of aging only in semelparous species. In other cases, programmed aging is taken to mean determination of aging patterns by genetic variation (Johnson, 1987). In general, these ambiguities of definition have probably been critical in keeping alive a metatheoretical concept that is either wrong, when defined precisely, or trivial, when defined broadly.

What of the other side of the dichotomy, stochastic theories of aging? Davies (1983, p. 24) suggests that such theories concern "*random damage* to *cellular structures* which leads eventually to tissue disorganization" (emphasis in the original). Davies (1983, pp. 27–36) includes the following types of theories under this heading: lipofuscin accumulation, collagen cross-linkage, free-radical damage, somatic mutation, and translation error catastrophe. Yet it must be wondered whether or not cells are simply programmed to develop in such a way that they forfeit repair options that would counter such forms of deterioration. After all, germ-cell lineages are potentially immortal.

No aspect of an organism's physiology can be wholly determined by a genetic program, while no form of random damage can be wholly independent of organism's repair and replacement capacities. The use of the terms *programmed* and *stochastic* fosters obscurity rather than clarity.

Perhaps a more constructive contribution to these metatheoretical debates can be made by evolutionary biology. The classic examples of programmed aging come from semelparous species. In such species, antagonistic pleiotropy has led to the evolution of an extreme sacrifice of later survival for initial reproduction. The physiological genetic means for this would be alleles that are actively fostered by natural selection to push for maximal reproduction, at the expense of the adult soma. This could be crudely described as a kind of "programming." Therefore, the former programmed–stochastic distinction could be better reformulated as a distinction between physiological mechanisms of aging involving dramatic antagonistic pleiotropy and those that do not.

## Further Theoretical Development

What has been offered here is not a final synthesis of theoretical issues pertaining to aging. There is a great deal of detailed work that could be done on any of the issues raised. Evidently, the point of view developed here presumes that further theoretical development of gerontology should be based on evolutionary foundations.

A particular focus for further theoretical development might be hybrids of physiological and evolutionary genetic theories. One form that such a hybrid might take is explicit modeling of the reaction kinetics of specific enzymes involved in particular mechanisms of aging. Results obtained from these enzyme models might then be plugged into a population-genetic model, possibly to generate effects on age-specific components of fitness, and thus ultimately effects on fitness values.

## Experimental Issues

In fields lacking conceptual coherence, there is also usually a lack of effective experimental programs. To some degree, this has not been true of gerontology. Much information has been gathered concerning the diverse forms of aging exhibited by multicellular organisms, particularly short-lived species such as those of *Drosophila* or *Mus*. Aging may now be one of the best documented of biological phenomena.

Yet such extensive documentation has led to few general and successful physiological theories of aging, as discussed. The critical point is that of causation. There is little important work in science that is not concerned with causation. But while gerontology has not lacked scientists who have directly sought the causal foundations of aging, they have had little success empirically. This raises the question of the appropriate experimental methods for causal research on aging. Three empirical methods will be discussed now, with a view to developing a methodological analysis of experimental gerontology founded upon evolutionary biology.

## Shortening Life Span

A classic method of causal analysis is to analyze circumstances in which the phenomena of interest are changed. In the context of aging, the easiest change to study is shortening life span. Many examples of such research have already been mentioned, particularly in Chapters 2, 3, and 6. There are two basic types of manipulation used to shorten life span: environmental and genetic. Each will be discussed in turn.

### ENVIRONMENTALLY REDUCING LIFE SPAN

Life span is readily truncated in irrelevant ways: decapitation, starvation, freezing, and so on. For the purposes of gerontological investigation, the attempt has usually been to find environmental treatments that do not abruptly kill, but instead give rise to survivorship curves of the same general form as those of control organisms. Radiation was one of the more frequently used treatments of this kind, as discussed in Chapter 7. In poikilotherms, particularly insects, elevation of ambient temperature often has a similar effect (Chapter 6).

Experiments of this kind have been performed for decades now, without yielding many profound insights. The problem is a virtually intractable one: whether or not the shortened life span is the result of the introduction of a novel mortality source that has nothing to do with the process of aging in the control organisms (Maynard Smith, 1966). In a sense, one has simply created a new empirical problem: What determines when the specially treated organisms die? Before the problem was only what determines the timing of death and reproduction in the control population. The assumption that both control and treated organisms die of the same causes, only at different times due to an acceleration of aging, is unwarranted unless the factors regulating aging are known at the outset and can then be shown to have accelerated aging in the treated organisms. Life-shortening environmental treatments, on their own, introduce new empirical puzzles without helping to solve extant puzzles.

### GENETICALLY REDUCING LIFE SPAN

Genetic manipulation that shortens life span might seem more defensible, on first inspection. After all, it is a standard method of genetic analysis of specific characters to create null mutants at loci to knock out subsidiary functions or steps that contribute to the character of interest. Obvious examples of such mutants are eye-color mutants in *Drosophila* or auxotrophic mutants in *Escherichia coli*. Since the pioneering work in Pearl's laboratory (Pearl, 1922; Pearl and Parker, 1922; Gonzalez, 1923), many mutants decreasing life span in organisms such as *Drosophila* have been found (e.g., Bozcuk, 1981). Then there are the various progeroid disorders in man, presumably genetic in nature (Martin, 1978), discussed in Chapter 2. It is also easy to create laboratory inbred stocks of differing mean longevities (Giesel, 1979; Giesel and Zettler, 1980; Sprott, 1983, 1985).

Unfortunately, the hope that such genetic studies would lead to the discovery of "longevity loci" has proved bankrupt. One reason for this is that genetic pathology can introduce novel causes of death, just as environmental manipulation can. Another reason is that patterns of survival and reproduction do not constitute well-defined characters in the same way that eye color or amino acid synthesis do. Some characters depend on a relatively well-defined and small set of biochemical processes, themselves determined by only a few loci, without too much environmental sensitivity. These characters can be profitably analyzed using mutagenesis, complementation tests, and the like. Other characters depend on many loci, at least in the sense that many mutations of major effect, such as null mutants, are likely to affect these characters, perhaps because such characters are dependent on the functioning of many organismal components. Examples of these characters are body mass, fecundity, developmental time, locomotor performance, and so on. Such characters are also almost invariably sensitive to diverse environmental influences, often quite recondite ones. Such characters are best analyzed using the tools of quantitative genetics (vide Falconer, 1981), along the lines illustrated in Chapters 3 and 4. Alleles of major deleterious effect do not provide opportunities to unravel the biological foundations of such characters, in most cases, and especially not when these characters are fitness related. If they did, then the history of population genetics would be quite different, since deleterious alleles are so easily generated by artificial mutagenesis, but have not proved useful in unraveling the genetics of fitness (Lewontin, 1974; Wright, 1977).

At this point, it seems fair to conclude that shortening life span will not normally be a useful method of studying aging. It might be when a great deal is known of the causes of aging in control populations, perhaps to refine knowledge of the causes of aging when such knowledge is sufficiently great that the introduction of artifactual sources of mortality would be readily detected. In any case, shortening life span will not break ground for investigations leading to such knowledge.

## The Use of the Comparative Method

From all that has been said here about the ultimate cause of aging being evolutionary, it might be supposed that the comparative method would be offered as the highway to certain knowledge concerning the physiology of aging. But there are many traps into which the comparative method may lead an investigation. Three of these traps seem particularly germane to the use of the comparative method in gerontology.

The first, and most important, of these traps is that a correlation between rates of aging and particular physiological characters could arise from *either* selective or physiological associations between senescence and the physiological characters.

For example, Sacher (1959) demonstrated statistical correlations between maximum longevity and body size or cephalization in mammals, and he explained this correlation in terms of "regulatory" and "homeostatic" systems (e.g., Sacher, 1978). An alternative possibility is that larger mammals are relatively less subject to death due to predation, starvation, climatic extremes, etc., particularly if they also have larger brain sizes, and therefore these species may have survivorship curves in the wild that do not decline very rapidly (Charlesworth, 1980, p. 221). This will give rise to a slower decline in the force of natural selection with respect to age after the onset of reproduction, compared with that of small mammals. This in turn will then lead to the evolution of slower rates of aging, all other things being equal. There is some degree of physiology in this alternative hypothesis, but it is the physiology of survival and reproduction, instead of the physiology of aging. In this view, there need not be any relationship between body size and rates of aging that is inherent in the physiology of the organism. The relationship instead may depend on ecological associations. It should be emphasized, though, that this physiological ecology is that obtaining in the species' original habitat, not that obtaining under the conditions of careful husbandry used in appropriate assays of longevity or age-specific reproduction.

The second major problem is that of confounding variables, particularly body size. It is well known that a host of biological variables evolve in association with body size, for whatever reasons, so that comparative analyses must allow for the effects of body size on the evolution of the characters concerned (Clutton-Brock and Harvey, 1979). Evidently, maximum longevity is a species characteristic that is positively correlated with body size, for whatever reason, especially in mammals (Prothero and Jürgens, 1987). Therefore, it is naive to perform statistical analyses of comparative patterns of cell proliferation or cell physiology without using multivariate regression techniques to mitigate the problem of simply testing for associations between species body size and cell characteristics. Hart and Setlow's (1974) work on DNA repair or Röhme's (1981) work on cell proliferation limits are cases in point. Elephants, men, and horses are quite large, as well as long-lived, relative to rodents, so that the lack of allowance for this confounding variable of size—which need have no direct physiological connection with rates of aging—must call into question studies of this kind that rely entirely on bivariate regressions. The solution to this problem is to use the kind of multivariate regression now common in evolutionary biology (e.g., Stearns, 1983), in which the dependent character is regressed on body size first, and then regressions using the other variables are performed on the residuals. These methods can largely alleviate the problem of body-size effects.

Third, there is the problem of phylogenetic independence. In looking for comparative patterns in the association of characters, it is tacitly assumed that each taxon constitutes an evolutionarily independent unit. If this is invalid, the number of degrees of freedom in a statistical analysis of comparative patterns will be gravely overestimated. Consider an extreme example, correlation between limb number and skeletal structure, specifically the endoskeleton–exoskeleton contrast. If 80 insect species and 60 mammalian species are used in a linear regression, with $-1$ scored for an endoskeleton, 0 scored for no skeleton, and $+1$ scored for possession of an exoskeleton, then the resulting pattern will be that of a straight line between two points, because all the species pile up on one or the other of two points, $(-1,4)$ or $(1,6)$ in Cartesian coordinates, and the regression is perfect, with enormous statistical significance, there being 138 degrees of freedom, supposedly. Obviously, there are only two independent data points, and no degrees of freedom, two points always allowing a perfect fit to a straight line.

Likewise, consider a comparative study that uses five rodent species (say two

*Mus,* a *Peromyscus,* and two *Rattus*), an ungulate (say *Equus*), as well as two primates (*Homo* and *Pan*). The ungulate is large and herbivorous. The primates are both medium sized and omnivorous, as well as relatively biped. The rodents are all very small by comparison with the other two groups and subsist on broadly similar omnivorous diets, quite different from those of the two primate omnivores. A bivariate regression between maximum longevity and some physiological variable has only one defensible degree of freedom, since two degrees of freedom are used up in estimating the slope and intercept of the regression line, with the means over each of the three groups of species used as single data points. What had seemed like a reasonably powerful comparative test in fact is remarkably weak. This makes the selection of species for comparative analysis, as well as the use of data from groups of related species, a matter requiring some attention to phylogeny. [See also Huey (1987).]

None of the foregoing strictures should be read as simple condemnations of the use of the comparative method in gerontology. Indeed, it could well be one of the most valuable methods for winnowing the great mass of still undigested, which is to say untested, physiological theories of aging. Such value as the method has, however, is confined to studies in which it is more or less correctly used, such as Stearns (1983). At present, such studies are rather sparse where aging is concerned.

## Postponing Aging

Ultimately, the power of empirical knowledge is revealed in its ability to help us accomplish difficult, often amazing, feats. Few could doubt that modern physics was really on to something after the events of the summer of 1945 had taken place. For gerontology, the acid test is clear: Once gerontologists are able to postpone aging in man, the standing of the discipline will be firmly established.

A surprising feature of gerontological research since 1950 is the lack of research on means of postponing aging. This may be due in part to the scientist's natural desire to avoid any connotation of quackery, which of course abounds where the postponement of aging is concerned. Another reason may be that it has simply proved hard to postpone aging in mammals, leaving aside nutritional restriction of adult rodents, which was clearly demonstrated only in the 1980s (Chapter 6). This situation is now changing, and the prospects are there for a major realignment of research. Before these are discussed, some of the finer distinctions between methods of postponing aging should be discussed.

Many aspects of the postponement of aging have already been discussed, especially in Chapters 2, 3, and 6. Those chapters should have made it clear that, in principle, there are many different ways to postpone aging. One obvious distinction is that between environmental and genetic manipulation to postpone aging. Running orthogonal to the genetic–environmental dichotomy are distinctions that hinge on the effects on fitness of postponing aging.

### EFFECTS ON FITNESS

The first type of effect is postponement of aging in conjunction with enhancement of early fitness components. In environments that are *not* novel, evolutionarily, it can be presumed that natural selection normally would have maximized the mean fitness, and thus produced high values for early fitness components in most organisms. Therefore, opportunities for material enhancement of early fitness along with postponement of aging must normally hinge on the rescue of the organism from some type of pathology. Both genetic and environmental examples are readily given.

Inbred lines derived from outbred populations will often be subject to diminished early fitness components in association with accelerated aging. Crossing such lines produces hybrid vigor, in which both fitness and longevity are enhanced (Crow, 1948; Clarke and Maynard Smith, 1955). Such results are not to be expected in crosses of lines from organisms that normally inbreed, and indeed are not found (Johnson and Wood, 1982).

In cases in which a population is subjected to extreme environmental conditions, in which its maintenance from generation to generation is marginal, it may also exhibit accelerated aging. Radiation and extreme temperatures are examples of such regimes. Removal from these deleterious environments would then simultaneously enhance fitness and retard aging. Generally speaking, such cases of postponed aging are not of particular interest for gerontology.

The genetic or environmental imposition of functional pathology and subsequent rescue are of value in studies of organismal function in general, with the modulation of senescence by such methods usually not the most convenient character to study. This method, then, is unlikely to be particularly fruitful for gerontology, being the other side of the coin in studies in which life span is shortened.

The second type of effect on fitness involves postponement of aging in association with reduced fitness, in effect trading fitness for aging. Genetic examples of this are afforded by the work on laboratory *Drosophila* populations in which indirect selection for postponed aging has led to reduced early fitness components (Wattiaux, 1968a; Rose and Charlesworth, 1981b; Luckinbill et al., 1984; Rose, 1984b), as discussed in Chapter 4. The *age-1* allele of *C. elegans* also provides an example in which longevity is increased in conjunction with reduced reproduction (Friedman and Johnson, 1988). Environmental examples of this are also to be found in *Drosophila,* in which enhancement of life span at lower temperatures is associated with greatly reduced early reproductive rates (Chapter 6). In *C. elegans* this same effect has been noted from experiments in which vitamin E was used to prolong life span (Harrington and Harley, 1988). In nutritionally restricted rodents, early reproduction is reduced in conjunction with increased life span (Holehan and Merry, 1985). All these are instances of reproductive effort tradeoffs, which take the form of antagonistic pleiotropy in the case of genetic tradeoffs. Such tradeoffs should be of major concern to gerontologists, since they tie aging to adaptation in a way that they seem to take little account of. Specific experimental projects relating to potential antagonisms between aging and fitness will be discussed shortly.

The third type of effect on fitness arises when postponement of aging proceeds without material effects on fitness itself. In the genetic context, such opportunities arise when deleterious alleles with effects confined to older ages are prevalent. Then selection regimes that favor survival to, and reproduction at, later ages have no effect at earlier ages. As yet, there is only a little evidence for the existence of such alleles, as discussed in Chapter 4. In the environmental context, cases of postpone-ment of this kind would be most readily detected by experimental manipulation of organisms that had little "reproductive life" left, in that effects on fitness could be discounted in advance. No such techniques seem to have been found yet. In fact, this approach to the postponement of aging seems to be little appreciated.

It should be mentioned that selection regimes that select for postponed aging without simultaneous selection on early reproduction, such as culture methods that use older adults to produce the next generation, will select for alleles having a range of effects on fitness itself. But if the founding population(s) had already been selected for some time, in the same environment, with reproduction at early ages, almost all the alleles that would increase in frequency in the population(s) selected for postponed aging will be either neutral or deleterious in their effects on early reproduction. (In such cases, alleles that were always beneficial at all ages would already have approached fixation.) Thus such selection regimes may postpone aging by either of the remaining two options, depressing fitness or having no effect. Analogously, the effects on aging of environmental treatments throughout life that are compared with controls kept under good conditions may yield postponed aging in conjunction with reduced or unaltered fitness. A critical question for our under-standing of the physiology of aging is the extent to which postponement of aging entails reduced fitness. Experiments of these two kinds, in which either type of postponed aging may arise, could effectively address this question.

## ENVIRONMENTALLY POSTPONING AGING

While it has been well known for some time that the rate of aging of invertebrates can be readily altered by manipulation of adult or larval culture conditions, in ways that correspond to normal environmental variation, there has been surprisingly little research devoted to uncovering the physiological mechanisms that underlie such modulation of aging, the study of Miquel et al. (1976) being a salutary exception. Even such fundamental questions as the nature of the association between modula-tion of aging and effects on fitness are rarely addressed. A further point is the relationship between the physiological mechanisms controlling the modulation of aging by different environmental variables. Finally, there is the possibility of similar physiological mechanisms mediating *both* genetic and environmental postponement of aging. All these questions deserve concerted investigation using a well-studied, short-lived, invertebrate. *Drosophila* species have probably been more studied from this standpoint than those of any other genus, and therefore they constitute the organisms of choice. *C. elegans* would be another useful system with which to study this problem.

The experimental system for environmentally postponing aging that has re-ceived the most attention is restricted nutrition in rodents (Masoro, 1988; Chapter 6). The volume and quality of work on this system are approaching the awesome, at least by the standards of gerontology. The nagging problem remains that it is not clear whether the ad libitum fed rodent is a case of pathological aging, with the supposedly postponed aging of the restricted rodent then the normal aging pattern. This is a problem of profound importance for this body of research, a problem exacerbated by the use of inbred rodent stocks and their derivatives, because the

The Future of Gerontology

attributes of such stocks are very difficult to interpret from a selective standpoint. Here is an area in which evolutionary biology might be able to contribute a great deal, by work on more appropriate model systems.

For example, there is the possibility that an invertebrate metazoan system with well-worked-out genetics, like *Drosophila* or *C. elegans,* could be found to exhibit reproducible nutritional restriction effects like those in rodents. With the greater potential for rapid experimental investigation and genetic analysis in such a system, it might be possible to develop considerable insight into the role of energetic metabolism in the physiological genetics of aging. In particular, it would be interesting to test experimentally some of the evolutionary hypotheses (e.g., Harrison and Archer, 1988) that have been put forward to explain the nutritional restriction effect on life span. This could be done, for example, by creating laboratory selection regimes for different patterns of life-span modulation in response to diet.

SELECTIVELY POSTPONING AGING

As was shown in Chapter 3, there are few experimental projects easier than selecting for postponed aging in outbred populations, at least in principle. All that is needed is a culture procedure that denies effective reproductive opportunities to young adults. Direct artificial selection is not necessary. In effect, natural selection in the laboratory does the "work."

The "in principle" above reflects the fact that it is simply not practical to conduct an experiment of this kind with chimpanzees or elephants, to say nothing of oak, since the results would not be available for centuries. Thus an important constraint is the type of species that may be used in feasible experiments. The obvious choice is to work with relatively short-lived, small, iteroparous invertebrates, such as insects and nematodes. Indeed, there has been considerable success in the development of genetically longer-lived insect and nematode stocks (e.g., Rose and Charlesworth, 1981b; Luckinbill et al., 1984; Rose, 1984b; Johnson and Wood, 1982; Johnson, 1985). There are already several laboratories in North America that have stocks with genetically postponed aging together with appropriate control stocks.

The question then is, what should be done with such stocks? When they have been replicated independently, as in Rose (1984b), they provide material for testing hypotheses about the physiological basis of aging. Biological changes that are consistent over replicated lines exhibiting postponed aging can be presumed to reflect *either* the physiological changes required to postpone aging *or* the pleiotropic effects of the alleles responsible for such changes. In either case, both types of change are bound up with postponed aging, each being in a sense necessary.

This research strategy has already been started with *D. melanogaster* stocks selected for later reproduction (Rose, 1984b). [See also Arking et al. (1988), Luckinbill et al. (1988b), Graves, Luckinbill, and Nichols (1988), and Pretzlaff and Arking (1989) for work on similar, although less replicated, *D. melanogaster* stocks.] The gross morphological changes associated with postponed aging have been studied, including such characters as body weight, thorax weight, gonadal weight, digestive system weight, and head weight (Rose et al., 1984). The only reproducible change found was a twofold reduction in early adult ovary weight, corresponding to the reduction in early fecundity that had already been found to be associated with increased longevity (Rose and Charlesworth, 1981b; Rose, 1984b). Service et al. (1985) examined changes in stress resistance, finding increased resistance to starvation, low levels of ethanol, and desiccation, but not to heat stress or high levels of ethanol. (See Chapter 2 for more detail.) Such increased stress resistance was not age specific, for those characters that were tested, corresponding to the lack of age specificity in the mortality rate difference between the postponed aging stocks and their controls (Rose, 1984b). This work has been extended to some additional physiological characters: respiration rate, motor activity levels, and soluble lipid content (Service, 1987). There is a mixture of age-specific differences, some confined to early ages and some general over all ages, like the stress resistance differences. It should be noted that there is no reason to expect these findings to generalize to other experimental systems, like rodents or rotifers.

There is no limit to experiments of this kind, but one particular type deserves special mention: experiments that test for the type of differences predicted by one or another general physiological theory of aging. Evidently, a particular biological character or process cannot be "the pacemaker" of aging if it consistently exhibits no detectable change when aging itself has significantly changed. Thus stocks with postponed aging could be used to clear away a great deal of intellectual debris.

A question of considerable scientific interest is the number of loci that play a critical role in the modulation of aging (Cutler, 1982). As already discussed, postponed aging stocks provide material allowing an estimate of the minimum number of loci involved. There are two ways in which this can be done. One is to perform a quantitative-genetic gene-number estimate, as Luckinbill et al. (1987) and Hutchinson and Rose (1990) have done with *D. melanogaster* and Johnson (1987) with *C. elegans*. The net significance of these results, once problems of statistical bias are allowed for (Hutchinson and Rose, 1990), is that it is hard to show that the number of independently segregating factors contributing to postponed aging is smaller than the total number of chromosomes. The second approach is to test for the contributions of major chromosomes using balancer stocks. When this was done, a similar conclusion was obtained by Luckinbill et al. (1988a), who found that all the major chromosomes in *D. melanogaster* appear to contribute to the response to selection for postponed aging. This body of work indicates the importance of the quantitative-genetics framework for genetic studies of aging (vide Falconer, 1981).

## Experimental Systems

Having settled upon effective methods for the study of aging is not enough. The best experimental system(s) must also be chosen. To some extent, this will depend on the goals motivating the study.

### Reasoning from Cells to Organisms

Aging is an obvious feature of multicellular organisms, while cells are the primary building blocks of such organisms. An obvious reductionist strategy is to study cells in vitro, or under special in vivo conditions, in the hope of finding physiological causes of aging in a more readily manipulated object of study. The discovery of the Hayflick limit to in vitro cell proliferation in the early 1960s (Chapter 7) inflamed hopes that aging could be successfully unraveled by the study of cells, particularly in vitro. There are many difficulties with explaining organismal aging in terms of the Hayflick limit, as discussed in Chapter 7, and other cellular mechanisms of aging do not seem much more promising. Breakthroughs in our understanding of organismal aging have simply not been forthcoming from cell research.

Shifting attention to the molecular has hardly changed matters. Except for aging of the extracellular matrix, molecular mechanisms of aging should be effective among in vitro cells, yet the evidence that such cells senesce, per se, is controversial (vide Martin et al., 1974; Bell et al., 1978). Two of the best-studied molecular mechanisms of aging, DNA damage and error catastrophe, appear to be of low incidence and to have few consequences, as discussed in Chapter 7. Collagen undoubtedly ages, although the case that its aging is an important cause of mortality (Kohn, 1971) is not yet widely accepted. Unlike most biological fields, gerontology has not benefitted from the molecular revolution to any obvious extent, except perhaps in the availability of technology that allows falsification of erroneous molecular theories of aging. [An example of this would be the two-dimensional gel electrophoresis technique that has been used to such devastating effect against the error catastrophe theory (e.g., Parker et al., 1981).]

Nonetheless, the gerontological community has often persisted in a reductionist bent. Of 100 "key biomedical research goals in aging" listed by Strehler (1977, pp. 375–88), fewer than 20 involve research above the cellular level. Close inspection of the rest of this list reveals some interesting features of gerontological research strategies. Many of the research proposals involve basic questions of molecular or cellular biology: repression of mitosis by cell contact, neuronal cell biology, the fraction of the genome that is transcribed in differentiated cells, mechanisms of mRNA stabilization, the role of heterogeneous nuclear RNA, role of episomes in dosage maintenance, posttranscriptional modification of tRNAs in the control of gene expression. Further progress on aging is being tied to significant advances in our understanding of cell biology.

This entire research strategy implicitly denies the opportunities afforded by approaches that involve tools from evolutionary biology, quantitative genetics, and whole-organism physiology. That would hardly be regettable if reductionist gerontologists were going from success to success. But they have not been.

Instead, it would seem more reasonable for the considerable analytical talents of cellular and molecular gerontologists to be invested in systems that show promise of providing answers to questions about the mechanisms of aging, evolutionary, organismal, cellular, or molecular. In practical terms, this would mean performing those cellular or molecular experiments that offer some hope of an interpretable result. At present, there is no straightforward interpretation available for in vitro cell proliferation limits. This suggests that that system should receive less attention. Cytogerontologists might instead work on the cells of *Drosophila, Caenorhabditis,* or rodent stocks that have postponed aging, whether the postponement is environmental or genetic. Likewise, a molecular characterization of genetically longer-lived fruit flies or nematodes would seem to be of great potential value in testing general molecular theories of aging. Cellular and molecular research should not cease, although it should give up on finding "the cause" of aging, particularly as that goal seems to have been largely accomplished by evolutionary biology, to the extent that there is a "cause" to discover. Such research should instead be redirected towards unraveling the specific mechanisms that normally limit life span.

## How Many Invertebrate Systems Do We Need?

For the purpose of testing general physiological theories of aging experimentally, it is doubtful that there is any need for experimental systems other than small, short-lived, readily cultured invertebrates. Most plants and vertebrates live too long and are difficult to culture rapidly in large numbers. At present there are four important systems: *Drosophila, C. elegans,* rotifers, and yeast. Rotifers have seen a little use in aging research (e.g., Lansing, 1947; Meadow and Barrows, 1971; Enesco, Bozovic, and Anderson, 1989) but offer the potential for rapid cultivation of large populations of organisms that live for only brief periods. Yeast, that is *Saccharomyces cerevisiae,* is also extremely well known and readily manipulable genetically in aging research (e.g., Egilmez and Jazwinski, 1989). However, it is still uncertain that these two systems will prove to be indispensable.

The fate of rotifers and yeast as experimental systems notwithstanding, both *D. melanogaster* and *C. elegans* systems are indispensable. The two systems are among the best understood genetic models, and the genetic approach to aging is one that is attracting ever greater interest (Martin and Turker, 1988; Johnson, 1988a). An enormous amount of biology other than genetics is also known of both species. These are reasons for the retention of at least one of the two systems.

There are also important reasons for the retention of both together. First, *Drosophila* has giant polytene chromosomes, which allow in situ hybridization for gene mapping. On the other hand, *C. elegans* has a smaller genome, making the cloning and sequencing of it in its entirety much more feasible. Second, *C. elegans* has a strictly determined set of pathways for cell development, which could allow much greater power of cellular analysis (Johnson, 1984). On the other hand, such highly determinate patterns of cell development could be less widely representative than the less defined patterns of an organism like *D. melanogaster.* Third, *C. elegans* reproduces normally by self-fertilization; males are rare products of chromosomal nondisjunction. This has led to the evolution of low frequencies of recessive deleterious alleles and extensive homozygosity, which in turn forestall inbreeding depression for fitness-related characters (Johnson and Wood, 1982; Johnson, 1988a). This makes *C. elegans* the most powerful system for genetic analysis of *de novo* mutants affecting aging (e.g., Friedman and Johnson, 1988). On the other hand, such a genetic system makes the species unsuitable for population-genetic experiments involving natural selection in the laboratory, for which *D. melanogaster* has been the system of choice (e.g., Rose, 1984b). Furthermore, the genetic system of *D. melanogaster* is also more representative in this respect. There are a number of other points of relatively less significance, such as the fact that *C. elegans* can be frozen in liquid nitrogen and recovered intact, but they will not be listed further. [See also Johnson (1987).] It is clear enough that both of these invertebrate systems are well worth continued investigation from a gerontological standpoint.

## Postponing Human Aging

### MAMMALIAN SYSTEMS ARE REQUIRED

The choice of experimental systems with which to address basic science questions concerning aging is not the same as the choice of systems with which to address the task of postponing human aging. From an evolutionary standpoint, reasoning from the physiological particulars of aging in a nematode or insect to a mammal is unlikely to be valid, leaving aside the most general aspects of the evolution and genetics of aging. It would be just as valid as reasoning about the cellular physiology of vision from insect to octopus to mammal. Aging is as physiologically diverse as other whole-organism attributes, if not more so, because it is produced by evolutionary forces acting on the full range of genetic variability present in each species. (This is discussed further at the outset of this chapter.)

Therefore, an evolutionary biologist would have to emphasize the value of mammalian research on aging where biomedical research is concerned. Nonetheless, it is patently inefficient to seek to solve two problems at once and use mammalian systems for both basic science and medical research. Mammalian systems cannot remotely compete with invertebrate models in testing and refining fundamental theories of aging, whether evolutionary or physiological. Their only advantage lies in the spillover from medical knowledge, particularly where pathology is concerned. But that again returns to the context of medical research.

Given that mammalian systems are required for medically relevant research on aging, what particular kinds are appropriate? It would seem self-evident that the relevant systems are those in which aging has been postponed, whether environmentally or genetically. Each of these cases will be discussed in turn.

### FOOD RESTRICTION

The only means now known for postponing mammalian aging is food restriction of rodents (Masoro, 1988). The central question for interpreting this work is whether the food-restricted rodent is in fact just the normal control relative to a pathological rodent fed ad libitum. As discussed in Chapter 6, this question admits of no clear answer with inbred and other artificial laboratory stocks. Answering it is an important task, which may well require some research into the ecological physiology of rodent nutrition. Evolutionary biology and physiological ecology may be able to assist in this task. As discussed above, one form such assistance might take is unraveling the evolution of nutritional restriction responses in a more tractable system than a rodent. In the meantime, it is difficult to give a good interpretation of the food-restriction work.

### THE VALUE OF RODENTS WITH
### SELECTIVELY POSTPONED AGING

In principle, selection for postponed aging on replicated, outbred, rodent laboratory stocks does not face these same problems of interpretation. However, the creation of such stocks poses many practical problems of design (Johnson, 1988b; Rose, 1988; Charlesworth, 1988). In any case, with such selected stocks, it may be possible to obtain considerable knowledge of the physiological mechanisms involved in genetically postponed aging in a small mammal, after the fashion of the *Drosophila* research. To this point, indeed, the research program is wholly analogous to that being pursued now with *D. melanogaster*.

However, further work with such a system might take an entirely different direction. Knowledge of the physiology of postponed aging in a rodent model might then allow more direct physiological intervention by means of substances like hormones to trigger the action of such mechanisms without either selection or gross external alteration of rearing conditions. Such hormonal controls might be general to all mammals. In the view of aging presented here, this may be the best prospect for substantially postponing human senescence.

But, before this rodent research program should be undertaken, preparatory work on model systems must be pursued. In total, three phases of research would be needed to implement this program to postpone human aging. The first would be the study of postponed aging in the most tractable invertebrate systems, *D. melanogaster* and *C. elegans*. Such studies are in any case useful for addressing the basic scientific questions involving aging. Work with such systems would reveal whether or not the idea of intervening in organismal physiology to postpone aging, based on knowledge of genetically postponed aging, is practical. If it cannot be done with the best understood and most readily manipulated metazoa, then there is little reason to suppose that it could be done for mammals.

Second, if it does prove possible to postpone aging in small invertebrate metazoa by means analogous to those of medical intervention, the next phase of research should be to achieve the same goal in a rodent species. The research strategy could be just like that used for work on fruit flies, selection to postpone aging in a particular mammal, with subsequent research devoted to determining the physiological mechanisms underlying the successful postponement.

Of course, this experimental program will be much more difficult to prosecute with mammals. Obviously it will take more time, per generation, to select for late reproduction, on the order of a year per generation. If ten generations are required for a significant response to selection, then the project could take on the order of 6–8 years. A further complicating factor is the lack of a close association between cessation of reproduction in female mammals and their death. Perhaps the best prospect for mitigation of this problem would be if (1) later reproductive success in females is dependent on aging processes that bring about death much later, or (2) later male reproductive success is also made a primary target of selection. While the specific protocol for selection is difficult to determine *a priori*, it seems almost certain that selection for postponed rodent aging would eventually be successful.

The task would then be to develop some understanding of the physiological genetics underlying selectively postponed aging in rodents. This would require adventitious exploitation of a number of different avenues of whole-organism, cellular, and biochemical research. Once an appreciable understanding of the causal basis for selectively postponed aging has been developed in the rodent model, it may be possible to intervene in a medical fashion in order to postpone aging for such a mammal. If such methods of intervention are found, they could be tested on dogs or chimpanzees for the generality with which the technique of intervention can postpone senescence among mammalian species.

The third and final phase of research would involve the use of such techniques of intervention with normal human subjects. There is little reason to suppose that progeroid individuals would be appropriate test subjects, since their leading mechanisms of aging are probably quite different from those affecting the rest of the population.

Nothing in this prospect suggests the possibility of immediately postponing human aging. However, there do not seem to be any other proposals that are plausible strategies, particularly in view of the lack of credibility of all nonevolutionary theories of aging. If the fundamental thesis of this book is correct, that the evolutionary theory of aging is the only fundamental and valid theory of aging, then attempts to postpone human aging on the basis of other theories are not likely to be successful. It has been supposed by some (e.g., Sacher, 1978) that the acceptance of the evolutionary theory of aging should lead to despair of ever alleviating the miseries of human aging. On the contrary, the evolutionary theory suggests that there are no ineluctable physiological causes of aging, only a failure of natural selection to "pay attention" to the problem. With the help of natural selection in the laboratory and the technology of modern gerontology, there are no absolute constraints preventing the postponement of human aging, only practical ones. With diligence, future generations may see even these practical constraints overcome.

# BIBLIOGRAPHY

Abugov, R. (1986) Genetics of Darwinian fitness. III. A generalized approach to age struc-
tured selection and life history. *J. Theor. Biol.* 122:311–23.

Albertini, R. J., and R. DeMars (1973) Somatic cell mutation: Detection and quantification
of X-ray-induced mutation in cultured, diploid human fibroblasts. *Mutat. Res.* 18:199–
224.

Albin, R. L. (1988) The pleiotropic gene theory of senescence: Supportive evidence from
human genetic disease. *Eth. Sociobiol.* 9:371–82.

Allemand, R. (1977) Le potentiel reproducteur des adultes de *Drosophila melanogaster*.
Variations genétiques en réponse aux regimes lumineux. *Genetica* 47:1–7.

Allemand, R., Y. Cohet, and J. David (1973) Increase in the longevity of adult *Drosophila
melanogaster* kept in permanent darkness. *Exp. Gerontol.* 8:279–83.

Allemand, R., Y. Cohet, and O. Savolainen (1976) Effects of different light regimes on the
egg production and egg hatchability of *Drosophila melanogaster* adults. *Acta ent.
Bohemslov.* 73:76–85.

Alpatov, W. W., and R. Pearl (1929) Experimental studies in the duration of life. XII.
Influence of temperature during the larval period and adult life on the duration of life of
the imago of *Drosophila melanogaster*. *Am. Nat.* 63:37–67.

Altman, P. L., and D. S. Dittmer (1972) *Biology Data Book,* Second edition. Federation of
American Societies for Experimental Biology, Bethesda.

Ames, B. N. (1983) Dietary carcinogens and anticarcinogens. *Science* 221:1256–64.

Ames, B. N., W. E. Durston, E. Yamasaki, and F. D. Lee (1973) Carcinogens are mutagens:
A sample test system combining liver homogenates for activation and bacteria for
detection. *Proc. Natl. Acad. Sci. USA* 70:2281–85.

Anderson, O. R. (1988) *Comparative Protozoology: Ecology, Physiology, Life History*.
Springer-Verlag, Berlin.

Aristotle. *De Longitudine et Brevitate Vitae*. Trans. by G. R. T. Ross (1908), Clarendon
Press, Oxford.

Arking, R., S. Buck, R. A. Wells, and R. Pretzlaff (1988) Metabolic rates in genetically
based long lived strains of *Drosophila*. *Exp. Gerontol.* 23:59–76.

Asdell, S. A., and M. F. Crowell (1935) The effect of retarded growth upon the sexual
development of rats. *J. Nutr.* 10:13–24.

Balin, A. K., D. B. G. Goodman, H. Rasmussen, and V. J. Cristofalo (1977) The effect of
oxygen and vitamin E on the lifespan of human diploid cells in vitro. *J. Cell Biol.*
74:58–67.

Baltimore, D. (1981) Somatic mutation gains its place among the generators of diversity. *Cell*
26:295–96.

Barrows, Jr., C. H., and G. C. Kokkonen (1978) Diet and life extension in animal model
systems. *Age* 1:131–43.

Bell, A. E., C. H. Moore, and D. C. Warren (1955) The evaluation of new methods of
improvement for quantitative characters. *Cold Spring Harbor Symp. Quant. Biol.*
20:197–212.

Bell, E., L. F. Marek, D. S. Levinstone, C. Merrill, S. Sher, I. T. Young, and M. Eden

(1978) Loss of division potential in vitro: aging or differentiation? *Science* 202:1158–63.

Bell, G. (1984a) Measuring the cost of reproduction. I. The correlation structure of the life table of a plankton rotifer. *Evolution* 38:300–313.

Bell, G. (1984b) Measuring the cost of reproduction. II. The correlation structure of the life tables of five freshwater invertebrates. *Evolution* 38:314–26.

Bell, G. (1984c) Evolutionary and nonevolutionary theories of senescence. *Am. Nat.* 124:600–3.

Bell, G. (1988) *Sex and Death in Protozoa, The History of an Obsession.* Cambridge University Press, Cambridge.

Berrill, N. J. (1951) Regenerating and budding in tunicates. *Biol. Rev.* 26:456–75.

Bertrand, H. A. (1983) Nutrition–aging interactions: Life-prolonging action of food restriction. *Rev. Biol. Res. Aging* 1:359–78.

Beverton, R. J. H. (1987) Longevity in fish: some ecological and evolutionary considerations. In: *Evolution of Longevity in Animals,* A. D. Woodhead and K. H. Thompson (eds.). Plenum Press, New York, pp. 161–85.

Bidder, G. P. (1925) The mortality of plaice. *Nature* 115:495–96.

Bidder, G. P. (1932) Senescence. *Br. Med. J.* 115:5831.

Bierbaum, T. J., L. D. Mueller, and F. J. Ayala (1989) Density-dependent selection of life-history traits in *Drosophila melanogaster. Evolution* 43:382–92.

Birchenall-Sparks, M. C., M. S. Roberts, J. Staecker, J. P. Hardwick, and A. Richardson (1985) Effect of dietary restriction on liver protein synthesis in rats. *J. Nutr.* 115:944–50.

Bjorksten, J. (1974) Crosslinkage and the aging process. In: *Theoretical Aspects of Aging,* M. Rockstein (ed.). Academic Press, New York, pp. 43–59.

Bozcuk, A. N. (1972) DNA synthesis in the absence of somatic cell division associated with ageing in *Drosophila subobscura. Exp. Gerontol.* 7:147–56.

Bozcuk, A. N. (1976) Testing the protein error hypothesis of ageing in *Drosophila. Exp. Gerontol.* 11:103–12.

Bozcuk, A. N. (1981) Genetic longevity in *Drosophila.* V. The specific and hybridised effect of *Rolled, Sepia, Ebony* and *Eyeless* autosomal mutants. *Exp. Gerontol.* 16:415–27.

Bradley, A. J., I. R. McDonald, and A. K. Lee (1980) Stress and mortality in a small marsupial (*Antechinus stuartii,* Macleay). *Gen. Comp. Endocrinol.* 40:188–200.

Brandes, D. (1966) Lysosomes and aging pigment. In: *Topics in the Biology of Aging: A Symposium Held at the Salk Institute for Biological Studies,* San Diego, California, November 4–6, 1965. P. L. Krohn (ed.). Interscience Publishers, New York, pp. 149–57.

Brenner, S. (1974) The genetics of *Caenorhabditis elegans. Genetics* 77:71–94.

Brittnacher, J. G. (1981) Genetic variation and genetic load due to the male reproductive component of fitness in *Drosophila. Genetics* 97:719–30.

Brown, W. T. (1985) Genetics of human aging. *Rev. Biol. Res. Aging* 2:105–14.

Brown, W. T. (1987) Genetic aspects of aging in humans. *Rev. Biol. Res. Aging* 3:77–91.

Brown, W. T., and H. M. Wisniewski (1983) Genetics of human aging. *Rev. Biol. Res. Aging* 1:81–99.

Browne, R. A. (1982) The costs of reproduction in brine shrimp. *Ecology* 63:43–47.

Brown-Séquard, C. E. (1889) Du rôle physiologique et therapeutique d'un suc extrait de testicules d'animaux d'après nombre de faits observés chez l'homme (The physiological and therapeutic role of animal testicular extract based on several experiments in man). *Arch. Physiol. Norm. Pathol.* 1:739–46.

Bryant, D. M. (1979) Reproductive costs in the house martin (*Delichon urbica*). *J. Anim. Ecol.* 46:765–82.

Burcombe, J. V. (1972) Change in enzyme levels during ageing in *Drosophila melanogaster*. *Mech. Ageing Dev.* 1:213–25.

Burnet, F. M. (1974) *Intrinsic Mutagenesis: A Genetic Approach to Aging*. J. Wiley & Sons, New York.

Burnet, F. M. (1976) *Immunology, Aging, and Cancer: Medical Aspects of Mutation and Selection*. W. H. Freeman, San Francisco.

Buss, L. W. (1987) *The Evolution of Individuality*. Princeton University Press, Princeton.

Butlin, R. K., and T. H. Day (1985) Adult size, longevity and fecundity in the seaweed fly, *Coelopa frigida. Heredity* 54:107–10.

Cerami, A. (1985) Glucose as a mediator of aging. *J. Am. Geriatr. Soc.* 33:626–34.

Charlesworth, B. (1970) Selection in populations with overlapping generations. I. The use of Malthusian parameters in population genetics. *Theor. Popul. Biol.* 1:352–70.

Charlesworth, B. (1974) Selection in populations with overlapping generations. VI. Rates of change of gene frequency and population growth rate. *Theor. Popul. Biol.* 6:108–33.

Charlesworth, B. (1976) Natural selection in age-structured populations. In: *Lectures on Mathematics in the Life Sciences*, S. A. Levin (ed.). American Mathematical Society, Providence, pp. 69–87.

Charlesworth, B. (1979) Evidence against Fisher's theory of dominance. *Nature* 278:848–49.

Charlesworth, B. (1980) *Evolution in Age-Structured Populations*. Cambridge University Press, Cambridge.

Charlesworth, B. (1987) The heritability of fitness. In: *Sexual Selection: Testing the Alternatives*, J. W. Bradbury and M. B. Andersson (eds.), John Wiley & Sons, New York, pp. 21–40.

Charlesworth, B. (1988) Selection for longer-lived rodents. *Growth Dev. Aging* 52:211.

Charlesworth, B., and J. A. Williamson (1975) The probability of survival of a mutant gene in an age-structured population and implications for the evolution of life-histories. *Genet. Res.* 26:1–10.

Charlesworth, D., and B. Charlesworth (1987) Inbreeding depression and its evolutionary consequences. *Ann. Rev. Ecol. Syst.* 18:237–68.

Child, C. M. (1915) *Senescence and Rejuvenescence*. University of Chicago Press, Chicago.

Clare, M. J., and L. S. Luckinbill (1985) The effects of gene–environment interaction on the expression of longevity. *Heredity* 55:19–29.

Clark, A. G. (1987) Senescence and the genetic-correlation hang-up. *Am. Nat.* 129:932–40.

Clark, A. M., and M. H. Rubin (1961) The modification by X-irradiation of the life span of haploids and diploids of the wasp, *Harbrobrocon* sp. *Radiat. Res.* 15:224–53.

Clarke, J. M., and J. Maynard Smith (1955) The genetics and cytology of *Drosophila subobscura*. XI. Hybrid vigor and longevity. *J. Genetics* 53:172–80.

Clarke, J. M., and J. Maynard Smith (1961a) Independence of temperature of the rate of ageing in *Drosophila subobscura. Nature* 190:1027–28.

Clarke, J. M., and J. Maynard Smith (1961b) Two phases of ageing in *Drosophila subobscura. J. Exp. Biol.* 38:679–84.

Clarke, J. M., and J. Maynard Smith (1966) Increase in the rate of protein synthesis with age in *Drosophila subobscura. Nature* 209:627–29.

Clutton-Brock, T. H., F. E. Guiness, and S. D. Albon (1982) *Red Deer: Behavior and Ecology of Two Sexes*. University of Chicago Press, Chicago.

Clutton-Brock, T. H., and P. H. Harvey (1979) Comparison and adaptation. *Proc. R. Soc. Lond.* B205:547–65.

Comfort, A. (1953) Absence of a Lansing effect in *Drosophila subobscura. Nature* 172:83–84.

Comfort, A. (1956) *The Biology of Senescence*. Routledge & Kegan Paul, London.

Comfort, A. (1960) The effect of age on growth-resumption in fish (*Lebistes*) checked by food restriction. *Gerontologia* 4:177–86.

Comfort, A. (1961) The longevity and mortality of a fish (*Lebistes reticulatus* Peters) in captivity. *Gerontologia* 5:209–22.

Comfort, A. (1964) *Ageing: The Biology of Senescence.* Holt, Rinehart & Winston, New York, Chicago, and San Francisco.

Comfort, A. (1971) Antioxidants and the control of ageing. *Ned. Tijdschr. Gerontol.* 2:82–87.

Comfort, A. (1979) *The Biology of Senescence,* Third edition. Churchill Livingstone, Edinburgh and London.

Comfort, A., I. Youhotsky-Gore, and K. Pathmanathan (1971) The effects of ethoxyquin on the longevity of C3H strain mice. *Nature* 229:254–55.

Cowdry, E. V. (1942) *Problems of Ageing: Biological and Medical Aspects,* Second edition. Williams & Wilkins, Baltimore.

Cristofalo, V. J. (1970) Metabolic aspects of aging in diploid human cells. In: *Aging in Cell and Tissue Culture.* E. Holeckova and V. J. Cristofalo (eds.). Plenum Press, New York, pp. 83–119.

Crow, J. F. (1948) Alternative hypotheses of hybrid vigor. *Genetics* 33:477–87.

Crow, J. F., and M. Kimura (1970) *An Introduction to Population Genetics Theory.* Harper and Row, New York.

Crowley, C., and H. J. Curtis (1963) The development of somatic mutations in mice with age. *Proc. Natl. Acad. Sci. USA* 49:626–28.

Curtis, H. J. (1963) Biological mechanisms underlying the aging process. *Science* 141:686–94.

Curtis, H. J. (1966) The role of somatic mutations in aging. In: *Topics in the Biology of Aging,* P. L. Krohn (ed.). John Wiley, New York, pp. 63–81.

Cutler, R. G. (1976) Nature of aging and life maintenance processes. *Interdis. Topics Gerontol.* 9:83–133.

Cutler, R. G. (1982) Longevity is determined by specific genes: Testing the hypothesis. In: *Testing the Theories of Aging,* R. Adelman and G. Roth (eds.). CRC Press, Boca Raton, pp. 25–114.

Daniel, C. W. (1977) Cell longevity: In vivo. In: *Handbook of the Biology of Aging,* C. E. Finch and L. Hayflick (eds.). Van Nostrand Reinhold, New York, pp. 122–58.

Danielli, J. F., and Muggleton, A. (1959) Some alternative states of amoeba, with special reference to life-span. *Gerontologia* 3:76–90.

Darwin, C. (1859) *The Origin of Species by Means of Natural Selection: Or the Preservation of Favoured Races in the Struggle for Life.* John Murray, London.

David, J., Y. Cohet, and P. Fouillet (1975) The variability between individuals as a measure of senescence: A study of the number of eggs laid and the percentage of hatched eggs in the case of *Drosophila melanogaster. Exp. Gerontol.* 10:17–25.

Davies, I. (1983) *Ageing.* Edward Arnold, London.

Davies, I., and A. P. Fotheringham (1981) Lipofuscin—Does it affect cellular performance? *Exp. Gerontol.* 16:119–25.

Denckla, W. D. (1974) Role of the pituitary and thyroid glands in the decline of minimal $O_2$ consumption with age. *J. Clin. Invest.* 53:572–81.

Denckla, W. D. (1975) A time to die. *Life Sci.* 16:31–44.

De Steven, D. (1980) Clutch size, breeding success, and parental survival in the tree swallow (*Iridoprocne bicolor*). *Evolution* 34:278–91.

De Witt, R. M. (1954) Reproductive capacity in a pulmonate snail, *Physagyrina Say. Am. Nat.* 88:159–64.

Dingley, F., and J. Maynard Smith (1969) Absence of a life-shortening effect of amino-acid analogues on adult *Drosophila*. *Exp. Gerontol.* 4:145–49.

Dobzhansky, Th. (1937) *Genetics and the Origin of Species.* Columbia University Press, New York.

Dobzhansky, Th. (1973) Nothing in biology makes sense except in the light of evolution. *Am. Biol. Teacher* 35:125–29.

Dobzhansky, Th., R. C. Lewontin, and O. Pavlovsky (1964) The capacity for increase in chromosomally polymorphic and monomorphic populations of *Drosophila pseudo-obscura*. *Heredity* 19:597–614.

Doolittle, W. F., and C. Sapienza (1980) Selfish genes, the phenotype paradigm and genome evolution. *Nature* 284:601–603.

Doyle, R. W., and W. Hunte (1981) Demography of an estuarine amphipod (*Gammarus lawrencianus*) experimentally selected for high "r": A model of the genetic effects of environmental change. *Can. J. Fish. Aquat. Sci.* 38:1120–27.

Dublin, L. I., A. J. Lotka, and M. Spiegelman (1949) *Length of Life—A Study of the Life Table*, Revised Edition. Ronald Press, New York.

Duesberg, P. H. (1983) Retroviral transforming genes in normal cells? *Nature* 304:219–26.

Duesberg, P. H. (1985) Activated proto-*onc* genes: Sufficient or necessary for cancer? *Science* 228:669–77.

Dueul, T. F., J. S. Huang, S. S. Huang, P. Stroobant, and M. D. Waterfield (1983) Expression of a platelet-derived growth factor-like protein in simian sarcoma virus transformed cells. *Science* 221:1348–50.

Duffy, P. H., J. A. Feuers, J. A. Leakey, K. D. Nakamura, A. Turturro, and R. W. Hart (1989) Effect of chronic caloric restriction on physiological variables related to energy metabolism in the male Fischer 344 rat. *Mech. Ageing Dev.* 48:117–33.

Edelman, P., and J. Gallant (1977) On the translational error theory of aging. *Proc. Natl. Acad. Sci. USA* 74:3396–98.

Edmondson, W. T. (1944) Ecological studies of sessile Rotatoria. I. Factors affecting distribution. *Ecol. Monogr.* 14:31–66.

Edmondson, W. T. (1945) Ecological studies of sessile Rotatoria. II. Dynamics of populations and social structures. *Ecol. Monogr.* 15:141–72.

Edney, E. B., and R. W. Gill (1968) Evolution of senescence and specific longevity. *Nature* 220:281–82.

Egilmez, N. K., and S. M. Jazwinski (1989) Evidence for the involvement of a cytoplasmic factor in the aging of the yeast *Saccharomyces cerevisiae*. *J. Bacteriol.* 171:37–42.

Elner, R. W., and R. N. Hughes (1978) Energy maximization in the diet of the shore crab, *Carcinus maervas*. *J. Anim. Ecol.* 47:103–16.

Enesco, H. E., V. Bozovic, and P. D. Anderson (1989) The relationship between lifespan and reproduction in the rotifer *Asplanchna brightwelli*. *Mech. Ageing Dev.* 48:281–89.

Epstein, C. J., G. M. Martin, A. L. Schultz, and A. G. Motulsky (1966) Werner's syndrome: A review of its symptomatology, natural history, pathologic features, genetics and relationship to the natural aging process. *Medicine* 45:177–221.

Etges, W. J. (1989) Chromosomal influences on life-history variation along an altitudinal transect in *Drosophila robusta*. *Am. Nat.* 133:83–110.

Ewens, W. J. (1979) *Mathematical Population Genetics.* Springer-Verlag, Berlin.

Failla, G. (1960) The aging process and somatic mutations. In: *The Biology of Aging*, AIBS Symp. Publ. No. 6, Washington, D.C., pp. 170–75.

Falconer, D. S. (1981) *Introduction to Quantitative Genetics*, Second edition. Longman, London.

Feramisco, J. R., M. Gross, T. Kamata, M. Rosenberg, and R. W. Sweet (1984) Microinjection of the oncogene form of the human H-*ras* (T-24) protein results in rapid proliferation of quiescent cells. *Cell* 38:109–17.

Feuers, R. J., P. H. Duffy, J. A. Leakey, A. Turturro, R. A. Mittelstaedt, and R. W. Hart (1989) Effect of chronic caloric restriction on hepatic enzymes of intermediary metabolism in the male Fischer 344 rat. *Mech. Ageing Dev.* 48:179–89.

Finch, C. E. (1987) Neural and endocrine determinants of senescence: Investigation of causality and reversibility by laboratory and clinical interventions. In: *Modern Biological Theories of Aging,* H. R. Warner, R. N. Butler, R. L. Sprott, and E. L. Schneider (eds.). Raven Press, New York, pp. 261–308.

Finch, C. E., and R. G. Gosden (1986) Animal models for the human menopause. In: *Aging, Reproduction and the Climacteric,* L. Mastroianni and C. A. Palulsen (eds.). Plenum Press, New York, pp. 3–34.

Fisher, R. A. (1928a) The possible modification of response of the wild type to recurrent mutation. *Am. Nat.* 62:115–26.

Fisher, R. A. (1928b) Two further notes on the origin of dominance. *Am. Nat.* 62:571–74.

Fisher, R. A. (1930) *The Genetical Theory of Natural Selection.* Clarendon Press, Oxford.

Fisher, R. A. (1958) *The Genetical Theory of Natural Selection,* Second revised edition. Dover Publications, New York.

Fleming, J. E., E. Quattrocki, G. Latter, J. Miguel, R. Marcuson, E. Zuckerkandl, and K. G. Bensch (1986) Age-dependent changes in proteins of *Drosophila melanogaster. Science* 231:1157–59.

Francis, A. A., W. H. Lee, and J. D. Regan (1981) The relationship of DNA excision repair of ultraviolet-induced lesions to the maximum lifespan of mammals. *Mech. Ageing Dev.* 16:181–89.

Freeman, J. T. (1938) The history of geriatrics. Ann. Med. Hist. 10:324–35.

Friedman, D. B., and T. E. Johnson (1988) A mutation in the *age-1* gene in *Caenorhabditis elegans* lengthens life and reduces hermaphrodite fertility. *Genetics* 118:75–86.

Fry, M., L. A. Loeb, and G. M. Martin (1981) On the activity and fidelity of chromatin-associated hepatic DNA polymerase-B in aging murine species of different life spans. *J. Cell. Physiol.* 106:435–44.

Fulder, S. J. (1975) The measurement of spontaneous mutation in mammalian somatic cells. *Nucleus* 18:98–107.

Fulder, S. J., and G. M. Tarrant (1975) Possible changes in gene activity during the ageing of human fibroblasts. *Exp. Gerontol.* 10:205–11.

Futuyma, D. J. (1986) *Evolutionary Biology,* Second edition. Sinauer Associates, Sunderland.

Gallant, J. (1981) Error catastrophe theory of cellular senescence. In: *Biological Mechanisms in Aging,* R. T. Schimke (ed.). U.S. Government Printing Office, Washington, D.C., pp. 373–81.

Gallant, J., and L. Palmer (1979) Error propagation in viable cells. *Mech. Ageing Dev.* 10:27–38.

Gallant, J. A., and J. Prothero (1980) Testing models of error propagation. *J. Theor. Biol.* 83:561–78.

Ganetzky, B., and J. R. Flanagan (1978) On the relationship between senescence and age-related changes in two wild-type strains of *Drosophila melanogaster. Exp. Gerontol.* 13:189–96.

Georgiadis, N. (1985) Growth patterns, sexual dimorphism and reproduction in African ruminants. *Afr. J. Ecol.* 23:75–88.

Gershon, H., and D. Gershon (1970) Detection of inactive enzyme molecules in aging of the organism. *Nature* 227:1214–17.

Herrewege, J. (1974) Nutritional requirements of adult *Drosophila melanogaster:* The influence of the casein concentration on the duration of life. *Exp. Gerontol.* 9:191–98.

Herrewege, J. (1975) Besoins nutritionnels de la *Drosophile* adulte: Influence des lecithines et du chlorure de choline sur la fecondité, la fertilité et la taille des oeufs. *Arch. Int. Physiol. Biochim.* 75:893–904.

Hiraizumi, Y. (1961) Negative correlation between rate of development and female fertility in *Drosophila melanogaster. Genetics* 46:615–24.

Hiraizumi, Y. (1985) Genetics of factors affecting the life history of *Drosophila melanogaster.* I. Female productivity. *Genetics* 110:453–64.

Hirsch, G. P. (1978) Somatic mutations and aging. In: *The Genetics of Aging,* E. L. Schneider (ed.). Plenum Press, New York and London, pp. 91–134.

Hoffman, G. W. (1974) On the origin of the genetic code and the stability of the translation apparatus. *J. Mol. Biol.* 83:349–62.

Hogarth, P. J. (1978) *The Biology of Reproduction.* John Wiley, New York.

Hogstedt, G. (1981) Should there be a positive or negative correlation between survival of adults in a bird population and clutch size? *Am. Nat.* 118:568–71.

Holehan, A. M., and B. J. Merry (1985) Lifetime breeding studies in fully fed and dietary restricted female CFY Sprague-Dawley rats. I. Effects of age, housing conditions and diet on fecundity. *Mech. Ageing Dev.* 33:19–28.

Holland, J. J., D. Kohne, and M. V. Doyle (1973) Analysis of virus replication in ageing human fibroblast cultures. *Nature* 245:316–19.

Holliday, R. (1989) Food, reproduction and longevity: Is the extended lifespan of calorie-restricted animals an evolutionary adaptation. *Bioessays* 10:125–27.

Holliday, R., and G. M. Tarrant (1972) Altered enzymes in ageing human fibroblasts. *Nature* 238:26–30.

Hollingsworth, M. J. (1966) Temperature and the rate of ageing in *Drosophila subobscura. Exp. Gerontol.* 1:259–67.

Hollingsworth, M. J. (1968) Environmental temperature and life span in poikilotherms. *Nature* 218:869–70.

Hollingsworth, M. J. (1969) The effect of fluctuating environmental temperatures on the length of life of adult *Drosophila. Exp. Gerontol.* 4:159–67.

Hood, L. E., I. L. Weissman, and W. B. Wood (1982) *Immunology,* Second edition. Benjamin-Cummings, Menlo Park.

Huey, R. B. (1987) Phylogeny, history, and the comparative method. In: *New Directions in Ecological Physiology,* M. E. Feder, A. F. Bennett, W. W. Burggren, and R. B. Huey (eds.). Cambridge University Press, Cambridge, pp. 76–101.

Hughes, D. M., and A. G. Clark (1988) Analysis of the genetic structure of life history of *Drosophila melanogaster* using recombinant extracted lines. *Evolution* 42:1309–20.

Hutchinson, E. W., and M. R. Rose (1990) Quantitative genetic analysis of postponed aging in *Drosophila melanogaster.* In: *Genetic Effects on Aging II,* D. E. Harrison (ed.). Telford Press, Caldwell, pp. 66–87.

Ingle, L., T. R. Wood, and A. M. Banta (1937) A study of the longevity, growth, reproduction and heart rate in *Daphnia longispina* as influenced by limitations in quantity of food. *J. Exp. Zool.* 76:325–52.

Johnson, T. E. (1984) Analysis of the biological basis of aging in *Caenorhabditis elegans.* In: *Invertebrate Models in Aging Research,* T. E. Johnson and D. H. Mitchell (eds.). CRC Press, Boca Raton, pp. 59–93.

Johnson, T. E. (1985) Aging in *Caenorhabditis elegans:* Update 1984. *Rev. Biol. Res. Aging* 2:45–60.

Johnson, T. E. (1986) Molecular and genetic analyses of a multivariate system specifying behavior and life span. *Behav. Genet.* 16:221–35.

Johnson, T. E. (1987) Aging can be genetically dissected into component processes using long-lived lines of *Caenorhabditis elegans. Proc. Natl. Acad. Sci. USA* 84:3777–81.

Johnson, T. E. (1988a) Genetic specification of life span: Processes, problems, and potentials. *J. Gerontol.* 43:B87–92.

Johnson, T. E. (1988b) Thoughts on the selection of longer-lived rodents. *Growth Dev. Aging* 52:207–9.

Johnson, T. E., W. L. Conley, and M. L. Keler (1988) Long-lived lines of *Caenorhabditis elegans* can be used to establish predictive biomarkers of aging. *Exp. Gerontol.* 23:281–95.

Johnson, T. E., and P. S. Hartman (1988) Radiation effects on life span in *Caenorhabditis elegans. J. Gerontol.* 43:B137–41.

Johnson, T. E., and G. McCaffrey (1985) Programmed aging or error catastrophe? An examination by two-dimensional polyacrylamide gel electrophoresis. *Mech. Ageing Dev.* 30:285–97.

Johnson, T. E., and W. B. Wood (1982) Genetic analysis of life-span in *Caenorhabditis elegans. Proc. Natl. Acad. Sci. USA* 79:6603–7.

Kato, H., M. Harada, K. Tsuchiya, and K. Moriwaki (1980) Absence of correlation between DNA repair in ultraviolet irradiated mammalian cells and life span of the donor species. *Jpn. J. Genet.* 55:99–108.

Kimura, M. (1983) *The Neutral Theory of Molecular Evolution.* Cambridge University Press, Cambridge.

King, C. E., and M. R. Miracle (1980) A perspective on ageing in rotifers. *Hydrobiologia* 73:13–19.

Kirkwood, T. B. L. (1977) Evolution of aging. *Nature* 270:301–4.

Kirkwood, T. B. L. (1980) Error propagation in intracellular information transfer. *J. Theor. Biol.* 82:363–82.

Kirkwood, T. B. L. (1981) Repair and its evolution: Survival versus reproduction. In: *Physiological Ecology: An Evolutionary Approach to Resource Use,* C. R. Townsend and P. Calow (eds.). Blackwell Scientific Publications, London and Boston, pp. 165–89.

Kirkwood, T. B. L., and T. Cremer (1982) Cytogerontology since 1881: Reappraisal of August Weismann and a review of modern progress. *Hum. Genet.* 60:101–21.

Kirkwood, T. B. L., and R. Holliday (1975) The stability of the translation apparatus. *J. Mol. Biol.* 97:257–65.

Kirkwood, T. B. L., and R. Holliday (1979) The evolution of ageing and longevity. *Proc. R. Soc. Lond.* B205:531–46.

Klass, M. R. (1977) Aging in the nematode *Caenorhabditis elegans:* Major biological and environmental factors influencing life span. *Mech. Ageing Dev.* 6:413–30.

Klekowski, E. J., Jr., and P. J. Godfrey (1989) Ageing and mutation in plants. *Nature* 340:389–91.

Kloek, G. P., D. B. Ralin, and G. C. Ridgel (1976) Survivorship and gene frequencies of *Drosophila melanogaster* populations in abnormal oxygen atmospheres. *Aviat. Space Environ. Med.* (March):272–79.

Koehn, R. K. (1987) The importance of genetics to physiological ecology. In: *New Directions in Ecological Physiology,* M. E. Feder, A. F. Bennett, W. W. Burggren, and R. B. Huey (eds.). Cambridge University Press, Cambridge, pp. 170–85.

Koehn, R. K., A. J. Zera, and J. G. Hall (1983) Enzyme polymorphism and natural selection.

In: *Evolution of Genes and Proteins,* M. Nei and R. K. Koehn (eds.). Sinauer Associates, Sunderland, Massachusetts, pp. 115–36.

Kohn, R. R. (1963) Human aging and disease. *J. Chronic. Dis.* 16:5.

Kohn, R. R. (1971) *Principles of Mammalian Aging.* Prentice-Hall, New Jersey.

Kohn, R. R., and E. Rollerson (1958) Relationship of age to swelling properties of human diaphragm tendon in acid and alkaline solutions. *J. Gerontol.* 13:241–47.

Kolta, M. G., R. Holson, P. Duffy, and R. W. Hart (1989) Effect of long-term caloric restriction on brain monoamines in aging male and female Fischer 344 rats. *Mech. Ageing Dev.* 48:191–98.

Kosuda, K. (1985) The aging effect on male mating activity in *Drosophila melanogaster. Behav. Genet.* 15:297–303.

Krebs, C. J. (1985) *Ecology: The Experimental Analysis of Distribution and Abundance,* Third edition. Harper & Row, New York.

Krebs, J. R., and N. B. Davies (1981) *An Introduction to Behavioural Ecology.* Blackwell Scientific Publications, London and Boston.

Krohn, P. L. (1962) Heterochronic transplantation in the study of ageing. *Proc. R. Soc. Lond.* B157:128–47.

Krohn, P. L. (1966) Transplantation and aging. In: *Topics in the Biology of Aging: A Symposium Held at the Salk Institute for Biological Studies,* San Diego, California, November 4–6, 1965, P. L. Krohn (ed.). Interscience Publishers, New York, pp. 125–39.

Kuhn, T. S. (1970) *The Structure of Scientific Revolutions,* Second edition. University of Chicago, Chicago.

Laganiere, S., and B. P. Yu (1989a) Effect of chronic food restriction in aging rats. I. Liver subcellular membranes. *Mech. Ageing Dev.* 48:207–19.

Laganiere, S., and B. P. Yu (1989b) Effect of chronic food restriction in aging rats. II. Liver cytosolic antioxidants and related enzymes. *Mech. Ageing Dev.* 48:221–30.

Lakatos, I. (1970) Falsification and the methodology of scientific research programmes. In: *Criticism and the Growth of Knowledge,* I. Lakatos and A. Musgrave (eds.). Cambridge University Press, Cambridge, pp. 91–196.

Lamb, M. J. (1964) The effects of radiation on the longevity of female *Drosophila subobscura. J. Insect Physiol.* 10:487–97.

Lamb, M. J. (1968) Temperature and lifespan in *Drosophila. Nature* 220:808–9.

Lamb, M. J. (1977) *Biology of Ageing.* Blackie, Glasgow and London.

Lamb, M. J. (1978) Ageing. In: *The Genetics and Biology of Drosophila,* Vol. 2C, M. Ashburner and T. R. F. Wright, (eds.). Academic Press, London, pp. 43–104.

Land, N., L. F. Parada, and R. A. Weinberg (1983a) Tumorigenic conversion of primary embryo fibroblasts requires at least two cooperating oncogenes. *Nature* 304:596–602.

Land, N., L. F. Parada, and R. A. Weinberg (1983b) Cellular oncogenes and multistep carcinogenesis. *Science* 222:771–78.

Lansing, A. I. (1947) A transmissible, cumulative and reversible factor in aging. *J. Gerontol.* 2:228–39.

Lansing, A. I. (1948) Evidence for aging as a consequence of growth cessation. *Proc. Natl. Acad. Sci. U.S.A.* 34:304–10.

Lansing, A. I., ed. (1952) *Problems of Ageing.* Williams & Wilkins, New York.

Laudan, L. (1977) *Progress and its Problems: Towards a Theory of Scientific Growth.* Routledge and Kegan Paul, London and Henley.

Law, R. (1979) The cost of reproduction in annual meadow grass. *Am. Nat.* 113:3–16.

Law, R., A. D. Bradshaw, and P. D. Putwain (1977) Life-history variation in *Poa annua. Evolution* 31:233–46.

Leakey, J. E. A., H. C. Cunny, J. Bazare, Jr., P. J. Webb, R. J. Feuers, P. H. Duffy, and R. W. Hart (1989a) Effects of aging and caloric restriction on hepatic drug metabolizing enzymes in the Fischer 344 rat. I: The cytochrome P-450 dependent monooxygenase system. *Mech. Ageing Dev.* 48:145–55.

Leakey, J. E. A., H. C. Cunny, J. Bazare, Jr., P. J. Webb, J. C. Lipscomb, W. Slikker, Jr., R. J. Feuers, P. H. Duffy, and R. W. Hart (1989b) Effects of aging and caloric restriction on hepatic drug metabolizing enzymes in the Fischer 344 rat. II: Effects on conjugating enzymes. *Mech. Ageing Dev.* 48:157–66.

Leffelaar, D., and T. A. Grigliatti (1984) A mutation in *Drosophila* that appears to accelerate aging. *Dev. Genet.* 4:199–210.

Leopold, A. C. (1961) Senescence in plant development. *Science* 134:1727–32.

Leopold, A. C. (1980) Aging and senescence in plant development. In: *Senescence in Plants*, K. V. Thimann (ed.). CRC Press, Boca Raton, pp. 1–12.

Lewis, C. M., and R. Holliday (1970) Mistranslation and ageing in *Neurospora. Nature* 228:877–80.

Lewontin, R. C. (1955) The effects of population density and composition on viability in *Drosophila melanogaster. Evolution* 9:27–41.

Lewontin, R. C. (1974) *The Genetic Basis of Evolutionary Changes.* Columbia University Press, New York.

Lindop, P. J., and J. Rotblat (1961) Long term effects of a single whole body exposure of mice to ionizing radiation. *Proc. R. Soc. London* B154:332–49.

Lindsley, D. L., and E. H. Grell (1968) Genetic variations of *Drosophila melanogaster.* Publication 627. Carnegie Institution of Washington.

Lindstedt, S. L., and W. A. Calder III (1981) Body size, physiological time and longevity of homeothermic animals. *Q. Rev. Biol.* 56:1–16.

Linn, S., M. Kairis, and R. Holliday (1976) Decreased fidelity of DNA polymerase activity isolated from aging human fibroblasts. *Proc. Natl. Acad. Sci. USA* 73:2818–22.

Lints, F. A. (1978) *Interdisciplinary Topics in Gerontology.* Vol. 14, *Genetics and Ageing.* H. P. von Haln (series ed.). S. Karger, New York.

Lints, F. A. (1983) Genetic influences on lifespan in *Drosophila* and related species. *Rev. Biol. Res. Aging* 1:51–72.

Lints, F. A., and C. Hoste (1974) The Lansing effect revisited. I. Life-span. *Exp. Gerontol.* 9:51–69.

Lints, F. A., and C. Hoste (1977) The Lansing effect revisited. II. Cumulative and spontaneously reversible parental age effects on fecundity in *Drosophila melanogaster. Evolution* 31:387–404.

Lints, F. A., and C. V. Lints (1969) Influence of preimaginal environment on fecundity and ageing in *Drosophila melanogaster* hybrids. I. Preimaginal population density. *Exp. Gerontol.* 4:231–44.

Lints, F. A., J. Stoll, G. Gruwez, and C. V. Lints (1979) An attempt to select for increased longevity in *Drosophila melanogaster. Gerontology* 25:192–204.

Lipman, J. M., A. Turturro, and R. W. Hart (1989) The influence of dietary restriction on DNA repair in rodents: A preliminary study. *Mech. Ageing Dev.* 48:135–143.

Lippman, R. D. (1983) Lipid peroxidation and metabolism in aging: A biological, chemical, and medical approach. *Rev. Biol. Res. Aging* 1:315–42.

Liu, R. K., and R. L. Walford (1975) Mid-life temperature-transfer effects on life-span of annual fish. *J. Gerontol.* 30:129–31.

Loeb, J., and J. H. Northrop (1916) Is there a temperature coefficient for the duration of life? *Proc. Natl. Acad. Sci. USA* 2:456–57.

Loeb, J., and J. H. Northrop (1917) On the influence of food and temperature upon the duration of life. *J. Biol. Chem.* 32:103–21.

Luckinbill, L. S., R. Arking, M. J. Clare, W. C. Cirocco, and S. A. Buck (1984) Selection for delayed senescence in *Drosophila melanogaster. Evolution* 38:996–1003.

Luckinbill, L. S., and M. J. Clare (1985) Selection for life span in *Drosophila melanogaster. Heredity* 55:9–18.

Luckinbill, L. S., M. J. Clare, W. L. Krell, W. C. Cirocco, and P. A. Richards (1987) Estimating the number of genetic elements that defer senescence in *Drosophila. Evol. Ecol.* 1:37–46.

Luckinbill, L. S., J. L. Graves, A. H. Reed, and S. Koetsawang (1988a) Localizing the genes that defer senescence in *Drosophila melanogaster. Heredity* 60:367–74.

Luckinbill, L. S., J. L. Graves, A. Tomkiw, and O. Sowirka (1988b) A qualitative analysis of some life-history correlates of longevity in *Drosophila melanogaster. Evol. Ecol.* 2:85–94.

Luckinbill, L. S., T. A. Grudzien, S. Rhine, and G. Weisman (1989) The genetic basis of adaptation to selection for longevity in *Drosophila melanogaster. Evol. Ecology* 3:31–39.

MacArthur, J. W., and W. H. T. Baillie (1929) Metabolic activity and duration of life. I. Influence of temperature on longevity in *Daphnia magna. J. Exp. Zool.* 53:221–42.

Manton, K., M. Woodbury, and E. Stallard (1989) Forecasting the limits to life expectancy: Modelling mortality from epidemiological and medical data. In: *Aging and Dying: The Biological Foundations of Human Longevity,* S. Ryan Johansson (ed.). University of California Press, Berkeley, in press.

Martin, G. M. (1978) Genetic syndromes in man with potential relevance to the pathobiology of aging. *Nat. Found.* 14:5–39.

Martin, G. M., A. C. Smith, D. J. Ketterer, C. E. Ogburn, and C. M. Disteche (1985) Increased chromosomal aberrations in first metaphases of cells isolated from the kidneys of aged mice. *Isr. J. Med. Sci.* 2:296–301.

Martin, G. M., C. A. Sprague, and C. J. Epstein (1970) Replicative lifespan of cultivated human cells: Effect of donor's age, tissue and genotype. *Lab. Invest.* 23:86–92.

Martin, G. M., C. A. Sprague, T. H. Norwood, and W. R. Pendergrass (1974) Clonal selection, attenuation and differentiation in an in vitro model of hyperplasia. *Am. J. Pathol.* 74:137–54.

Martin, G. M., C. A. Sprague, T. H. Norwood, W. R. Pendergrass, P. Bornstein, H. Hoehn, and W. P. Arend (1975) Do hyperplastoid cell lines "Differentiate themselves to death"? *Adv. Exp. Med. Biol.* 53:67–90.

Martin, G. M., and M. S. Turker (1988) Model systems for the genetic analysis of mechanisms of aging. *J. Gerontol.* 43:B33–39.

Maslansky, C. J., and G. M. Williams (1985) Ultraviolet light-induced DNA repair synthesis in hepatocytes from species of differing longevities. *Mech. Ageing Dev.* 29:191–203.

Masoro, E. J. (1984) Nutrition as a modulator of the aging process. *The Physiologist* 27:98–101.

Masoro, E. J. (1988) Food restriction in rodents: An evaluation of its role in the study of aging. *J. Gerontol.* 43:B59–64.

Masoro, E. J., M. S. Katz, and C. A. McMahan (1989) Evidence for the glycation hypothesis of aging from the food-restricted rodent model. *J. Gerontol.* 44:B20–22.

Maynard Smith, J. (1958) The effects of temperature and of egg-laying on the longevity of *Drosophila subobscura. J. Exp. Biol.* 35:832–42.

Maynard Smith, J. (1959) Sex-limited inheritance of longevity in *Drosophila subobscura. J. Genet.* 56:1–9.

Maynard Smith, J. (1962) Review lectures on senescence. I. The causes of ageing. *Proc. R. Soc. Lond.* B157:115–27.

Maynard Smith, J. (1963) Temperature and the rate of ageing in poikilotherms. *Nature* 199:400–2.

Maynard Smith, J. (1966) Theories of aging. In: *Topics in the Biology of Aging,* P. L. Krohn (ed.). Interscience, New York.

Maynard Smith, J. (1978) *The Evolution of Sex.* Cambridge University Press, London.

Maynard Smith, J., A. N. Bozcuk, and S. Tebbutt (1970) Protein turnover in adult *Drosophila. J. Insect Physiol.* 16:601–13.

Mayr, E. (1982) *The Growth of Biological Thought: Diversity, Evolution, and Inheritance.* Belknap Press of Harvard University Press, Cambridge and London.

McCay, C. M., and M. F. Crowell (1934) Prolongation of lifespan. *Sci. Mon.* 39:405–14.

McCay, C. M., M. F. Crowell, and L. A. Maynard (1935) The effect of retarded growth upon the length of lifespan and upon the ultimate body size. *J. Nutr.* 10:63–79.

McCay, C. M., L. A. Maynard, G. Sperling, and L. L. Barnes (1939) Retarded growth, lifespan, ultimate body size and age changes in the albino rat after feeding diets restricted in calories. *J. Nutr.* 18:1–13.

McCay, C. M., F. Pope, and W. Lunsford (1956) Experimental prolongation of the life span. *Bull. N.Y. Acad. Med.* 32:91–101.

McCay, C. M., G. Sperling, and L. L. Barnes (1943) Growth, ageing, chronic diseases, and life span in rats. *Arch. Biochem. Biophys.* 2:469–79.

McGrath, J. P., D. J. Capon, D. V. Goeddel, and A. D. Levinson (1984) Comparative biochemical properties of normal and activated human *ras* p21 protein. *Nature* 310:644–49.

Meadow, N. D., and C. H. Barrows (1971) Studies on aging in a bdelloid rotifer. II. The effects of various environmental conditions and maternal age on longevity and fecundity. *J. Gerontol.* 26:302–9.

Medawar, P. B. (1946) Old age and natural death. *Mod. Quart.* 1:30–56.

Medawar, P. B. (1952) *An Unsolved Problem of Biology.* H. K. Lewis, London.

Medawar, P. B. (1955) The definition and measurement of senescence. In: *Ciba Foundation Colloquia on Ageing,* Vol. 1, *General Aspects,* G. E. W. Wolstenholme, M. P. Cameron, and J. Etherington (eds.). J&A Churchill, London, pp. 4–15.

Medawar, P. B., and J. S. Medawar (1983) *Aristotle to Zoos: A Philosophical Dictionary of Biology.* Harvard University Press, Cambridge, pp. 5–8, 145–146.

Mertz, D. B. (1975) Senescent decline in flour beetle strains selected for early adult fitness. *Physiol. Zool.* 48:1–23.

Metchnikoff, E. (1904) *The Nature of Man.* Heinemann, London.

Metchnikoff, E. (1908) *The Prolongation of Life: Optimistic Studies.* G. P. Putnam's Sons, New York and London.

Mets, T., and G. Verdank (1981a) Variations in the stromal cell population of human bone marrow during aging. *Mech. Ageing Dev.* 15:41–49.

Mets, T., and G. Verdank (1981b) In vitro aging of human bone marrow-derived stromal cells. *Mech. Ageing Dev.* 16:81–89.

Mildvan, A. S., and B. L. Strehler (1960) A critique of theories of mortality. In: *The Biology of Aging,* AIBS Symp. Publ. No. 6:216–35.

Miller, D. S., and P. R. Payne (1968) Longevity and protein intake. *Exp. Gerontol.* 3:231–34.

Milne, C. P. (1985) An estimate of the heritability of worker longevity or length of life in the honey bee. *J. Apicult. Res.* 24:140–43.

Miquel, J., A. C. Economos, J. Fleming, and J. E. Johnson, Jr. (1980) Mitochondrial role in cell aging. *Exp. Gerontol.* 15:575–91.

Miquel, J., P. R. Lundgren, K. G. Bensch, and H. Atlan (1976) Effects of temperature on the life span, vitality and fine structure of *Drosophila melanogaster*. *Mech. Ageing Dev.* 5:347–70.

Molisch, H. (1938) *The Longevity of Plants*. Botanical Garden, New York.

Moment, G. B. (1978) The Ponce de Leon trail today. In: *The Biology of Aging*, J. A. Behnke, C. E. Finch, and G. B. Moment (eds.). Plenum Press, New York, pp. 1–17.

Moment, G. B. (1982) Theories of aging: An overview. In: *Testing the Theories of Aging*, R. C. Adelman and G. S. Roth (eds.). CRC Press, Boca Raton, pp. 1–23.

Mortimer, R. K., and J. R. Johnston (1959) Life span of individual yeast cells. *Nature* 183:1751–52.

Mousseau, T. A., and D. A. Roff (1987) Natural selection and the heritability of fitness components. *Heredity* 59:181–97.

Mueller, L. D. (1985) The evolutionary ecology of *Drosophila*. *Evol. Biology* 19:37–98.

Mueller, L. D. (1987) Evolution of accelerated senescence in laboratory populations of *Drosophila*. *Proc. Natl. Acad. Sci. USA* 84:1974–77.

Muller, H. J. (1959) One hundred years without Darwinism are enough. *School Science and Mathematics* April:304–16.

Muller, R., and E. F. Wagner (1984) Differentiation of F9 tetracarcinoma stem cells after transfer of c-*fos* proto-oncogenes. *Nature* 311:438–42.

Murphy, P. A., J. T. Giesel, and M. N. Manlove (1983) Temperature effects on life history variation in *Drosophila simulans*. *Evolution* 37:1181–92.

Nagel, J. E. (1983) Immunology. *Rev. Biol. Res. Aging* 1:103–60.

Nagylaki, T. (1977) The evolution of one- and two-locus systems. II. *Genetics* 85:347–54.

Nakamura, K. D., P. H. Duffy, M.-H. Lu, A. Turturro, and R. W. Hart (1989) The effect of dietary restriction on *myc* protooncogene expression in mice: A preliminary study. *Mech. Ageing Dev.* 48:199–205.

Nesse, R. M. (1988) Life table tests of evolutionary theories of senescence. *Exp. Gerontol.* 23:445–53.

Newbold, R. F., and R. W. Overell (1983) Fibroblast immortality is a prerequisite for transformation by EJ C-Ha-*ras* oncogene. *Nature* 304:648–51.

Noodén, L. D. (1980) Senescence in the whole plant. In: *Senescence in Plants*, K. V. Thimann (ed.) CRC Press, Boca Raton, pp. 219–58.

Noodén, L. D. (1988) Whole plant senescence. In: *Senescence and Aging in Plants*, L. D. Noodén and A. C. Leopold (eds.). Academic Press, San Diego, pp. 392–439.

Noodén, L. D., and A. C. Leopold (1988) *Senescence and Aging in Plants*. Academic Press, New York.

Northrop, J. (1917) The effect of prolongation of the period of growth on the total duration of life. *J. Biol. Chem.* 32:123–26.

Norton, H. T. J. (1928) Natural selection and Mendelian variation. *Proc. Lond. Math. Soc.* 28:1–45.

Orgel, L. E. (1963) The maintenance of the accuracy of protein synthesis and its relevance to ageing. *Proc. Natl. Acad. Sci. USA* 49:517–21.

Orgel, L. E. (1970) The maintenance of the accuracy of protein synthesis and its relevance to ageing: A correction. *Proc. Natl. Acad. Sci. USA* 67:1476.

Orgel, L. E., and F. H. C. Crick (1980) Selfish DNA: The ultimate parasite. *Nature* 284:604–7.

Packer, L., and J. R. Smith (1974) Extension of the lifespan of cultured normal diploid cells by vitamin E. *Proc. Natl. Acad. Sci. USA* 71:4763–67.

Palumbi, S. R., and J. B. C. Jackson (1983) Aging in modular organisms: Ecology of zooid senescence in *Steginoporella* sp. (Bryozoa; Cheilostomata). *Biol. Bull.* 164:267–78.

Parker, J., J. Flanagan, J. Murphy, and J. Gallant (1981) On the accuracy of protein synthesis in *Drosophila melanogaster. Mech. Ageing Dev.* 16:127–39.

Parsons, P. A. (1978) The effect of genotype and temperature on longevity in natural populations of *Drosophila melanogaster. Exp. Gerontol.* 13:167–69.

Partridge, L. (1980) Mate choice increases a component of offspring fitness in fruit flies. *Nature* 283:290–91.

Partridge, L. (1986) Sexual activity and life span. In: *Insect Aging, Strategies and Mechanisms*, K. G. Collatz and R. S. Sohal (eds.). Springer-Verlag, Berlin, pp. 45–54.

Partridge, L. (1987) Is accelerated senescence a cost of reproduction? *Funct. Ecol.* 1:317–20.

Partridge, L., and M. Farquhar (1981) Sexual activity reduces lifespan of male fruitflies. *Nature* 294:580–82.

Partridge, L., K. Fowler, S. Trevitt, and W. Sharp (1986) An examination of the effects of males on the survival and egg-production rates of female *Drosophila melanogaster. J. Insect Physiol.* 32:925–29.

Partridge, L., A. Green, and K. Fowler (1987) Effects of egg-production and of exposure to males on female survival in *Drosophila melanogaster. J. Insect Physiol.* 33:745–749.

Pearl, R. (1922) *The Biology of Death, Being a Series of Lectures Delivered at the Lowell Institute in Boston in December 1920.* J. B. Lippincott, Philadelphia and London.

Pearl, R. (1928) *The Rate of Living.* Alfred A. Knopf, New York.

Pearl, R., T. Park, and J. R. Miner (1941) Experimental studies on the duration of life. XVI. Life-tables for the flour beetle *Tribolium confusum* Duval. *Am. Nat.* 75:5–19.

Pearl, R., and S. L. Parker (1922) Experimental studies on the duration of life. II. Hereditary differences in duration of life in live-breed strains of *Drosophila. Am. Nat.* 56:174–87.

Pearl, R., and S. L. Parker (1924) Experimental studies on the duration of life. IX. New life-tables for *Drosophila. Am. Nat.* 58:71–82.

Pearson, O. P. (1945) Longevity of the short-tailed shrew. *Am. Midl. Nat.* 34:531.

Pegram, R. A., W. T. Allaben, and M. W. Chou (1989) Effect of caloric restriction and associated factors in Fischer 344 rats: Preliminary findings. *Mech. Ageing Dev.* 48:167–177.

Perry, J. S. (1953) The reproduction of the African elephant, *Loxodonta africana. Philos. Trans. R. Soc. Lond.* B237:93–149.

Phelan, J. P., and S. N. Austad (1989) Natural selection, dietary restriction, and extended longevity. *Growth Dev. Aging* 53:4–5.

Phillips, P. D., and V. J. Cristofalo (1983) Cell biology. *Rev. Biol. Res. Aging* 1:225–51.

Phillips, P. D., and V. J. Cristofalo (1987) A review of recent research on cellular aging in culture. *Rev. Biol. Res. Aging* 3:385–415.

Pierson, B. F. (1938) Relation of mortality after endomixis to the prior interendomitotic interval in *Paramecium aurelia. Biol. Bull.* 74:235–43.

Popp, R. A., E. G. Bailiff, G. P. Hirsch, and R. A. Conrad (1976) Errors in human hemoglobin as a function of age. *Interdis. Topics Gerontol.* 9:209–18.

Popper, K. R., (1959) *The Logic of Scientific Discovery.* Hutchinson, London.

Powers, D. A. (1987) A multidisciplinary approach to the study of genetic variation within species. In: *New Directions in Ecological Physiology*, M. E. Feder, A. F. Bennett, W. W. Burggren, and R. B. Huey (eds.). Cambridge University Press, Cambridge, pp. 102–29.

Pretzlaff, R., and R. Arking (1989) Patterns of amino acid incorporation in long-lived genetic strains of *Drosophila melanogaster. Exp. Gerontol.* 24:67–81.

Price, T. D., and P. R. Grant (1984) Life history traits and natural selection for small body size in a population of Darwin's finches. *Evolution* 38:483–94.

Prothero, J., and K. D. Jürgens (1987) Scaling of maximum life span in mammals: A review. *Basic Life Sci.* 42:49–74.

Provine, W. B. (1971) *The Origins of Theoretical Population Genetics.* University of Chicago Press, Chicago and London.

Pryor, W. A. (1987) The free-radical theory of aging revisited: A critique and a suggested disease-specific theory. In: *Modern Biological Theories of Aging,* H. R. Warner, R. N. Butler, R. L. Sprott, and E. L. Schneider (eds.). Raven Press, New York, pp. 89–112.

Rasmuson, M. (1956) Recurrent reciprocal selection. Results of three model experiments on *Drosophila* for improvement of quantitative characters. *Hereditas* 42:397–414.

Reznick, D. N., E. Perry, and J. Travis (1986) Measuring the cost of reproduction: A comment on papers by Bell. *Evolution* 40:1338–44.

Richardson, A., and M. C. Birchenall-Sparks (1983) Age-related changes in protein synthesis. *Rev. Biol. Res. Aging* 1:255–73.

Richardson, A., M. C. Birchenall-Sparks, and J. L. Staecker (1983) Aging and transcription. *Rev. Biol. Res. Aging* 1:275–94.

Richardson, A., J. A. Butler, M. S. Rutherford, I. Semsei, M.-Z. Gu, G. Fernandes, and W.-H. Chiang (1987) Effect of age and dietary restriction on the expression of alpha$_{2u}$-globulin. *J. Biol. Chem.* 262:12821–25.

Richardson, A., and I. Semsei (1987) Effect of aging on translation and transcription. *Rev. Biol. Res. Aging* 3:467–83.

Rinderer, T. E., A. M. Collins, and M. A. Brown (1983) Heritabilities and correlations of the honey bee: Response to *Nosema apis,* longevity, and alarm response to isopentyl acetate. *Apidologie* 14:79–86.

Robbins, K. C., H. N. Antoniades, S. G. Devare, M. W. Hunkapiller, and S. A. Aaronson (1983) Structural and immunological similarities between simian sarcoma virus gene product(s) and human platelet-derived growth factor. *Nature* 305:605–8.

Robertson, F. W., and J. H. Sang (1944) The ecological determinants of population growth in a *Drosophila* culture. I. Fecundity of adult flies. *Proc. R. Soc. Lond.* B132:258–77.

Robertson, O. H. (1961) Prolongation of the life span of kokanee salmon (*Oncorhynchus nerka kennerlyi*) by castration before beginning of gonad development. *Proc. Natl. Acad. Sci. USA* 47:609–21.

Rockstein, M. (1959) The biology of aging in insects. In: *CIBA Foundation Colloquia on Ageing* 5:247–63.

Rockstein, M. (1966) Biology of aging in insects. In: *Topics in the Biology of Aging,* P. L. Krohn (ed.). John Wiley, New York, pp. 43–61.

Rockstein, M. (1974) The genetic basis for longevity. In: *Theoretical Aspects of Aging,* M. Rockstein (ed.). Academic Press, New York, pp. 1–10.

Rockstein, M., and H. M. Lieberman (1958) Survival curves for male and female house-flies (*Musca domesticus* L.). *Nature* 181:787–88.

Roff, D. A., and T. A. Mousseau (1987) Quantitative genetics and fitness: Lessons from *Drosophila. Heredity* 58:103–18.

Röhme, D. (1981) Evidence for a relationship between longevity of mammalian species and life spans of normal fibroblasts *in vitro* and erythrocytes *in vivo. Proc. Natl. Acad. Sci. USA* 78:5009–13.

Rose, M. R. (1982) Antagonistic pleiotropy, dominance, and genetic variation. *Heredity* 48:63–78.

Rose, M. R. (1983) Evolution of aging. *Rev. Biol. Res. Aging* 1:19–24.

Rose, M. R. (1984a) Genetic covariation in *Drosophila* life history: Untangling the data. *Am. Nat.* 123:565–69.

Rose, M. R. (1984b) Laboratory evolution of postponed senescence in *Drosophila melanogaster*. *Evolution* 38:1004–10.

Rose, M. R. (1985) Life history evolution with antagonistic pleiotropy and overlapping generations. *Theor. Popul. Biol.* 28:342–58.

Rose, M. R. (1988) Response to "Thoughts on the selection of longer-lived rodents"— rejoinders. *Growth Dev. Aging* 52:209–11.

Rose, M., and B. Charlesworth (1980) A test of evolutionary theories of senescence. *Nature* 287:141–42.

Rose, M. R., and B. Charlesworth (1981a) Genetics of life history in *Drosophila melanogaster*. I. Sib analysis of adult females. *Genetics* 97:173–86.

Rose, M. R., and B. Charlesworth (1981b) Genetics of life history in *Drosophila melanogaster*. II. Exploratory selection experiments. *Genetics* 97:187–96.

Rose, M. R., M. L. Dorey, A. M. Coyle, and P. M. Service (1984) The morphology of postponed senescence in *Drosophila melanogaster*. *Can. J. Zool.* 62:1576–80.

Rose, M. R., and J. L. Graves, Jr. (1989) What evolutionary biology can do for gerontology. *J. Gerontol.* 44:B27–29.

Rose, M. R., and P. M. Service (1985) Evolution of aging. *Rev. Biol. Res. Aging* 2:85–98.

Rose, M. R., P. M. Service, and E. W. Hutchinson (1987) Three approaches to trade-offs in life-history evolution. In: *Genetic Constraints on Adaptive Evolution,* V. Loeschcke (ed.). Springer-Verlag, Berlin, pp. 91–105.

Rosen, R. (1978) Feedforwards and global system failure: A general mechanism for senescence. *J. Theor. Biol.* 74:579–90.

Rosenberg, B., G. Kemeny, L. G. Smith, I. D. Skurnick, and M. J. Bandwiski (1973) The kinetics and thermodynamics of death in multicellular organisms. *Mech. Ageing Dev.* 2:275–94.

Ross, G. R. T. (1908) Translation of Aristotle's *De Longitudine et Brevitate Vitae.* Clarendon Press, Oxford.

Ross, M. H. (1961) Length of life and nutrition in the rat. *J. Nutr.* 75:197–210.

Ross, M. H. (1976) Nutrition and longevity in experimental animals. *Curr. Concepts Nutr.* 4:61–76.

Rothstein, M. (1983) Enzymes, enzyme alteration, and protein turnover. *Rev. Biol. Res. Aging* 1:305–14.

Rothstein, M. (1987) Evidence for and against the error catastrophe hypothesis. In: *Modern Biological Theories of Aging,* H. R. Warner, R. N. Butler, R. L. Sprott, and E. L. Schneider (eds.). Raven Press, New York, pp. 139–54.

Rudzinska, M. A. (1961) The use of a protozoan for studies on aging. I. Differences between young and old organisms of *Tokophyra infusionum* as revealed by light and electron microscopy. *J. Gerontol.* 16:213–24.

Ruley, H. E. (1983) Adenovirus early region 1A enables viral and cellular transforming genes to transform primary cells in culture. *Nature* 304:602–06.

Russell, E. S. (1966) Lifespan and aging patterns. In: *Biology of the Laboratory Mouse,* E. L. Green (ed.). McGraw-Hill, New York, pp. 511–19.

Russell, R. L. (1987) Evidence for and against the theory of developmentally programmed aging. In: *Modern Biological Theories of Aging,* H. R. Warner, R. N. Butler, R. L. Sprott, and E. L Schneider (eds.). Raven Press, New York, pp. 35–61.

Sabbadin, A. (1979) Colonial structure and pattern in ascidians. In: *Biology and Systematics of Colonial Organisms,* G. Larwood and B. R. Rosen (eds.). Academic Press, New York, pp. 433–44.

Sacher, G. A. (1957) Dependence of acute radiosensitivity on age in adult female mouse. *Science* 125:1039–40.

Sacher, G. A. (1959) Relation of lifespan to brain weight and body weight in mammals. In: *CIBA Foundation Colloquia on Ageing,* G. E. W. Wolstenholme and M. O'Connor (eds.). Churchill, London, pp. 115–33.

Sacher, G. A. (1968) Molecular versus systemic theories on the genesis of aging. *Exp. Gerontol.* 3:265–71.

Sacher, G. A. (1978) Longevity and aging in vertebrate evolution. *Biol. Sci.* 28:497–501.

Sacher, G. A. (1982) Evolutionary theory in gerontology. *Perspect. Biol. Med.* 25:339–53.

Sacher, G. A., and R. W. Hart (1978) Longevity, aging, and comparative cellular and molecular biology of the house mouse, *Mus musculus,* and the white-footed mouse, *Peromyscus leucopus. Birth Defects* 14:71–96.

Sacher, G. A., and E. F. Staffeldt (1974) Relation of gestation time to brain weight for placental mammals: Implications for the theory of vertebrate growth. *Am. Nat.* 108:593–615.

Salk, D. (1982) Werner's syndrome: A review of recent research with an analysis of connective tissue metabolism, growth control of cultured cells, and chromosomal aberrations. *Hum. Genet.* 62:1–15.

Samis, H. V. (1978) Molecular genetics of aging. In: *The Genetics of Aging,* E. L. Schneider (ed.). Plenum Press, New York and London, pp. 7–25.

Sang, J. H. (1949a) The ecological determinants of popultion growth in a *Drosophila* culture. III. Larval and pupal survival. *Physiol. Zool.* 22:183–202.

Sang, J. H. (1949b) The ecological determinants of population growth in a *Drosophila* culture. IV. The significance of successive batches of larvae. *Physiol. Zool.* 22:202–10.

Sang, J. H. (1949c) The ecological determinants of population growth in a *Drosophila* culture. V. The adult population count. *Physiol. Zool.* 22:210–23.

Sapolsky, R. M., L. C. Krey, and B. S. McEwen (1986a) The adrenocortical axis in the aged rat: Impaired sensitivity to both fast and delayed feedback inhibition. *Neurobiol. Aging* 7:331–35.

Sapolsky, R. M., L. C. Krey, and B. S. McEwen (1986b) The neuroendocrinology of stress and aging: The glucocorticoid cascade hypothesis. *Endocr. Rev.* 7:284–301.

Sartin, J. L. (1983) Endocrine physiology. *Rev. Biol. Res. Aging* 1:181–93.

Scheiner, S. M., R. L. Caplan, and R. F. Lyman (1989) A search for trade-offs among life history traits in *Drosophila melanogaster. Evol. Ecol.* 3:51–63.

Schnebel, E. M., and J. Grossfield (1988) Antagonistic pleiotropy: An interspecific *Drosophila* comparison. *Evolution* 42:306–11.

Schwab, M., K. Alitalo, M. E. Varmus, J. M. Bishop, and D. George (1983) A cellular oncogene (c-ki-ras) is amplified, over expressed, and located within karyotypic abnormalities in mouse adrenocortical tumour cells. *Nature* 303:497–501.

Service, P. M. (1987) Physiological mechanisms of increased stress resistance in *Drosophila melanogaster* selected for postponed senescence. *Physiol. Zool.* 60:321–26.

Service, P. M. (1989) The effect of mating status on lifespan, egg laying, and starvation resistance in *Drosophila melanogaster* in relation to selection on longevity. *J. Insect Physiol.* 35:447–52.

Service, P. M., E. W. Hutchinson, M. D. MacKinley, and M. R. Rose (1985) Resistance to environmental stress in *Drosophila melanogaster* selected for postponed senescence. *Physiol. Zool.* 58:380–89.

Service, P. M., E. W. Hutchinson, and M. R. Rose (1988) Multiple genetic mechanisms for the evolution of senescence in *Drosophila melanogaster. Evolution* 42:708–16.

Service, P. M., and M. R. Rose (1985) Genetic covariation among life-history components: The effect of novel environments. *Evolution* 39:943–45.

Shapiro, J. A. ed. (1983) *Mobile Genetic Elements.* Academic Press, New York.

Shaw, R. F., and B. L. Bercaw (1962) Temperature and lifespan in poikilothermous animals. *Nature* 196:454–57.

Shock, N. W. (1987) The evolution of gerontology as a science. *Rev. Biol. Res. Aging* 3:3–12.

Simmons, M. J., and J. F. Crow (1977) Mutations affecting fitness in *Drosophila* populations. *Annu. Rev. Genet.* 11:49–78.

Simmons, M. J., C. R. Preston, and W. R. Engels (1980) Pleiotropic effects on fitness of mutations affecting viability in *Drosophila melanogaster*. *Genetics* 94:467–75.

Sinex, F. M. (1974) The mutation theory of aging. In: *Theoretical Aspects of Aging*, M. Rockstein, M. L. Sussman, and J. Chesky (eds.). Academic Press, New York, pp. 23–31.

Smith, J. N. M. (1981) Does high fecundity reduce survival in song sparrows? *Evolution* 35:1142–48.

Smith-Sonneborn, J. (1983) Aging in protozoa. *Rev. Biol. Res. Aging* 1:25–28.

Sohal, R. S. (1986) The rate of living theory: A contemporary interpretation. In: *Insect Aging, Strategies and Mechanisms*, R. S. Sohal and K. G. Collatz (eds.). Springer-Verlag, Berlin, pp. 23–44.

Sohal, R. S. (1987) The free radical theory of aging: A critique. *Rev. Biol. Res. Aging* 3:431–49.

Sohal, R. S., and J. H. Runnels (1986) Effect of experimentally-prolonged life span on flight performance of houseflies. *Exp. Gerontol.* 21:509–14.

Sokal, R. R. (1970) Senescence and genetic load: Evidence from *Tribolium*. *Science* 167:1733–34.

Sonneborn, T. M. (1957) Breeding systems, reproductive methods, and species problems in Protozoa. In: *The Species Problem: A Symposium Presented at the Atlanta Meeting of the American Association for the Advancement of Science, December 28–29, 1955*, E. Mayr (ed.). Publication No. 50 of the American Association for the Advancement of Science, Washington, D.C., pp. 155–324.

Sonneborn, T. M. (1960) Enormous differences in length of life of closely related ciliates and their significance. In: *Biology of Ageing*, B. L. Strehler (ed.). Waverly Press, Baltimore, p. 289.

Sonneborn, T. M. (1978) The origin, evolution, nature, and causes of aging. In: *The Biology of Aging*, J. A. Behnke, C. E. Finch, and G. B. Moment (eds.). Plenum Press, New York.

Spedding, J., R. L. Ellis, and D. D. Heath (1889) *The Works of Francis Bacon*, Vol. 5, *Instauratio Magna. Or Historia Vitae et Mortis*. Longman & Co., London.

Sprott, R. L. (1983) Genetic aspects of aging in *Mus musculus:* January 1981–February 1982. *Rev. Biol. Res. Aging* 1:73–80.

Sprott, R. L. (1985) Genetic aspects of aging in *Mus musculus*. *Rev. Biol. Res. Aging* 2:99–104.

Sprott, R. L. (1987) Genetic aspects of aging in *Mus musculus*. *Rev. Biol. Res. Aging* 3:71–76.

Stanley, J. F., D. Pye, and A. MacGregor (1975) Comparison of doubling numbers attained by cultured animal cells with life span of species. *Nature* 255:158–59.

Stanulis-Praeger, B. M. (1987) Cellular senescence revisited: A review. *Mech. Ageing Dev.* 38:1–48.

Stearns, S. C. (1976) Life-history tactics: A review of the ideas. *Q. Rev. Biol.* 51:3–47.

Stearns, S. C. (1977) The evolution of life history traits: A critique of the theory and a review of the data. *Ann. Rev. Ecol. Syst.* 8:145–77.

Stearns, S. C. (1983) The influence of size and phylogeny on patterns of covariation among life-history traits in the mammals. *OIKOS* 41:173–87.

Stern, C. (1973) *Principles of Human Genetics,* Third edition. Freeman, San Francisco.

Stewart, T. A., P. K. Kattengale, and P. Leder (1984) Spontaneous mammary adenocarcinomas in transgenic mice that carry and express MTV/*myc* fusian genes. *Cell* 38:627–637.

Storer, J. B. (1966) Longevity and gross pathology in 22 inbred mouse strains. *J. Gerontol.* 21:404–9.

Strehler, B. L. (1961) Studies on the comparative physiology of aging. II. On the mechanism of temperature life-shortening in *Drosophila melanogaster. J. Gerontol.* 16:2–12.

Strehler, B. L. (1962) *Time, Cells and Aging.* Academic Press, New York.

Strehler, B. L. (1977) *Time, Cells and Aging,* Second edition. Academic Press, New York.

Strehler, B. L., G. Hirsch, D. Gusseck, R. Johnson, and M. Bick (1971) Codon-restriction theory of aging and development. *J. Theor. Biol.* 33:429–74.

Stuchlíková, E., M. Juricobá-Horaková, and Z. Deyl (1975). New aspects of the dietary effect of life prolongation in rodents. What is the role of obesity in aging? *Exp. Gerontol.* 10: 141–144.

Szilard, L. (1959) On the nature of the aging process. *Proc. Natl. Acad. Sci. USA* 45:30–45.

Taub, R., C. Moulding, J. Battery, W. Murphy, T. Vasicek, G. M. Lenoir, and P. Leder (1984) Activation and somatic mutations of the translocated c-*myc* gene in Burkitt lymphoma cells. *Cell* 36:339–48.

Taylor, C. E., and C. Condra (1980) r- and K-selection in *Drosophila pseudoobscura. Evolution* 34:1183–93.

Taylor, C. E., C. Condra, M. Conconi, and M. Prout (1981) Longevity and male mating success in *Drosophila pseudoobscura. Am. Nat.* 117:1035–39.

Temin, R. G. (1966) Homozygous viability and fertility loads in *Drosophila melanogaster. Genetics* 53:27–56.

Templeton, A. R. (1980) The evolution of life histories under pleiotropic constraints and r-selection. *Theor. Popul. Biol.* 18:279–89.

Templeton, A. R. (1983) The evolution of life histories under pleiotropic constraints and K-selection. In: *Lecture Notes in Biomathematics.* Vol. 52. *Proceedings, Edmonton 1982,* H. I. Freedman and C. Strobeck (eds.). Springer-Verlag, Berlin.

Templeton, A. R., T. J. Crease, and F. Shah (1985) The molecular through ecological genetics of *abnormal abdomen* in *Drosophila mercatorum.* I. Basic genetics. *Genetics* 111:805–18.

Templeton, A. R., and M. A. Rankin (1978) Genetic revolutions and control of insect populations. In: *The Screwworm Problem,* R. H. Richardson (ed.). University of Texas Press, Austin, pp. 81–111.

Thimann, K. V., ed. (1980) *Senescence in Plants.* CRC Press, Boca Raton.

Tice, R. R. (1978) Aging and DNA-repair capacity. In: *The Genetics of Aging,* E. L. Schneider (ed.). Plenum Press, New York and London, pp. 53–89.

Tonegawa, S. (1983) Somatic generation of antibody diversity. *Nature* 302:575–81.

Trout, W. E., and W. D. Kaplan (1970) A relation between longevity, metabolic rate, and activity in shaker mutants of *Drosophila melanogaster. Exp. Gerontol.* 5:83–92.

Tucić, N., D. Cvetković, and D. Milanović (1988) The genetic variation and covariation among fitness components in *Drosophila melanogaster* females and males. *Heredity* 60:55–60.

Verzar, F., and H. Thoenen (1960) Die Wirkung von Elektrolyten auf die thermische Kontraktion von Collagenfaden. *Gerontologia* 4:112–19.

Visscher, M. B., J. T. King, and Y. C. P. Lee (1952) Further studies on influence of age and diet upon reproductive senescence in strain A female mice. *Am. J. Physiol.* 170:72–76.

Walford, R. L. (1962) Auto-immunity and aging. *J. Gerontol.* 17:281–85.

Walford, R. L. (1966) Generalizing biologic hypotheses and aging: An immunological approach. In: *Topics in the Biology of Aging: A Symposium Held at the Salk Institute for Biological Studies, San Diego, California, November 4–6, 1965,* P. L. Krohn (ed.). Interscience Publishers, New York, pp. 163–69.

Walford, R. L. (1969) *The Immunologic Theory of Aging.* Munksgaard, Copenhagen.

Walford, R. L., G. S. Smith, P. J. Meredith, and K. E. Cheney (1978) Immunogenetics of aging. In: *The Genetics of Aging,* E. L. Schneider (ed.). Plenum Press, New York and London, pp. 383–401.

Waterfield, M. D., G. T. Scrace, N. Whittle, P. Stroobant, A. Johnsson, A. Wasteson, B. Westermark, C. H. Heldin, J. S. Huang, and T. F. Deuel (1983) Platelet-derived growth factor is structurally related to the putative transforming protein p28sis of simian sarcoma virus. *Nature* 304:35–39.

Wattiaux, J. M. (1968a) Cumulative parental effects in *Drosophila subobscura. Evolution* 22:406–21.

Wattiaux, J. M. (1968b) Parental age effects in *Drosophila pseudoobscura. Exp. Gerontol.* 3:55–61.

Weindruch, R., and R. L. Walford (1982) Dietary restriction in mice beginning at 1 year of age: Effect on life-span and spontaneous cancer incidence. *Science* 215:1415–18.

Weindruch, R., and R. L. Walford (1988) *The Retardation of Aging and Disease by Dietary Restriction.* Charles C. Thomas, Springfield, Illinois.

Weismann, A. (1889) *Essays Upon Heredity and Kindred Biological Problems.* Clarendon Press, Oxford.

Wertz, R. L., G. B. Hartwig, A. P. Frost, J. J. Brophy, S. K. Atwater, and A. D. Roses (1981) Patients with myotonic dystrophy, a possible segmental progeroid syndrome, and Duchenne muscular dystrophy have fibroblasts with normal limits for in vitro lifespan and growth characteristics. *J. Cell Physiol.* 107:255–60.

Western, D., and J. Ssemakula (1982) Life history patterns in birds and mammals and their evolutionary interpretation. *Oecologia* 54:281–90.

Widdowson, E. M., and G. C. Kennedy (1962) Rate of growth, mature weight, and lifespan. *Proc. R. Soc. Lond.* B156:96–108.

Williams, G. C. (1957) Pleiotropy, natural selection, and the evolution of senescence. *Evolution* 11:398–411.

Williams, G. C. (1960) Pleiotropy, natural selection, and the evolution of senescence. In: *The Biology of Aging,* B. L. Strehler (ed.). American Institute of Biological Sciences, Washington, D.C., pp. 332–37.

Williams, G. C. (1966a) Natural selection, the costs of reproduction, and a refinement of Lack's principle. *Am. Nat.* 100:687–90.

Williams, G. C. (1966b) *Adaptation and Natural Selection, A Critique of Some Current Evolutionary Thought.* Princeton University Press, Princeton.

Wilson, D. L. (1974) The programmed theory of aging. In: *Theoretical Aspects of Aging,* M. Rockstein, M. L. Sussman, and J. Chesky (eds.). Academic Press, New York, pp. 11–21.

Wise, P. M. (1983) Aging of the female reproductive system. *Rev. Biol. Res. Aging* 1:195–222.

Witkowski, J. (1985) The myth of cell immortality. *Trends Biochem. Sci.* 10:258–60.

Woodhead, A. D., and S. Ellett (1969a) Endocrine aspects of ageing in the guppy, *Lebistes reticulatus* (Peters). III. The testis. *Exp. Gerontol.* 4:17–25.

Woodhead, A. D., and S. Ellett (1969b) Aspects of ageing in the guppy, *Lebistes reticulatus* (Peters). IV. The ovary. *Exp. Gerontol.* 4:197–205.

Woodhead, A. D., R. B. Setlow, and E. Grist (1980) DNA repair and longevity in three species of cold-blooded vertebrates. *Exp. Gerontol.* 15:301–4.

Wright, S. (1929a) Fisher's theory of dominance. *Am. Nat.* 63:274–79.

Wright, S. (1929b) Evolution of dominance (Comments on Dr. Fisher's reply). *Am. Nat.* 63:556–61.

Wright, S. (1968) *Evolution and the Genetics of Populations.* Vol. 1. *Genetic and Biometric Foundations.* University of Chicago Press, Chicago.

Wright, S. (1977) *Evolution and the Genetics of Populations: A Treatise in Four Volumes,* Vol. 3, *Experimental Results and Evolutionary Deductions.* University of Chicago Press, Chicago.

Wright, S. (1980) Genic and organismic selection. *Evolution* 34:825–43.

Yu, B. P. (1985) Recent advances in dietary restriction and aging. *Rev. Biol. Res. Aging* 2:435–43.

Yu, B. P. (1987) Update on food restriction and aging. *Rev. Biol. Res. Aging* 3:495–505.

Yu, B. P., E. J. Masoro, and C. A. McMahan (1985) Nutritional influences on aging of Fischer 344 rats: I. Physical, metabolic, and longevity characteristics. *J. Gerontol.* 40:657–70.

Yuasa, Y., S. K. Srivastava, C. Y. Dunn, J. S. Rhim, E. P. Reddy, and S. A. Aaronson (1983) Acquisition of transforming properties by alternative point mutations within c-*bas/has* human protooncogene. *Nature* 303:775–79.

# AUTHOR INDEX

# SUBJECT INDEX